Vladimir Putin and the Evolution of Russian Foreign Policy

CHATHAM HOUSE PAPERS

The Royal Institute of International Affairs, at Chatham House in London, has provided an independent forum for discussion and debate on current international issues for over eighty years. Its resident research fellows, specialized information resources and range of publications, conferences and meetings span the fields of international politics, economics and security. The Institute is independent of government and other vested interests.

Chatham House Papers address contemporary issues of intellectual importance in a scholarly yet accessible way. In preparing the papers, authors are advised by a study group of experts convened by the RIIA, and publication of a paper indicates that the Institute regards it as an authoritative contribution to the public debate. The RIIA is, however, precluded by its Charter from having an institutional view. Opinions expressed in this publication are the responsibility of the author.

Vladimir Putin and the Evolution of Russian Foreign Policy

Bobo Lo

THE ROYAL INSTITUTE OF INTERNATIONAL AFFAIRS | Russia and Eurasia Programme

Blackwell Publishing

© The Royal Institute of International Affairs, 2003

The Royal Institute of International Affairs
Chatham House
10 St James's Square
London SW1Y 4LE
http://www.riia.org
(Charity Registration No: 208223)

Blackwell Publishing Ltd
350 Main Street, Malden, MA 02148-5018, USA
108 Cowley Road, Oxford OX4 1JF, UK
550 Swanston Street, Carlton South, Melbourne, Victoria 3053, Australia
Kurfürstendamm 57, 10707 Berlin, Germany

First published 2003 by Blackwell Publishing Ltd

Library of Congress Cataloging-in-Publication Data has been applied for

ISBN 1-4051-0299-3 (hardback); ISBN 1-4051-0300-0 (paperback)

A catalogue record for this title is available from the British Library.

Set in 10.5 on 12 pt Caslon with Stone Sans display
By Koinonia, Manchester
Printed and bound in the United Kingdom
by MPG Books Ltd, Bodmin, Cornwall

For further information on
Blackwell Publishing, visit our website:
http://www.blackwellpublishing.com

Contents

Contents

Acknowledgments

The cover of this book credits to one person the work of many. This has been very much a collective enterprise, and I owe an immense debt to numerous friends and colleagues. It is perhaps invidious to single out individuals, but I should like to thank three people in particular. Tania Keefe was an exceptional research assistant, unearthing a rich seam of information about contemporary Russian foreign policy as well as undertaking the ugly task of reading through the initial draft. Ole Lindeman brought to the project the indispensable perspective of the insider, offering critical insights and suggestions while shepherding me through lengthy periods of self-doubt. Finally, Roy Allison was the moving spirit behind the book, a never-ending source of ideas, energy and analytical rigour.

Two outstanding institutions have played central roles in this enterprise. The Royal Institute of International Affairs has provided inspiration and intellectual support from the outset. I shall always be grateful to the distinguished members of the Chatham House study group for their extremely constructive and perceptive comments on the draft text, and to James Nixey and Margaret May for their logistical and moral support. When I was living in Russia, the Carnegie Moscow Center became something of a home from home, and I am especially grateful to Dmitri Trenin and Bob Nurick without whom this book would never have been completed. Thank you, also, to Gareth Meyer and Timofei Bordachev for their invaluable suggestions on individual chapters.

It has been said that 'no man is a failure who has good friends', and I have been unusually blessed in this regard. Lizzy Fisher, Alex Pravda and Riitta Heino, Chris and Antonia Davis, Roy Allison, Ole and Berit Lindeman, and Laetitia Spetschinsky have had the dubious pleasure of putting me up in recent months, during which they offered friendship and support far exceeding any reasonable expectations. More generally, I should like to recognize the contribution of all my friends in helping me to get through some difficult

Acknowledgments

times. Thank you to Lyn and Bruce Minerds, Stephen Shay and Nicola Cade, Linda Kouvaras and Richard Ward, Gareth Meyer and Penny Xirakis, Justine Braithwaite and David Peebles, Glenn and Agnes Waller, Ros and Simon Harrison, Emily Gale, Jill Colgan, Rohi Jaggi, Tatiana Parkhalina, Kostya Eggert, and David and Lena Waterhouse. Last but certainly not least, I am indebted to my family: my mother, to whom this book is dedicated, my father, Helen, Hsiao, Didi and Ping.

December 2002   B.L.

About the author

Dr Bobo Lo is an Associate Fellow at the Royal Institute of International Affairs at Chatham House, and the Visiting Fellow at the Carnegie Moscow Center. He has written extensively on Russian foreign and security policy as an independent researcher and, previously, as First Secretary and then Deputy Head of Mission at the Australian Embassy in Moscow (1995–99). He is the author of *Soviet Labour Ideology and the Collapse of the State* (2000) and *Russian Foreign Policy in the Post-Soviet Era: Reality, Illusion and Myth-making* (2002).

To my mother
for keeping the faith

1

The Putin phenomenon

The phenomenon of Vladimir Vladimirovich Putin stands as one of the most remarkable of our times. In the space of three short years he has emerged from near-total obscurity to become one of the most talked-about figures in world politics. This metamorphosis, striking in itself, is all the more singular for having occurred with a minimum of fanfare. It is in many respects the triumph of an 'unexceptional' man. In contrast to his immediate predecessors, Putin has made a virtue out of appearing ordinary. He offers no compelling public persona, nor is he the purveyor of memorable ideas. If the West thinks of Yeltsin as 'the man on the tank' during the failed putsch of August 1991, and of Gorbachev as the statesman who brought us *glasnost*, *perestroika* and 'new thinking' in foreign policy, then Putin comes across as just another more or less respectable, more or less 'normal', international leader.

And yet the paradox is that this apparent blandness, the lack of obvious distinction, has struck a real chord both domestically and in Russia's relations with the outside world. Vladimir Putin is in a critical sense a man of his time, when larger-than-life personalities like Yeltsin, Clinton, Kohl and Mitterrand have given way to a generation of unspectacular but businesslike leaders – George W. Bush, Tony Blair, Gerhard Schröder. To most Russians, tired of the turbulence of the post-Soviet decade, he represents the promise of a return to an idealized world of order and stability. His appeal to the international community, although more qualified, is similar: for the first time in years there is hope that Russian foreign policy is moving out of the vicious cycle of stagnation and unpredictability that characterized its conduct under Yeltsin. It is no surprise that Margaret Thatcher's famous description of Gorbachev, as someone with whom the West could 'do business', has been applied to Putin more than once since his advent to power.

This image of ordinariness and relative normality is, however, only part of the story. Contrary to appearances, Russia's president is an exceptionally complex and elusive figure. When he was first designated as Yeltsin's successor,

Russian and Western commentators alike were quick to ask the question, 'who is Mr Putin?', and just as quick to try to supply answers. KGB apparatchik, authoritarian, reactionary, statist, advocate of law and order, Cold War warrior, progressive, modernizer, champion of liberal economic reform – the labels piled on top of one another, as people struggled to define and make sense of a man whose coming no one predicted and whose views were shrouded in the mystery of a secret past. Three years later, we are little the wiser. Putin the president is the most public of politicians, making clever use of every type of information media to outline government policies and project a carefully nurtured image of strength, reasonableness and enlightenment. Putin the man, however, remains an enigma who defies ready characterization and whose exterior serves to obscure multiple contradictions: at once accessible and distant, personable and intimidating, dispassionate and emotional.

This dichotomy between the public and the private recalls one of the dominant historical figures of the 20th century, Josef Stalin, with whom there are a number of striking parallels. Not, of course, in terms of psychological disposition but in explaining some of the reasons behind their astonishing political success. Like Stalin, Putin has transcended the limitations of an unfashionable administrative background to reach the summit.[1] In the course of his ascent, he has also enjoyed the good fortune to be underestimated by peers and outsiders alike, the insight to tap into the popular and institutional mood, and the talent to capitalize on the weaknesses of others ostensibly better qualified to hold the highest office. He has managed to make an understated personal charisma disarming to his political rivals and attractive to the general public. Importantly, Putin has adopted an unsentimental attitude to ideological issues; not without beliefs, he nevertheless understands their instrumental uses and the need for flexibility and expediency when considerations of power are paramount. Like the shapeshifter of science fiction imagination, he has the rare ability to be all things to all people, as illustrated, for example, in his judicious use of the nationalist card. On the other hand, Putin has sought to use power not just for its own sake, but to promote an ambitious domestic and external policy agenda.[2] He has demonstrated an enviable ability to get things done, assisted by a real interest in and grasp of detail – an attribute possessed by Stalin but notably absent in subsequent Soviet and Russian leaders.

The outcome of this mix of characteristics and circumstances is that Putin now commands an authority unprecedented since the death of Stalin in 1953. It is somewhat ironic that the post-Soviet era, with its powerful images of democracy and freedom, should give rise to a man whose political standing and control over policy exceeds that of more 'authoritative' figures of the past, such as Khrushchev, Gorbachev and Yeltsin.[3] While the temper of his era as well as personal disinclination have meant that Putin is far from being an absolutist tyrant, for the first time in decades the occupant of the Kremlin Palace embodies both the development of policy *and* a superior capacity to bring it to fruition. He may prefer to rule by consensus rather than fiat, but it is a consensus overwhelmingly on his terms.[4] Recalling Louis XIV's famous aphorism, '*l'Etat, c'est moi*' ('The state, I am the state'), government under Putin might be said to operate according to the principle, '*le consensus, c'est moi*'. Those who challenge, or are seen to threaten, his authority face extinction – albeit political rather than personal. It is no surprise, therefore, that something of a modern-day 'cult of personality' has grown around him. Putin's representation in the Russian media is much more benign than the intimidating and unquestioning idolatry that surrounded Stalin, but it nevertheless exudes an aura of mastery, often of near infallibility.[5] Whereas Stalin's instrument of choice, the mass rally, was very much a product of the 1930s, Putin has opted for contemporary but equally effective means of self-projection and image-making – an 'impromptu' exhibition of his judo prowess, slick one-liners with world leaders and the foreign press, relaxed question-and-answer sessions on the internet or with Russian and foreign students, soundbites of meetings with government ministers in which he dispenses reasoned, but critical, opinions about their performance.

Present-day Russian foreign policy mirrors many of these realities. More so than other areas of government, it is intimately associated with Putin the individual. If the Yeltsin administration's conduct of international relations revealed the primacy of competing sectional agendas over a consensus vision of the 'national interest',[6] then today it is appropriate to speak about a genuinely 'presidential' foreign policy, one that reflects the characteristics of Putin himself. In the first instance, it combines the projection of selected images with the pursuit of substance. It is no coincidence that public diplomacy has become one of the key priorities of his administration, and not only in connection with Chechnya. Putin *is* the face of Russian foreign policy at home and abroad. There is no risk that current Foreign Minister Igor Ivanov, or indeed any other figure, will absorb some of the international limelight as Andrei Kozyrev and Yevgenii Primakov did under Yeltsin, and Eduard Shevardnadze under Gorbachev. Indeed, Ivanov's profile is lower even than that of Maxim Litvinov and Vyacheslav Molotov, foreign ministers under Stalin. The common notion that Putin is almost solely responsible for the pro-Western orientation in Russia's external relations post-11 September is less a reflection of policy reality (see Chapter 7) than a measure of his political dominance, substantive and symbolic.

Russian foreign policy is also, in the most generous understanding of the term, 'universalist' – inclusive, multifaceted, and flexible as to means.

Although the confrontation of Soviet times has given way to a strong desire for expanded cooperation with the West, the Kremlin's world-view remains expansive and ambitious, and the vision of a powerful and self-confident Russia as seductive as ever. At the same time, disparate attitudes and interests are united under the all-embracing rubric of 'pragmatism' – the nearest thing to a state ideology that exists today, a 'one-size-fits-all' device that glosses over numerous underlying contradictions. At home this 'pragmatic' foreign policy is directed at all constituencies – liberal and conservative, 'normal' and 'great power', pro-Western and 'centrist' – while it is similarly eclectic in the face it presents to the world. Depending on the time and the setting, Russia is European, Asian, Eurasian, a regional power, a global player, one of the poles in the emergent multipolar world order. Putin has visited an exceptionally wide range of countries and received a proportionately large number of world leaders.[7] He has striven to inject substance into many previously flagging or neglected relationships; unlike Yeltsin, he cannot be accused of simply going through the motions. For all his supposed Eurocentrism and attention to domestic and regional priorities, Putin's perspective on the world is globalist; there is nothing modest about his conception of Russia's place in the world, even if the packaging and modalities differ greatly from those of the Stalin era.

Crucially, Moscow's conduct of external affairs is more centralized, coordinated and professional than at any time in the recent past. The epithet 'presidential' reflects not only Putin's policy predilections but also his way of managing business. For better or worse, the Russian government speaks with one voice; the institutional anarchy and ad-libbing of the Yeltsin period have given way to a much more disciplined approach. These days the apparent logical inconsistencies in pursuing closer or 'strategic' relations with, say, both the United States and Iran are the product of deliberate policy rather than of bureaucratic chaos and infighting. A long-term vision for Russian foreign policy may still be lacking, but it is difficult to argue that this is the result of the mutually neutralizing impact of rival sectional interests, as was the case under Yeltsin.[8] Significantly, too, much of the calm self-confidence evident in the public Putin has been transferred more generally to the exposition of Russian views on international issues. The insecurities are still there, but Moscow has become better at putting a brave face on its fears and disappointments. The complaints about 'lack of respect' and affronts to Russian 'dignity' so characteristic of foreign policy pronouncements during the 1990s have become a rarity.

But if it is a comparatively straightforward matter to identify certain differences between the foreign policy of the Yeltsin and Putin periods, then the same cannot be said about making sense of the overall character and direction of change. While the *modus operandi* of the administration has altered radically, in all aspects of government and not just external relations, it is not clear whether we are witnessing a seismic shift in Russian foreign policy or merely a sophisticated reinterpretation of standard themes. Does Vladimir Putin represent a new order of thinking for a post-Soviet, post-industrial Russia, or is he mainly a creature of spin who understands the techniques and language of the new age but subscribes to few of its values? Is it appropriate to speak about a 'revolution', albeit presidential rather than democratic, or has much of the dynamism of the past three years been more apparent than real? Are we deceived by Putin's unprepossessing manner, his 'ordinariness', into underestimating the significance of the real changes that are taking place? Or, alternatively, is his relative popularity in the West yet another example of our wishful thinking about Russia?

This book sets out to address these questions by examining several key dimensions of Russian foreign policy-making. The first of these, discussed in Chapter 2, centres on the cultural, ideological and institutional context Putin inherited, and the diverse challenges that confronted him. Russia's president is not an isolated, freak phenomenon. He is a product of his environment, and his instincts and beliefs have been shaped by direct personal experience and upbringing, by the enormous transformations in Russian society and in the world over the past 15 years, and by his predecessors' successes and failures in domestic and foreign policy. Despite his dispassionate exterior, Putin is man not automaton. He is susceptible to emotions and biases, even if he perhaps masks this better than most. To understand his 'inheritance' – historical, psychological, political – is therefore to open a window on why he acts the way he does, sometimes in conflict with the national interest as in the West we might view it.

Context, but of a different kind, is likewise the subject of Chapter 3 on the policy-making environment. One of the perennial curses of Russian government throughout history has been the gulf between the formulation and development of policy on the one hand and its implementation on the other. In the end, the answer to the conundrum 'stasis, evolution or revolution?' in relation to Russian foreign policy lies in the administration's capacity to translate intent into action. It is vital therefore to establish the *kto est kto* ('who's who') and *kto kogo* ('who wins over whom')[9] of decision-making. We know Putin wields the ultimate power, but who has his ear? Who are the influential individual and institutional actors? How is policy developed and realized? Finding answers to these questions helps us to differentiate between real and 'virtual' change, and to make informed judgments about the future course of Russian foreign policy.

Western opinions about Putin tend to fall into two broad categories: those that see him as a modernizer – a latter-day Peter the Great – seeking to drag Russia kicking and screaming into a new epoch of globalization and interdependency; and those that suspect him of remaining a Cold War warrior at heart, albeit with a civilized veneer. Inevitably, many of these judgments are simplistic and founded in false hope or ingrained prejudice rather than sober analysis. At a time when many things are still evolving or remain unclear, it is all the more essential to consider the Putin administration's approach to the substance of foreign policy – the subject of the chapters on 'The Economic Agenda' and 'Security and Geopolitics'.

The first of these, Chapter 4, highlights the greatly increased importance of economic priorities in Russia's external relations, focusing on four themes in particular: the nexus between foreign economic policy and domestic socio-economic reform; Russia's integration into global economic structures and mechanisms; the heightened influence of profit considerations in determining policy; and the conflation between geoeconomics and geopolitics. More generally, this chapter assesses how far Russian foreign policy has moved in an 'economizing' direction, and considers the prospects for the emergence of a more 'normal', more functionally balanced, approach to international affairs.

Chapter 5 makes the case that security and geopolitical priorities have retained their primacy on the Putin external agenda, notwithstanding the growing significance of economic interests. For the most part the Russian establishment continues to view foreign relations principally through the prism of national security. At the same time, there has been a considerable evolution in thinking about basic strategic constructs – zero-sum, balance of power, spheres of influence – as well as in relation to concrete threat perceptions and interests such as international terrorism, issues of geopolitical disadvantage, strategic stability, and conflict resolution. This chapter analyses thinking and policy in an area that is crucial not only in itself, but also as a barometer of the extent to which Russian foreign policy as a whole is changing under Putin. In this context, an especially critical issue concerns the degree to which the Kremlin subscribes to the current positive-sum rhetoric of cooperative security in response to common threats and challenges.

One of the catchphrases of the Putin administration in recent times has been that Russia is an integral part of 'world civilization' and, as such, faces many of the same problems as the West. Conversely, however, old notions of Russia's individuality, its *spetsifika* (or 'special-ness'), have proved highly resilient. Chapter 6, 'Identity, Values and Civilization', looks at the whole question of civilizational convergence and association. It is obvious that Russia under Putin wishes to develop better and more substantive relations with the West. But does it really picture itself as part of this world, living according to the values and mores of Western humanism? Or is it the case that 'civilization', like 'democracy' and 'the civil society', is one of those handy labels that serves to justify the otherwise inexcusable? Can we speak of a rapprochement with the West in the fullest sense, or will there continue to be a gulf in moral and philosophical perceptions, one that will prevent Russia from becoming a fully-fledged member of a wider, Western-centred community anytime soon? On a slightly less abstract plane, Putin's purported Eurocentrism has emerged as one of the characteristics distinguishing his foreign policy approach from that of his predecessor. The matter, however, is far from clear. Putin may be European by emotional and intellectual affinity – although this is debatable – but the strategic culture in which he grew up is one that has always taken the United States as its basic point of reference. Furthermore, Washington remains the dominant player in the areas of prime policy interest to Moscow: the fight against international terrorism; integration into the global economy; the strategic disarmament agenda. The question arises, then, as to whether Putin has managed to reconcile the civilizational and strategic dimensions in Russian foreign policy thinking and, if so, how.

The final chapter considers the '11 September effect'. In the West it has become official wisdom that the events of Black Tuesday marked the beginning of a new era in global politics. The world, it is said, 'will never be the same'. But opinion in Russia on this point is less categorical and more cynical. For many, 11 September and its aftermath did not so much establish a new set of realities as confirm old truths, in particular America's domination of international affairs and its propensity to throw its weight around. And even those who believe that Moscow now has a golden opportunity to recast its relationship with the West fear the moment could be lost unless Putin acts decisively to free Russian foreign policy from its ideological and conceptual shackles. Consequently, despite some promising signs, the jury is still very much out on the prospects for 'partnership'. How committed is Putin to this goal, or is his interpretation of partnership limited to a narrow materialism and tactical opportunism? And, assuming he has made a 'strategic choice' towards the West,[10] does he – for all his political mastery – have the wherewithal to achieve a transformation against the dead weight of decades of strategic and political tradition? Compared by some commentators to Gorbachev, will Putin share Gorbachev's fate of political frustration and, eventually, demise?

Some Western politicians and commentators, disillusioned by a decade of under-achievement in Russia, have sought to minimize its importance in the world.[11] Other observers, equally misguided, reiterate the tired old cliché about Russia's 'indispensability'. In these fluid and uncertain times, when image is so often confused for substance, it is therefore all the more critical to retain a sense of proportion. On the one hand, few would pretend that Russia is a great power in the same way that the Soviet Union was a global force. The extent of its political, strategic and economic decline has been such as to remove all reasonable doubt. But neither is it a post-Soviet version of 'Upper Volta with rockets' – the somewhat silly phrase coined during the 'stagnation' (*zastoi*) period of the 1970s and recently revived.[12] Many of the features that made the Soviet Union what it was remain relevant today. With its vast geographical extent adjoining several of the world's most unstable regions, its position as the second nuclear weapons power, as one of five permanent members of the UN Security Council, and as a major exporter of energy and natural resources, Russia merits our continuing attention. At the same time, it is undergoing an immense transformation that challenges many long-held preconceptions. While we may not approve of some of the changes, the bottom line is that Russia is a very different country to the one that existed a little over ten years ago. This combination of historical constants and rapid – and volatile – change takes the subject of Putin and his management of foreign policy well beyond the confines of idle intellectual discourse. However one assesses the record of the past few years, Russia *matters*, almost in spite of itself. To understand how it views and interacts with the contemporary world is therefore a task of the very first importance, and one that we underestimate at our cost.

2

The inheritance

It is a peculiar characteristic of politicians everywhere that they will often strive for office, no matter how difficult the circumstances and how onerous the responsibilities they take on in achieving their objective. Some justify this seemingly perverse behaviour by referring to a deep-felt sense of patriotic duty, coming to the aid of the nation in its time of need. Others are motivated more by naked personal ambition or a sense of individual destiny. In Russia, a third category comes to mind: those who have power thrust upon them and, finding the experience not unpleasant, decide to make the most of a good thing. As 'accidental' rulers they benefit from low expectation levels; their contemporaries tend to dismiss them as short-term appointments and/ or as manipulatable figures hostage to the play of special interests. Since they come to office when the affairs of state appear more than usually unmanageable, they are not seen to threaten established patterns of political behaviour; it is assumed they will be too vulnerable and preoccupied with everyday priorities to attempt far-reaching change.

This was the situation facing Vladimir Putin upon his selection as Boris Yeltsin's heir-apparent in September 1999. Although he was not quite the novice depicted in the Russian and Western media, his curriculum vitae did not conform to the usual one of Soviet and Russian leaders. Gorbachev and Yeltsin, for example, were established political figures by the time they came to the Kremlin, and their rise to the top had been logical and well documented. Both had been Communist Party First Secretaries of their respective regions – in Yeltsin's case also of Moscow – and were intimately involved with the Politburo, the supreme policy-making body of the Soviet Union. Yeltsin had also been President of the Russian Soviet Federated Socialist Republic (RSFSR). Compare this to Putin's credentials: a reasonably good KGB career, including a posting in East Germany; Deputy Mayor of St Petersburg with responsibility for the city's foreign relations; and, at the tail-end of the Yeltsin presidency, Head of the Federal Security Service (*Federalnaya sluzhba bezopasnosti* – FSB) and Secretary of the Presidential Security Council. The relative modesty of Putin's credentials was accentuated by the near farcical circumstances of his appointment as prime minister. In the 18 months between March 1998 and September 1999, five different men – Viktor Chernomyrdin, Sergei Kiriyenko, Yevgenii Primakov, Sergei Stepashin, and finally Putin himself – filled the position, succeeding each other at ever diminishing intervals.[1] By the time Putin became head of government, Yeltsin, his regime, and the office of prime minister itself had become a laughing-stock. Putin, portrayed as the most nondescript of nonentities, appeared to many as Yeltsin's last desperate attempt to stave off political and personal disgrace.[2]

At the end of the 1990s Russia found itself in a state of profound crisis. Although the socio-economic consequences of the August 1998 financial crash proved to be less catastrophic than had first seemed likely,[3] the land-scape revealed a society riven by fundamental cleavages, chronic decay and a collective lack of self-confidence. Russia, while not yet a 'failed state' in the classical sense, certainly looked to be heading that way. The extent of its weakness was manifest in four areas in particular: (i) the search for a post-Soviet identity and sense of purpose; (ii) a dysfunctional political system; (iii) rampant corruption; and (iv) in the handling of concrete policy priorities. For most of the decade attention, in Russia and abroad, focused principally on the domestic dimension of these issues. Thus, much of the debate over identity centred on polarized conceptions of the type of society Russia should aspire to create following the Soviet demise. The political struggle was reflected in the enduring contest between the executive and the legislature, dramatized most spectacularly in the October 1993 battle for control of the White House.[4] Corruption showed itself in innumerable shady financial dealings – such as the fire-sales of formerly state-owned enterprises for knock-down prices (the so-called 'sham privatization')[5] – as well as more routinely in daily life where great and small alike exploited the system's lacunae to enrich themselves or simply to survive. Finally, the Yeltsin years were a time of frequent and high-profile policy failures. Russia struggled along the path towards democratization, a market economy and a civil society, but in haphazard and often self-destructive fashion.

This chapter relates the tale of the less publicized foreign policy dimen-sion of these problems and how they established a context for the evolution of a distinctly Putin approach to Russia's relations with the outside world. Identity and self-perception, then, become issues not so much about societal development but about Russia's place in the post-Cold War international environment. Similarly, the workings of a dysfunctional political system are relevant here not for what they tell us about the evident shortcomings of the post-Soviet polity, but more directly because of their paralysing impact on policy-making in external relations. Corruption in the foreign policy sphere is not about theft or dubious transactions, but refers to an overall venal mind-set that ensured the primacy of sectional agendas over any larger conception of the national interest. And the Yeltsin administration's management of specific international issues concerns us because of its implications for the state of play in Russia's relations with key countries, regions and institutions on the eve of Putin's assumption of power. The common denominator binding these disparate aspects is that in each of them the challenges facing Russia's new president appeared truly daunting, the tools for addressing them distressingly inadequate, and the domestic and international climate unpromising in the extreme.

And yet, in the face of seemingly insuperable odds, the Putin regime has been able to pull off a modern-day alchemist's trick, succeeding within a very short space of time in re-establishing Russian foreign policy on a new, self-confident footing, and transforming multiple poisoned chalices into surprisingly solid foundations of power and policy. In place of the former bitter conflict of identities and ideologies, there is a broad church consensus – imperfect to be sure, but nevertheless workable; in lieu of ongoing struggles between executive and legislature, the political climate is one of stability and cooperation; whereas post-Soviet governance used to be mainly characterized by chaotic dealings between openly competing institutions and agencies, the bureaucratic atmosphere is now one of calm and relative compliance; and whereas the main features of the Kremlin's handling of concrete priorities were inconsistency and lack of balance and perspective, this now exudes an underlying common sense and level-headedness. It is testament to the remarkable conversion that has occurred that Russian foreign policy, formerly notable for its 'surprises' and shock value, has become almost 'boringly normal'.

Identity and self-perception

During the first post-Soviet decade, conceptions of Russian identity revolved around two key questions. The first was that of civilizational location. Where did Russia belong, physically, historically, culturally? The second related to its place in the post-Cold War world. Granted that it was now a very different country, what sort of role should Russia seek to play, taking into account the co-existence of old constants and radically changed realities? Such open-ended questions would have been controversial in any emergent nation. In Russia, however, they acquired an extra edge in the circumstances of the USSR's sudden collapse from a position of apparent invulnerability. The sense of national disorientation was palpable, provoking sharply contradictory emotions among the elite and population at large – bewilderment, anger, embarrassment, humiliation, relief, optimism. At the same time, the destruction of so many 'givens' offered something of an open canvas. Within fairly generous parameters, identity could be whatever one wanted to make of it. The downside was that the multiplicity of possible identities exacerbated the potential for discord. In such a hothouse atmosphere, the likelihood of consensus was slight.

Of course, there was nothing new about discussions of identity. Since the time of Peter the Great the political class had been engaged in an intense debate about Russia's place and mission in the world. Initially, this had centred on whether it should look to develop into a strong and prosperous nation on the basis of its own, specifically Russian values, or, alternatively, whether this could only be done with the assistance of Western technological and intellectual expertise. The corollary of such polarized perspectives was the emergence of very different ideas about Russia's civilizational location. Proponents of the innate superiority of 'native' values stressed the 'uniqueness' of the Russian situation, its *spetsifika*, with its own rules and characteristics. Believers in the utility of the Western experience, on the other hand, identified Russia as an inalienable part of a common European civilization. This clash of self-perceptions reached its height in the middle of the 19th century with the division between Slavophiles and Westernizers, one that extended well beyond intellectual discourse to materially influencing contrasting approaches to government in the tumultuous decades preceding the Russian Revolution.

With the advent of communist rule and the rise of the Soviet Union as a world power, new conceptions entered the melting-pot. The issue of national identity was no longer confined to one of regional association (or not) with Europe, but acquired a global dimension. Although Russia had been an empire since at least the 18th century, it was not until the Soviet period that the idea of a universalist approach to the world prevailed. Originally derived from purist notions of a communist 'world revolution', this universalism became increasingly less ideological and more nationalistic in the course of the 20th century. It became accepted wisdom that Moscow's vision could not be limited to any one region, but must involve the pursuit of foreign policy on many fronts – as was the case with other global powers such as the United States, Britain and France. By the time of the Soviet collapse, the world-view of the larger part of the ruling class had become grounded in a strategic Eurasianism that argued that Russia transcended continental boundaries to absorb multiple and mutually reinforcing identities: at once Slavic, European, Asian, Eurasian, imperial and global.

Events in the post-Soviet decade undermined many of these 'truths', but did not destroy them. And it was unrealistic to expect that they could have done so. In the first place, the elite had been brought up with a globalist world-view, and to assume that Russian foreign policy would always be 'multi-vectored'.[6] Given this had been the case for over half a century, it was asking a lot for it to jettison this mindset out of hand. Second, the country's domestic and international decline had been so precipitous that there was a natural tendency to deny reality. Instinctively, the political class felt the need to cling on to something. Even if most people understood that the bipolar world had disappeared for good, they were unwilling to accept that Russia had, virtually overnight, been relegated to the ranks of just another regional power. As a result, what became known as *derzhavnost* ('great power-ness') – based on the assumption that Russia had been, was and would always be a 'great power' (*velikaya derzhava*) – emerged as one of the most popular foreign policy ideologies of the Yeltsin period. In keeping with this belief, it followed that Russia was, in spite of any 'temporary difficulties',[7] a transcontinental entity: neither exclusively Slavic, European or Asian, but Eurasian and global. This mindset was reinforced by a powerful imperial syndrome. The disintegration of the Soviet empire into 15 sovereign republics provoked an elite reaction similar to that engendered by the decline of Russia's international position more generally: an upsetting actual state of affairs was 'counterbalanced' by a refusal to believe that all had been lost. Although this imperial syndrome did not envisage the physical recovery of lost lands, it manifested itself in an enduring conviction that the former Soviet Union (FSU) remained part of Moscow's 'sphere of influence'.

At the same time, the Yeltsin administration attempted to convert a negative – Russia's fall from strategic eminence – into a positive through close engagement with the West. Convinced that the fate of the country and the regime itself depended on Western political and economic support, it sought to present Russia in a cooperative light as a vital strategic partner of the West and, more broadly, as a constructive member of the international community, partaking in common values and interests. In this way, a redefined Russia would retain its status and influence as a great power, but on an altogether different basis. In place of the fear that had underpinned the international 'respect' of the past, a new attitude towards it would arise, welcoming its like-mindedness and positive contribution to resolving a range of global problems. Nevertheless, for many so-called 'liberals' or Westernizers the ultimate goal differed little from that of the *derzhavniki* and quasi-imperialists. Russia would remain a great power, one way or another, and other countries, including the most powerful, should continue to treat it as such.[8]

The problem, however, was that during the 1990s the gap between Russian expectations – of all ideological types – and realities widened at an alarming rate. It soon became clear that other powers, foremost among them the United States, would not accord Moscow the status and role it felt it deserved. World leaders regularly pronounced on Russia's importance in global affairs, but in practice the latter's concerns were seen to count for little. Early hopes of a post-Cold War bipolar condominium with America were exposed as far-fetched, and the limits of Russia's influence soon became evident – in the Balkans, over NATO enlargement, in the Middle East, and even in its supposed backyard, the FSU.

The Yeltsin administration responded to these setbacks in increasingly desperate and angry fashion. It complained bitterly about its marginalization from international decision-making and the West's failure to consult,[9] and insisted that Russia remained a great power that would not sit idly by while others ignored its interests. However, its dependence on Western assistance and its inability to influence proceedings meant that such claims were not credible, and the disjunction between rhetoric and reality assumed embarrassing proportions. Abroad, Yeltsin's Russia acquired the reputation of a has-been with a negative, anachronistic attitude towards the world, while at home an increasing band of critics found plentiful ammunition to support their accusations of administration incompetence and impotence. Advocates of a liberal foreign policy agenda lamented the inconstancy in Moscow's approach towards the West, one that seemed to fluctuate randomly between cooperation and confrontation. Others spoke instead of 'national humiliation', demanded that the government pursue a more geographically 'balanced' approach based on the resolute defence of Russia's 'national interests', and called for the adoption of 'counter-measures' against 'hostile' Western actions such as the eastwards expansion of NATO.[10]

In a fraught political atmosphere, the civilizational dimension acted to fuel already powerful animosities over policy. For many, pursuit of the liberal foreign policy agenda signalled not only a belief in the utility of, say, accession to international economic and financial institutions, but also a wider commitment to a particular choice of identity – Russia as an intrinsic part of European, that is Western, civilization. Conversely, regime attempts to 'diversify' Moscow's foreign policy approach – a commendable strategy in itself – were motivated by more than a desire to finalize the 4,000 km common border with China or stabilize the security environment in Northeast Asia. The 'strategic partnership' with Beijing was, for key figures in the Yeltsin administration, primarily important in order to 'counterbalance' American 'hegemonism' and thereby ensure a greater status and influence for Moscow than would have been possible had it tried to achieve this on its own. Foreign

Minister Primakov, the architect of a 'multipolar' foreign policy under Yeltsin, was clear about its essential rationale: only in this way would Russia receive its due as a Eurasian, global power, and be able to protect its strategic and other interests.[11] At a more subliminal level, the anti-Westernism prevalent in some circles extended to a wider, quasi-philosophical rejection of Western values in favour of the 'Russian way' – a recast version of the 19th-century Slavophile-Westernizer debate, only this time in a more volatile domestic and external environment.

The existence of conflicting conceptions of national identity and purpose made for incoherence and disarray. By a cruel trick of fate, the country of multiple identities appeared to metamorphose into a nation of no particular identity: not European, nor Asian, nor even Eurasian, and certainly not global; equally, not empire, nor great power, nor normal nation-state. The mixture of frustration, resentment, and feelings of dependency translated into a wildly erratic approach to Russia's foreign relations. In contrast to the Soviet era when the issue of identity had supplied a focal point for consensus, under Yeltsin it acted in precisely the opposite way, exacerbating and 'legitimizing' bitter rivalries. It seemed that the only point of agreement was that Russia's niche in the post-Cold War world remained as distant as ever.

This, then, was the conundrum facing Putin on his accession: how to transform the discussion of identity into a unifying force in society, while ensuring a plausible concordance between ambitious self-perceptions and uncomfortable realities. It is a tribute to his political skills, as well as good luck, that he has managed to achieve a balance between what, on the face of things, are incompatible objectives. A number of societal and personal factors have contributed to this turnaround. The first was the exhaustion of the political class at the end of the 1990s. Somewhat analogous to the situation in the West where a growing Russia-fatigue became evident, the ups and downs in the domestic struggles of the time took a heavy toll on its protagonists. By the end of the decade, many in the political elite were looking for a respite during which they might hope to consolidate their gains or lick their wounds. In the circumstances, few saw much mileage in pursuing the ideological and civilizational arguments that had been such a feature of the Yeltsin era. Relatedly, the retirement of a figure on which so much political spite had been concentrated removed, almost at a stroke, much of the intensity surrounding Russia's present and future identity. Depersonalization of the debate brought with it a large degree of neutralization.

That said, these trumps could have been jeopardized by a successor with a different character and background. For example, it is probable that had Yevgenii Primakov succeeded Yeltsin – as seemed likely in the autumn of 1999 – then the debate over civilizational choice would have been reinvigorated

15

with predictable results. Putin's somewhat anonymous background, referred to earlier, was crucial in this respect because it allowed him to begin with a fairly clean slate. Moreover, such history as he did possess was nicely balanced in terms of appealing to a wide spectrum of political opinion. He had impeccable European (or Westernizing) credentials from having served as Anatolii Sobchak's deputy in a liberal St Petersburg city hall. At the same time, as a career KGB officer he could hardly be accused of being soft on the West, especially given that he had returned to the security apparatus after his St Petersburg period. In short, Putin could appeal to very contrasting perceptions of Russian identity – and be credible. To an extent unimaginable in the case of Yeltsin, assuming the latter had been so inclined, he had the opportunity to develop a synthesized vision of Russia's place and role in the world, incorporating elements from different ideological strands. And, in doing so, he could in some measure restore the consensus on such questions not witnessed since the Soviet period.

From the outset, Putin demonstrated a healthy appreciation of his position – something for which his education and bureaucratic training had prepared him well. It is a curiosity of 20th-century Russian history that the security apparatus has, from time to time, supplied leaders of reformist bent. Felix Dzerzhinsky, the head of the original Soviet secret service, the Cheka, was one of the most prominent figures in the New Economic Policy (NEP) under Lenin, while much later Yurii Andropov, head of the KGB for 15 years and infamous for his role as Soviet Ambassador in Budapest during the crushing of the 1956 Hungarian uprising, embarked as General Secretary on decentralizing and liberalizing economic reforms while smoothing the way for Gorbachev's political ascent.[12]

Putin, with his mixture of semi-authoritarian and reformist urges, is far from unrepresentative of his security and intelligence milieu. On the one hand, he was brought up in a strong spirit of law and order, and of patriotism and conviction in his country's essential 'greatness'. On the other hand, he enjoyed good access, by Soviet standards, to the outside world. As an external intelligence officer, and particularly while serving in East Germany in a dynamic period (1985–90), he could hardly avoid noticing the widening economic, technological and strategic gap with the West, and drawing appropriate conclusions. Unlike someone from the military establishment – a much more closed part of society – or his contemporaries climbing their way up the Soviet Communist Party hierarchy, he developed a first-hand appreciation of the growing disjunction between the virtual world of communist mythology and the grim realities of Soviet life and the nation's declining capabilities.[13] This inculcated in him a belief in the need for managed change, a middle way between the systemic complacency and graft of the

Brezhnev-generation *nomenklatura* (or elite) and the anarchy of the late Gorbachev and Yeltsin years. Translated in terms of identity, this meant absorbing many of the lessons of the Western experience – including that a sound economic foundation is a prerequisite of military power and international influence – while remaining sceptical about many of its underpinning values.[14] This dichotomy appears to have been reinforced by the triumphs and reversals of his St Petersburg government experience. For a time, he breathed the heady air of a reformist city administration, one strongly committed to engagement with the West. But by 1996 corruption scandals surrounding Sobchak and the latter's defeat in the mayoral elections reinforced Putin's dislike of the Moscow-based special interests so closely associated with a freewheeling pro-Westernism.

It is largely in response to this mix of political circumstances and personal inclinations that Putin has embraced virtually every conceivable type of national identity, but in flexible and undogmatic fashion. He has been especially careful to apply identity according to context and moment. Having early on announced his conviction that Russia was first and foremost a European nation,[15] Putin has proceeded to reiterate this during his frequent trips to Europe as well as more generally in discussions on European security and economic integration. So convincing has this 'pro-European' campaign been that many commentators have argued that the principal feature of his conduct of foreign policy is its Eurocentrism, in contrast to the America-centrism of his predecessor. But Putin has also been very successful in tapping into other conceptions of national identity. For example, Moscow's approach to the FSU is far more activist these days: the number of bilateral and multilateral meetings with regional leaders has multiplied, while the content of these interactions is more focused and productive than before. Putin has assuaged those in Russia resentful of the independence (and 'ingratitude') of the former Soviet republics, yet has refrained for the most part from quasi-imperialist ventures that might lose valuable support from liberals at home and in the West.[16] Globally, he has largely eschewed the tendentious rhetoric of 'multipolarity' while pursuing a more 'multi-vectored' foreign policy in practice. For all his alleged Eurocentrism, it has been Putin who has concluded friendship and cooperation agreements with China and North Korea, given new impetus to relations with India, and increased Russian involvement in Asia-Pacific regional structures such as APEC (Asia-Pacific Economic Cooperation), the ARF (the ASEAN Regional Forum) and the Shanghai Cooperation Organization (SCO).

As a result of this multifaceted approach, he has managed to restore credibility to Russia's international position – and mostly in a non-threatening way. He does not go on interminably about its 'rights' as a 'great power', and he rarely complains when the West is seen to pursue policies hostile to Russian interests. In this connection, his calm reaction to Washington's decision to withdraw from the 1972 Anti-Ballistic Missile Defense (ABM) Treaty was instructive. Describing the decision as a 'mistake', he noted nevertheless that the government had been prepared for this eventuality and that, in any case, American plans to develop a ballistic missile defence system did not threaten Russia's power of deterrence.[17] By avoiding overly committal language about Russian 'greatness', Putin has relieved much of the pressure on the administration to demonstrate this on the ground. Expectations all round have been lowered, with Moscow working instead to realize more accessible goals. The guiding principle of a deliberate policy in expectation management has been that it is better to aim (relatively) low and achieve, than reach for the sky and miss by a mile – as was often the case under Yeltsin. None of this is to suggest that a consensus over national identity has emerged, but at least the issue is no longer one that is tearing the elite apart. Many Russians continue to harbour strong anti-Western sentiments, but these days talk of government impotence and 'national humiliation' is sporadic and half-hearted.

The political context

It is a truism that foreign policy in any country cannot be viewed outside its domestic political context. However, in few countries has the fusion between the two been so intimate as in post-Soviet Russia. In the 1990s the conduct of Russia's international relations often became a mere extension of the domestic struggle, with the competition for power between the executive and the legislature creating a highly fractious setting for the foreign policy debate. The Dumas of that era, dominated by the Communists and their allies, took every opportunity to undermine a president who stood for everything they abhorred – and who reciprocated their hate cordially. In such a hostile climate there was no prospect of a foreign policy consensus, even on issues, like START-2 ratification, where there was little substantive disagreement.[18] Contrary to conventional wisdom, Russian foreign policy became increasingly politicized, as the President's personal fortunes became inextricably entwined with Western assistance and a so-called pro-Western line. The perception grew that the management of Moscow's relations with the outside world was directed not to the service of wider societal goals such as democratization, the transition to a market economy and the development of a civil society, but to narrow political ends, namely the preservation of the Yeltsin regime. As a consequence, many in the elite came to view the West as an accomplice in the domestic struggle, instead of as a partner in post-Cold War international security cooperation.

The presence of such a backdrop affected foreign policy-making in several ways. First, the public became more engaged in the debate over foreign policy as a result of the democratization that began in the later Gorbachev period. This participation, though indirect, influenced the presentation and dynamics of policy-making. Popular attention may have focused overwhelmingly on domestic issues such as falling living standards, but the overall climate of uncertainty – accentuated at election time – could not help but constrain the conduct of external relations as well. Typically, the administration's response to pressure, real or imagined, was to revert to a conservative and often demagogic approach that highlighted themes such as Russia's 'great power' status, the pursuit of a 'national interests' foreign policy, and criticisms of Western actions. On a more tangible level, electoral setbacks arising from domestic dissatisfaction had adverse consequences for the liberalization of foreign policy. For example, the outcomes of the 1993 and 1995 Duma elections led to the discrediting and removal of the reformist politicians who might have spearheaded a more imaginative response to the challenges of, say, NATO enlargement and conflict resolution in the Balkans. It was indicative of the administration's risk-averse mentality that Yeltsin should have reacted to communist and nationalist gains in the 1995 elections by appointing the 'centrist' Yevgenii Primakov in a (successful) attempt to eliminate foreign policy as an issue in the 1996 presidential campaign.[19]

More generally, the uncertainty of the times undermined Yeltsin's already weak resolve to pursue a consistent external line of any kind. A regime with greater political self-confidence might have been able to insulate foreign policy from the periodic domestic crises that afflict most governments. In post-Soviet Russia, however, the fragmentation of political life and the inability of any single group or sectional interest, including the presidency, to dominate for long militated against the development, let alone implementation, of policy. The situation was aggravated by Yeltsin's penchant for playing off various interests (including within government) against one another – a tactic born of deep personal and political insecurity. At the broad conceptual level, the combination of anarchy and petty politicking resulted in a foreign policy that equivocated between a fragile pro-Westernism and a competitive vision of multipolarity. Meanwhile, on specific issues such as NATO enlargement, conflict resolution in the Balkans and the strategic disarmament agenda (e.g., START-2 ratification), Moscow oscillated between accommodation and confrontation. Throughout this confusion, however, one message emerged clearly: the vulnerability and incapacity of the Yeltsin administration. Few were fooled by the old ruse of 'compensating' for policy weakness and failure at home with an assertive attitude in external relations. On the contrary, the resultant erratic swings only reinforced the general impression of aimlessness and chaos in domestic and foreign policy alike.

Putin's task, then, was a multiple one. First, it was vital to depoliticize the conduct of foreign policy by minimizing its instrumental, party political, aspects. And this required achieving some kind of broader political and societal consensus that might allow issues to be considered on their own merits. Second, he needed to turn the democratization of post-Soviet society to his advantage by enlisting it in support of the government's line. Appealing to the public and not just to the elite was important in ensuring a more reliable base for the conduct of foreign affairs. In this way, even if matters did not always unfold ideally, he would be less vulnerable to the influence and/or pressure of special interests. Third, it was essential to provide discipline and constancy in leadership, but without uniting opposition from quarters either fearful or resentful of the power of a resurgent presidency – in other words, to convey the impression at once of strength *and* collegiality. This meant co-opting diverse political interests by giving them a stake in either selected aspects of external policy and/or in the overall outcome, for example, the image of a self-confident Russia able once again to play the part of a serious global actor.

As with the representation of identity, Putin has been very successful in achieving his aims. It is true that he began with some undoubted political advantages: the freshness of his face and reputation; the public's desire for order and predictability in government; his close association with the successful early stages of the second post-Soviet Chechen war. But Putin has also been determined and skilful enough to make the best of his luck. Most importantly, he has gone out of his way to be politically welcoming. The comparative colourlessness of the current domestic environment in Russia is a tribute principally to his skills of alliance-building. He has come to dominate the political class through stealth and guile, in not dissimilar fashion to Stalin who in the 1920s was able to split his potential rivals by playing on their mutual suspicions while, initially at least, appearing inoffensive.[20] At the same time, Putin has seized on the popular desire for order and 'legality' to secure a wider legitimacy and freedom of manoeuvre. In this connection, his personal animosity towards the financial-industrial interest groups that shaped political proceedings under Yeltsin and the hatred of the public towards the same have coincided nicely. Finally, he has been able to demonstrate that increased central (or 'statist') control translates into dividends for many different constituencies: for supporters of a liberal foreign policy agenda, it offers the promise of increased security and economic integration with the West; for quasi-imperialists, an activist approach in the FSU; and for everyone, an increasingly plausible projection of Russia as a major player in international affairs. In sum, the emergence of a more stable political context has become the closest thing to a positive-sum game in the post-Soviet period. Certain individuals and group interests may not win as big as they did under Yeltsin, but only the most recalcitrant, outspoken or unpopular actually lose out. Taking into account the natural cravenness and venality of the political elite, this ensures the Putin regime a significant safety margin if and when things go wrong in Russia's external relations. Just as critically, it provides the regime with the political space to take longer-term decisions about strategic orientation.

The institutional context

One of the most striking characteristics of post-Soviet foreign policy has been the proliferation of individual and institutional actors. In Soviet times, the duopoly of the Ministry of Foreign Affairs (MFA) and Communist Party Central Committee had supplied a stable if unimaginative basis for decision-making. But with the end of the USSR, and the accompanying democratization and marketization of society, these institutional certainties evaporated. Although the end of Party control meant that in nominal terms the primacy of the Foreign Ministry was now unchallenged, in practice the reverse was true. It appeared that anyone could, if they wished, play some part in foreign policy. And they were certainly not averse to seizing the opportunity. In much the same way that sectional groups exploited the chaos of domestic political and economic transition to promote their private interests, so they sought to do the same in the sphere of external affairs. Over the course of the decade, the number of foreign policy actors grew steadily, as did the range of competing policy agendas. Even within government, the MFA found itself regularly contradicted or, worse still, ignored by other ministries and agencies. Among the most persistent of these 'offenders' were the Ministry of Defence (MOD), the Ministry of Atomic Energy (MINA-TOM), the Ministry of Economic Development and Trade (MEDT), and the Presidential Administration apparatus (the foreign policy adviser, the Security Council). And although these bureaucratic actors involved them-selves only selectively – the MOD in policy towards the FSU and the Balkans, MINATOM in exports of dual technology to Iran, the Trade Ministry over Caspian Sea energy projects, the Presidential Administration in the relationship with Japan – the cumulative outcome was a comprehensive usurpation of the MFA's management of foreign policy. Furthermore, new interests entered the scene: the Duma with its four key external policy committees (international affairs, defence, geopolitics, security); the natural monopolies, in particular Gazprom and Lukoil; and the military-industrial complex, represented most visibly by Rosvooruzhenie, the state arms export body.

More critical still than the diminution of the MFA's importance was that no clear successor emerged to take over its former coordinating role. Early hopes that the Security Council might do so were soon belied, while President Yeltsin himself was never able to make good on the official cliché that Russian foreign policy was 'presidential' in character. Instead, the conduct of external relations became characterized by a collective indiscipline. Various agencies failed to consult, bickered publicly, issued conflicting statements, and acted independently. Even on issues where there was substantial agreement in principle – the relationship with China, NATO enlargement, the alliance's military interventions over Bosnia and Kosovo – the Russian government was only rarely able to maintain a unified policy stance. This state of affairs worsened steadily during Yeltsin's second term (1996-9), with Kremlin 'control' being typified by wild lurches in policy. Increasingly, the President's failing health, his political gamesmanship and his growing indifference to policy detail conveyed the impression of the inmates running the asylum.

By the time Yeltsin retired, it seemed matters could scarcely deteriorate any further – an impression that proved to Putin's advantage. Just as public and elite alike craved a measure of political normality, so there was strong demand for a return to professionalism in governance in general, and in the conduct of foreign relations specifically. The image of a rudderless Russia was a disturbing one, while the disorder (*bezporyadok*) in decision-making was anathema to a generation that had long taken for granted that there would be one state foreign policy only. As a result, the need for some semblance of a coordinated, centralized approach to the outside world became ever more compelling, with even rival sectional interests seeking a greater predictability and continuity. A new president, one less partial to the politics of an antagonistic divide-and-rule, offered the prospect of restoring discipline – not so much as to threaten the power of special interests, but enough so that everyone would know where they stood.

Putin's administrative inexperience at the highest levels made his task here especially challenging. It was one thing for people to acknowledge the need for greater coordination and direction; quite another to accept the consequent constraints on their behaviour from a relative greenhorn. Despite the difficulties, however, Putin has been able to manage this delicate balancing act by attracting the support of vested interests, exploiting the popular mood to impose greater central control and, where necessary, coercing those unwilling to comply. Specifically, he has relied on a narrow but trusted circle of friends and former colleagues among his St Petersburg

KGB and city hall connections, while also giving the old Yeltsin guard – such as Presidential Chief-of-Staff Alexander Voloshin, Foreign Minister Igor Ivanov, former Prime Minister Viktor Chernomyrdin – a stake in the new regime by retaining their services.

Meanwhile, the balance of power in two other key relationships has altered significantly. Putin's convincing popular mandate from the 1999 Duma and 2000 presidential elections has emasculated parliament's ability to materially influence (or obstruct) the Kremlin's conduct of foreign policy.[21] In addition, economic actors and instrumentalities are now beholden to the executive rather than the other way round. Although big business continues to influence the handling of the economic agenda (see Chapter 3), there is no doubt about who is master and who is subordinate. The harsh treatment meted out to tycoons Boris Berezovsky and Vladimir Gusinsky, and to regional governors such as former Vice-President Alexander Rutskoi, has had a chastening effect on the elite in general. While the fall of such high-profile figures had nothing to do with foreign policy as such,[22] the message is clear and applicable everywhere: toe the line or face the consequences. The new president's methods of consolidating his authority may have been undemonstrative for the most part, but they are no less effective for all that.

Finally, Putin has been able to maintain control over various foreign policy actors because of his capacity, noted in Chapter 1, to get across the detail of issues. This is not to subscribe to the popular myth of him as the all-seeing and all-knowing leader. But there is ample evidence to indicate that he knows sufficient to make the risk of trying to defy or deceive him a foolish one. If the days of government ministries and agencies doing their own thing are not necessarily over, then at least they are now more inclined to observe the proprieties of government discipline.

The foreign policy panorama

The breath of fresh air represented by the public Putin might soon have dissipated had he been unable to point to some concrete foreign policy achievements. Here, he was fortunate in benefiting from the overwhelmingly negative perception of the Yeltsin administration's performance, where there appeared to be almost nothing positive to show for a decade of policy anarchy. 'direction' and vacillating attitudes towards the outside world. Across the political spectrum, from communists and nationalists to 'centrists' and liberals, there was a general consensus that Russia's international standing had hit rock bottom by the end of the 1990s, with the Kremlin's angry but wholly impotent response to the NATO military intervention over Kosovo confirming the magnitude of national decline. A brief survey of the state of play in Moscow's principal areas of geographic and functional interest highlights the depth of the crisis.

America

The relationship with the United States was, at the outset of the post-Cold War era, intended to be the flagship of Russian foreign policy. Yeltsin (and Gorbachev before him) viewed Washington as Moscow's natural partner in the new international politics. The rivalry of the Cold War would give way to a cooperative bipolarity in which both sides would work together as guarantors of global security.[23] At the same time, Yeltsin looked to America to assist Russia's political, economic and social transformation, as well as consolidate his personal hold on power. To some extent this did occur, and the balance-sheet of Russia–USA relations was by no means as negative as many of its critics alleged.

Nevertheless, two facts are incontrovertible: (i) the level of actual achievement fell well short of initial hopes and expectations on both sides; and (ii) the atmosphere of the bilateral relationship was considerably worse at the end of the decade than it was at its beginning. In terms of specifics, too, the picture was grim. In the nuclear field, for example, the quarrel over American strategic missile defence plans (NMD/BMD) and the Russian failure to ratify the START-2 treaty overshadowed positive developments such as the Nunn-Lugar Cooperative Threat Reduction (CTR) program,[24] the 1992 signing of the START-2 agreement, and the denuclearization of Ukraine, Belarus and Kazakhstan. In conflict resolution, the American-dominated NATO operations against Slobodan Milosevic in 1999 and, earlier, in the Bosnian conflict were memorable for all the wrong reasons, while joint Russia–NATO peacekeeping operations in the Balkans were notable as much for disagreements over command-and-control issues as for the effectiveness of on-the-ground cooperation.[25]

More generally, the nominally 'equal partnership'[26] between the two former superpower rivals became almost absurdly unequal. And while the growing gap between the two was obviously unavoidable, this reality was never a comforting one. The Yeltsin administration seemed incapable of demonstrating any dividends from its relationship with Washington, or of obtaining a *quid pro quo* for inevitable 'losses' or concessions in certain areas. American economic and technological assistance was dismissed as inadequate at best, while the advice of Harvard economists was widely blamed for contributing to the country's socio-economic troubles. Post-Soviet Russia might have become more 'democratic' and 'progressive', but few viewed the benefits in a favourable light. Meanwhile, even liberal observers were fiercely critical of NATO enlargement, the Kosovo operation, American strategic missile defence and Washington's increasing engagement with the newly independent republics of the former Soviet Union.[27] If Russia seemed in many respects a 'failed state', then the Russia–USA relationship became the epitome of a 'failed relationship'.

Western Europe

The verdict was not as drastic in the case of Moscow's interaction with Western European countries and institutions. But this was largely by default, a consequence of the essential Americacentrism of Russian foreign policy.[28] The comparatively minor status of Western Europe meant that, in a manner of speaking, there was less to actively dislike. But here too the scorecard read poorly. Far from making progress towards integration with Europe, Russia appeared more than ever to be a peripheral player, excluded from effective decision-making: neither strong enough to command respect, nor sufficiently like-minded to attract it. Although the picture was not all bad – as the growing volume of trade with the EU testified – there was not much to like either, with even achievements such as the 1997 Founding Act with NATO turning sour as its limitations were exposed by the Kosovo crisis.[29] In the end, the fundamental problem of the Yeltsin administration's European policy became one not so much of 'weakness' and inconstancy, as with the United States, but of neglect.

The former Soviet Union

If the relationship with the United States was seen by many as the greatest foreign policy failure of the Yeltsin period, then Moscow's handling of affairs in the former Soviet space came a close second. Irrespective of political orientation, the elite were unanimous in condemning Russian policy – and with good reason. Moscow failed to develop relations with the FSU states on a post-imperial basis; integration through bilateral (the Russia–Belarus 'Union') and multilateral channels (the Commonwealth of Independent States – CIS) was more nominal than real, with security and especially economic interaction falling away drastically;[30] and Moscow regularly upset the former republics by accusing them of mistreating the Russian diaspora, while doing nothing to support the latter.[31] Ironically, the one success in relation to the FSU – the fact that the extent and intensity of armed conflict in the region turned out to be less than many had originally feared – was more a product of default than of design. Indeed, the cases of Abkhazia, South Ossetia and Transdniestria suggested that Russian political and military involvement often fuelled rather than alleviated conflict. As in many other areas of foreign policy, the approach of the Yeltsin administration towards the FSU turned out to be neither one thing nor the other, with the inevitable outcome being that it failed to satisfy any constituency, liberal, quasi-imperialist, or 'great power'.

Asia

The exception to the general record of failure was the Kremlin's policy towards the Asia-Pacific region. In particular, the rapprochement with China emerged as arguably the finest policy achievement of the Yeltsin administration, while there was also significant improvement in the substance and atmospherics of ties with Tokyo. Other successes included the Shanghai Five agreement on security confidence-building measures along the former Sino-Soviet border, Russian accession to the APEC grouping, and growing participation in the ARF. Yet despite these gains, policy towards Asia was by no means an unqualified success. At decade's end Russia was no closer to being regarded as a primary actor on the continent; the emphasis on multipolarity in the 'strategic partnership' with Beijing suggested that rapprochement was primarily motivated by a desire to 'counterbalance' the United States;[32] hopes in 1997-8 that Moscow and Tokyo might finally resolve their territorial dispute proved premature, leading in turn to a serious loss of momentum in ties between the two; and India's importance narrowed down to three issues – arms sales, nuclear cooperation, and Soviet-era debt. For all the supposed equivalence of East and West in Moscow's world-view, Russian foreign policy continued to assign to Asia an all too evident second-class status.[33]

Middle East

The theme of neglect, apparent in relation to Western Europe and the FSU, repeated itself in other areas as well. Compared to the Soviet era, whole regions of the world effectively vanished from the foreign policy map. This retrenchment was not restricted to logical casualties such as Africa, Latin America and Southeast Asia – which had long been of secondary importance – but also included regions where Moscow's presence had until recently been quite strong, such as the Middle East. Although Russia maintained its formal position as co-sponsor of the Middle East Peace Process (MEPP), its contribution became increasingly negligible, a point noted by Arab leaders.[34] Moreover, when it did engage actively in the region, for example with Iran and Iraq, this often carried adverse consequences for its relationship with the United States, leading on several occasions to public and humiliating defeats.[35]

Eastern Europe

More striking still was the case of Eastern Europe, which had been an integral part of the Soviet empire until 1989. The Kremlin's approach towards the region revealed one of the hallmarks of post-Soviet Russian foreign policy: general passivity punctuated by frenetic bursts of activity in times of crisis. For the most part, Eastern Europe was a backwater, and Moscow devoted minimal resources to recasting relations with the countries of the region. But whenever a high-profile issue cropped up – such as NATO enlargement or Western military responses to developments in the Balkans – then the Kremlin threw itself into the fray, its new-found enthusiasm contrasting markedly with its former indifference. In this connection, a common denominator between the Middle East and Eastern Europe was that administration interest in both regions was fundamentally derivative: only if the West intervened did Russia seek to become involved. The real importance of Eastern Europe was therefore not intrinsic but as a 'stake' in Moscow's broader relationship with the West. Such an instrumentalist approach proved self-defeating in every way. Unwilling to alter the dynamics of interaction with the former Warsaw Pact members, the Yeltsin regime effectively converted the 'loss' of Eastern Europe to the West's principal security body into one of the most potent symbols of a weak and dysfunctional foreign policy.

In sum, on practically every front Russian foreign policy was seen to be in a state of abject retreat. The collective psychosis of defeat was such that few recognized that many so-called 'concessions' were actually beneficial, or that the administration had achieved some important gains. Perceptions often reflected the intrusion of intense personal and political biases rather than a proper understanding of the policy options actually available. Nevertheless, none of this alters the fact that an otherwise fractured political class was united in the conviction that Moscow's conduct of international relations had been almost uniformly disastrous, whether judged in its entirety or in relation to specific priorities. In attempting to satisfy opposing constituencies by offering a range of personas – Russia as a great power, Russia as an integral member of the community of 'civilized' states,[36] Russia as the dominant presence in the former Soviet space – the Yeltsin administration ended up satisfying no one. To liberal Westernizing opinion, Russia developed an undesirable reputation as an obstructive presence in the world, constantly standing on its 'dignity' and demanding 'respect' yet unwilling to contribute positively to the changed global environment. To the *derzhavniki* and quasi-imperialists, on the other hand, the distinguishing feature of the Yeltsin years was the administration's spinelessness that prevented it from defending *any* position effectively, no matter how vital. Meanwhile, the ageing president's increasingly erratic pronouncements[37] heightened the sense of things spiralling out of control. From whichever perspective one looked, the image of a feeble, marginalized and largely bereft nation appeared to encapsulate Russia on the eve of the Putin succession.

So poor was the outlook that almost any successor to Yeltsin would have been regarded as an improvement. Yet the task of sustaining this impression was by no means trivial. Putin faced a dual challenge: first, to effect positive changes in Russia's relations with key countries and international institutions; and, second, to transform its image by convincing a sceptical domestic audience as well as disenchanted interlocutors abroad that it was a serious international actor. It is testament to his considerable skills that he has achieved a degree of success that few could have anticipated. Long before the label 'sea-change' began to be applied to Russian foreign policy post-11 September,[38] its atmosphere changed radically. Beginning with the relationship with the West, this moved from an interaction imbued with a culture of mutual disappointment to one offering real hope. Although limited at first by the reluctance of the incoming Bush administration to engage with Russia,[39] Moscow's approach has increasingly reflected a desire for positive engagement wherever possible, including a much more mature attitude towards differences in policy and perception. Political and economic ties with the major European powers have become more substantive and the relationship with Washington has acquired new warmth, while cooperation with NATO has resumed after the extended hiatus provoked by the Kosovo crisis. Crucially, too, neither the Russian political class nor the public has interpreted these changes as signs of irretrievable weakness. Although there has been some low-level grumbling, Putin has been able to neutralize criticisms of his approach not only by virtue of his political authority, but also by demonstrating a simultaneous strengthening of Russian positions in other foreign policy areas. In the FSU, for example, an intensive programme of high-level visits and meetings, a more assertive stance on issues such as CIS debt and Caspian Sea energy development, and an active interest in the welfare of the Russian-speaking populations offer a compelling contrast to the passivity of the past. And even in the Asia-Pacific, the one region where the Yeltsin administration enjoyed relative success, Putin has produced tangible outcomes – such as the Friendship and Cooperation treaties with Beijing and Pyongyang – that eluded his predecessor.

But in the end, for all the substantive improvements, perhaps the main difference in the foreign policy of the Yeltsin and Putin administrations lies in the packaging and presentation. Previously, this had been one of the more conspicuous weaknesses in the Kremlin's management of international relations. Under Putin, however, public diplomacy has emerged as a definite strength. He has shown the benefits of a more dispassionate approach that conveys an impression of reasonableness, predictability and dignity – qualities notably lacking in Yeltsin (particularly during his second term). Furthermore, Putin has been able to ride out foreign policy setbacks or embarrassments such as Washington's abrogation of the ABM Treaty and the American security presence in Central Asia following 11 September. Part of the secret of his success lies in the (slightly) greater realism of an elite whose political and policy expectations are somewhat reduced these days. Thus, it was obvious from mid-1999 that Washington would develop a strategic missile defence system regardless of Russian objections, while 11 September created an exceptional set of circumstances that outweighed conventional geopolitical logic. But the real key to Putin's Teflon-like qualities is that he has known 'how to lose' or, more accurately, to convert necessity into a virtue; he has yet to fight a battle he cannot win. It is typical of his *modus operandi* that he dismissed ABM abrogation as a 'mistake' and not an insult, let alone a disaster, while taking an upbeat view of the American presence in Central Asia in the context of the war against international terrorism, linking it to the Russian military campaign in Chechnya.[40] The contrast with Yeltsin's handling of NATO enlargement and the Kosovo crisis – in which a vociferous but ineffectual opposition served only to highlight Russian weakness – could scarcely be more pronounced.

Conclusion

The genesis of Putin's foreign policy lies in the duality of his inheritance. On the one hand, he faced enormous challenges in developing a consensual vision of national identity, reforming a shambolic political system, restoring order in government and arresting the precipitous decline in Russia's international position. He appeared also to have few helpers in addressing these problems. A disillusioned public, a deeply corrupt elite, mounting Russia-fatigue abroad – these hardly seemed the building blocks of success. On the other hand, the accumulation of so many negatives opened up the opportunity for Putin, or someone like him, to make his mark. The widespread perception that matters had deteriorated so badly on virtually every front meant that, in a sense, there was only one way things could go.

Here, Putin's relative anonymity and inexperience at the top levels of government were more assets than hindrances. Unlike the 'usual suspects' he was not tainted by association with the Moscow-based power cliques or the policy failures of the Yeltsin period, and his service in the KGB's foreign intelligence arm (as opposed to its hated internal apparatus) and location in St Petersburg gave him a cleanskin image – a potential saviour in contrast to the general cess of politics. His lack of a high-profile constituency also meant that, initially at least, he was not perceived as a threat. Although in subsequent months media attention turned to the so-called St Petersburg KGB group, their influence at the time of Putin's appointment as president-designate was the subject of only passing comment. It is symptomatic of the complacent attitude of the power elites then that the tycoon Boris Bere-zovsky – now Putin's bitterest critic – welcomed his appointment as prime minister and worked hard to secure his election as president. In other words, his apparent weakness made him attractive – in contrast to personalities like former Prime Minister Primakov who many, including Yeltsin himself,[41] feared would seek to upset the established order of things. The common assumption was that Putin would offer a more presentable, more 'rational' approach, greater predictability, perhaps even make a few policy adjustments here and there – but do nothing dramatic.

So the legacy left to him was not as unpromising as it first looked. And in foreign policy the scope for visible improvement was even greater than in the domestic sphere. For all the Yeltsin administration's incompetent manage-ment, its biggest 'sin' was something far beyond anyone's capacity to influence: the gulf between a resurgent West and a Russia plummeting from the heights of superpower bipolarity. In wearing the consequences of decades of unbalanced Soviet economic development that were bound, eventually, to tell on the nation's military and strategic capabilities, the Yeltsin regime suffered principally from guilt by association. As a consequence, Putin did not need to do a great deal to convey the impression of a new era in Russian foreign policy, particularly given the general relief among the elite that Yeltsin – and much of the personal, ideological and political animus of the 1990s – had finally exited the stage. With image continuing to dominate substance in political life, it was almost enough for Putin just to behave in a professional and businesslike manner, and let things take care of themselves.

Yet if he was lucky in more ways than one to have had Yeltsin as his immediate predecessor, there was nothing inevitable about the *extent* of Putin's subsequent foreign policy success. He, too, has had to operate in a climate of unrealistic expectations, in which stereotyped images of Russia as a 'great power', an imperial mentality and inertial Cold War thinking continue to exert a hypnotic influence on much of the establishment. He may have been afforded considerable licence to entrench himself politically and to project a revised image for Russia, but it would be entirely wrong to underestimate the difficulty of his manifold tasks or the skill with which he has approached them. It has been Putin's great achievement – arguably the greatest of his presidency – to make the very best of his mixed inheritance.

3

The policy-making environment

The world of policy-making is rarely as it seems, even in the most liberal and transparent of Western democracies. For all their substantial institutional framework, relative openness of deliberative processes, and considerable grass-roots participation, the fact remains nevertheless that most of the important decisions are made by a tiny group of people. Furthermore, this elite subscribes to a culture of confidentiality that is protective not only of the information it holds but also of the processes through which conclusions are reached. It is not easy to determine who makes policy and how they make it. We can observe certain external phenomena – cabinet meetings, parliamentary proceedings, debates in the media, the electoral process – but we are often left none the wiser as a result of this knowledge.

In post-Soviet Russia, these problems are compounded severalfold. First, the sheer weight of centuries of autocratic governance has meant that there is no experience of transparent decision-making. At various stages in its history, Russia has had institutions bearing a fleeting resemblance to representative government, but without exception their influence has been much more formalistic than real. For over a thousand years, it has been individuals, not institutions, that have mattered.[1] Second, contrary to Western democracies, there has been almost no accountability by the elite to a wider public. In Russia the priority has been to keep the God-like (*vozhd*) figure of the Tsar and later Communist Party General Secretary happy, rather than a population denied – until recently – even the theoretical opportunity to call their rulers to account. As a result, policy-makers have concentrated their energies on court/party intrigues, manoeuvring for favour and position – a habit not at all conducive to open government. Third, the enormous systemic weaknesses, first of Tsarist and then Communist rule, have reinforced the reliance on individuals instead of institutions, and an accompanying tradition of great secretiveness. Frequently, the only way of getting things done was by circumventing the system and resorting to personal contacts and mutual favours.

The purpose of this preamble is to issue something of a disclaimer for what is to follow. In spite of the democratization of Russia over the past 15 years, the overall policy-making environment remains extremely murky. We can identify a growing number of actors and institutions; we can get a look-in on some of the mechanisms of decision-making; and we can from time to time make the link between cause and effect. But who counts, who does what, and how they do it, continue to be difficult questions for which, in many cases, there are either no or only unsatisfactory answers. This is particularly the case in foreign affairs. Because its impact on people's daily lives tends to be indirect at best, there has been little broader level interest in its doings – as reflected in its marginal profile during parliamentary and presidential elections. The truism that policy-making in Russia is an elite preserve is therefore especially applicable here. It is as though the public expects the establishment to run the show by itself, by whatever means the latter deems appropriate. Consequently, we can often make only educated guesses about the processes through which policy is managed and developed.

And yet the issue, hard to grasp as it is, cannot be sidestepped. If we are to make sense of the Putin administration's conduct of international affairs then we need to find some answers to these questions, no matter how rough and tentative. For in the end the viability and sustainability of Moscow's foreign policy course, and of individual policies, depends less on their 'objective' merits than on the alignment of supporters and opponents, their number, and above all their political and institutional weight. As noted in Chapter 1, one of the most crippling defects of Russian governance has been the disjunction between policy formulation and its implementation. There are countless examples of well-intentioned policies falling by the wayside, as bureaucrats and special interests effectively stripped them of all meaningful content. With this in mind, the purpose of the coming pages is threefold: (1) to introduce the players in Russian foreign policy-making, and assess their respective influence; (2) to offer some thoughts on the interplay between different individual and institutional actors, i.e., what passes for the policy process; and (3) to identify the essential characteristics of decision-making in the Putin administration's foreign policy.

A cast of thousands?

Chapter 2 observed that one of the main differences in the conduct of foreign policy between the Soviet and post-Soviet periods has been the explosion in the number of participants. The tight dual control exerted by the Foreign Ministry and the Communist Party Central Committee gave way to far looser arrangements in which an increasing number of parties became involved in various aspects of foreign policy. Although the Putin presidency has witnessed a partial return to institutional order and predictability, the number of actors shows no sign of diminishing – indeed, rather the reverse.[2] At the same time, the importance of these actors varies considerably; some individuals and institutions play a significant role across a wide range of issues, while others have bit (and somewhat forgettable) parts. In order to navigate our way through the confusion, then, it would be useful to begin our review with the major institutional players.

The Ministry of Foreign Affairs (MFA)

Over the past decade it has become increasingly fashionable to disparage the role of the Foreign Ministry. It has been accused – not always unfairly – of being hidebound, negative and incompetent. Perhaps most damningly, many critics characterize it as little more than a post-box, restricted to routine fetching and carrying tasks while others get on with the real business of policy-making.[3] The MFA's stature has also suffered from the unpalatable reputation of Russia's three Foreign Ministers in the post-Soviet period. The first, Andrei Kozyrev, was widely regarded as a limp-wristed, slavishly Westernizing liberal; the second, Yevgenii Primakov, welcomed by some as a centrist figure, was reviled by others who saw him as the arch-representative of Cold War geopolitical values; while the third and current incumbent, Igor Ivanov, although attracting nothing like the opprobrium levelled at his two predecessors, stands dismissed as a competent but colourless civil servant. Although many of these comments have been notable for their unfairness, the underlying point remains: for most observers the Foreign Ministry has fallen from its previous eminence in Soviet times to a second-class status.

In fact, this perception is flawed in several respects. It is one thing to affirm that the MFA's position is frequently (and publicly) overridden these days or that it is not the most important player in a number of foreign policy areas, but it is wrong to extrapolate from these truths that it is a secondary actor on the policy-making map in general. First, the size and breadth of the Foreign Ministry ensures that it cannot help but be influential. It is the one institution in today's Russia that boasts comprehensive coverage across the full gamut of external policy issues. Its expertise – concentrated in literally hundreds of area and functional specialists – is without parallel. No other actor has the resources to begin to address the raft of second-line foreign policy issues, ranging from the Asia-Pacific region, to the Middle East, to Latin America. And even on primary priorities, such as the key relationships with the United States, Western Europe and China, it still represents the main if no longer the only information database. The Foreign Ministry is the embodiment of the axiom that knowledge is power – albeit not the power of former times.

Second, we should not mistake an often negative or oppositional role for a lack of clout. While the MFA is rarely the source of creative ideas on international issues, it can and does exert a significant influence as a 'braking mechanism'.[4] Its innate conservatism taps into the mood of the political class, while also fuelling doubts within the administration. When the latter's resolve is at its highest, as for example over the decision to support the American campaign in Afghanistan after 11 September, this factor is not so significant. But when the issue is less clear-cut, such as in relation to the detail of strategic disarmament negotiations, the development of the political relationship with NATO, or the Russian attitude towards external military action in Iraq, this conservatism can be influential.

Third, the Foreign Ministry is *always there*. Whereas other actors flit across the stage, their star in a brief if showy ascendancy, it by contrast is an everlasting presence. It may be overruled on particular issues, or over foreign policy orientation, but such defeats are rarely decisive. Here, it is as well to recall the experience of the Yeltsin years, when at various times the Security Council, the Ministry of Defence, and the Presidential Administration, were said to have taken over the MFA's primary role in foreign policy. In the end, however, like 'old faithful' it reemerged, bloodied but unbowed. Given this history, it would be foolish to discount an institution that possesses enormous in-built resilience.

Fourth, like other policy institutions the Foreign Ministry is adapting to the changed political and institutional climate under Putin. Generally speaking, this has entailed concentrating on executive rather than advisory functions, such as performing the bureaucratic legwork for the May 2002 agreements with the USA on strategic offensive reductions and with NATO on the establishment of the NATO–Russia Council.[5] At a more administrative level, the MFA's evolution is reflected in the increase in Deputy Foreign Ministers, particularly from the security apparatus,[6] as well as in its close participation in a growing number of interdepartmental policy committees. Once again, we should be careful not to equate unspectacular with insignificant.

The Ministry of Defence (MOD)

The Defence Ministry was in many respects the largest beneficiary of the diversified and anarchic institutional environment of the early post-Soviet period. Previously excluded from foreign policy, it emerged as the primary actor in a number of important areas, most visibly in international conflict resolution in the former Soviet Union and the Balkans where it often acted without reference to the MFA and in conflict with its approach.[7] Under Putin, the MOD as foreign policy actor has experienced mixed fortunes. On the one hand, it remains a leading player in strategic disarmament, where its technical expertise has assured it an equal carriage and status with the MFA in negotiations with the Americans.[8] On the other hand, today's more ordered bureaucratic context has restricted its opportunities for foreign policy free-lancing, in the CIS and elsewhere. It is also noticeable that on security issues that are more 'political' than defence-oriented, such as the relationship with NATO, the Defence Ministry occupies a secondary position compared to the MFA.

Overall, its influence in the foreign policy process is hard to assess, not least because of the problem in disentangling the role of the Defence Ministry from the personal impact of Sergei Ivanov, Defence Minister and one of the President's closest confidants. There is a strong argument that the MOD *qua* institution has declined at the same time as the authority of its leading repre-sentative has grown – an illustration of the distinction between weak institu-tions and powerful individuals. Whatever the truth of the matter, one thing is clear: the Defence Ministry's importance in foreign policy is of a strictly partial nature. In marked contrast to the MFA, its influence is limited to a relatively small number of issues – conflict resolution, strategic disarmament, relations with NATO – a situation that is unlikely to change anytime soon.

The security apparatus

It is almost impossible to quantify the input of the security services in Putin's foreign policy since the tradition of extreme secrecy in such institutions ensures that reliable information on the subject is scarce indeed. Neverthe-less, some remarks are apposite. First, pursuing the theme touched on earlier, personalities and personal loyalties are central. It is logical that Putin should obtain much of his information about frontline issues from those he most trusts. It just so happens that this group includes some of his contemporaries and former colleagues from the security services. Thus Sergei Ivanov's chief quality in the eyes of his president is their long-time personal friendship, rather than the fact that he was formerly a career intelligence officer – although the two factors are obviously linked.

Second, based on his previous career experience, Putin may believe that he is more likely to receive reliable information about certain issues from the security and intelligence apparatus than from an MFA whose objectivity has increasingly been called into question, or from an academic community whose intellectual inflexibility greatly limits its capacity to provide useful policy advice. The security services – in particular the Foreign Intelligence Service (*Sluzhba vneshnei razvedki* – SVR) – have retained many of their analytical functions, and are arguably the one source in Russia that combines relative objectivity, access to highly sensitive sources and the ability to pro-vide a reasonable flow of in-depth analysis. Interestingly, in an interview to

US media bureau chiefs in June 2001, Putin suggested as much: '[the] ability to work with a large amount of information … is a skill that in analytical services, in security services is being cultivated, the skill to pick the most important items out of the huge flow of information, process them and use them efficiently'.[9]

Third, it is misleading to take a monolithic view of the security apparatus. Some people and institutions matter and others do not, while 'importance' itself can be a temporary commodity. For example, when Sergei Ivanov headed the Security Council the latter was a major participant in security-related foreign policy issues. But when he moved to the MOD and was succeeded by former Interior Minister Vladimir Rushailo, the Security Council reverted to an almost exclusive focus on Chechnya and effectively disappeared as a foreign policy player.[10] This underlines the point about personalities and institutions.[11] Furthermore, even within the external intelligence community, the primacy of personal and clan loyalties excludes many who might otherwise have a plausible claim to influence policy. In this connection, Putin has been accused of favouring *Pitertsy* (residents of St Petersburg) at the expense of Moscow-based political and security figures.[12]

The economic ministries

What the security services cannot do well is to advise on economic issues. And with the 'economization' of Russian foreign policy (see following chapter) proceeding apace, it has become imperative to make use of specialist expertise in an often highly technical field. To this purpose, Putin has resorted to a rising generation of 'young reformers' – German Gref, the Minister of Economic Development and Trade, Finance Minister Alexei Kudrin, presidential economic adviser Andrei Illarionov – while also consulting closely with some of the original Yeltsin-era reformers, in particular former Prime Minister Yegor Gaidar, Anatolii Chubais, the head of United Energy Systems (UES – Russia's electrical monopoly organization), and Boris Nemtsov, head of the neo-liberal party the Union of Rightist Forces (Soyuz pravykh sil – SPS).[13] In foreign policy, these figures are influential in two main areas: (i) Russia's interaction with Western economic and financial institutions, especially on flagship issues such as Soviet-era debt and accession to the World Trade Organization (WTO); and (ii) obtaining Western support for liberalizing reforms in the domestic economy, and recognition of Russia as a full 'market economy'.

The decision-making map in the sphere of foreign economic policy is exceptionally complicated, resembling a patchwork with often opposing interests running various aspects and agendas. For example, as will be seen in Chapter 4, there is powerful opposition within the government to WTO accession and, more generally, to Russia's integration into the Western economic and financial system. The protectionist philosophy of, say, the ministries that deal with precious metals (e.g., aluminium), agriculture and secondary industry – not to mention the Central Bank[14] – differs substantially from the more economic *laissez-faire* attitudes of the trade and finance ministries. At the same time, there are institutions such as the Ministry of Atomic Energy (MINATOM) whose main export strategy – to expand cooperation with countries like Iran and China – runs against the Westernizing integrationist world-view of the Gref-Kudrin team.

The economic ministries do not, then, constitute a unitary bloc of policy-makers, particularly as there is often a disjunction between the minister's line and the views of middle- and senior-level bureaucrats (as in the case of the trade ministry where some officials oppose opening up the economy to foreign competition). The reason for grouping them here is that together they represent the one branch of foreign policy where Putin's presidential control is least in evidence. His lack of an economics background, the complexity of the issues involved and the limited competence of his trusted standby – the security services – on economic questions means that he is dependent on sources of information and analysis whose reliability he cannot necessarily assume or verify. This is perhaps why he has sought refuge in diversity, and why in turn the area of foreign economic policy is the most 'anarchic' in the administration's conduct of external relations.

The Presidential Administration (apparat)

During the Yeltsin years, many observers considered the presidential *apparat* to be an alternative foreign ministry – and with some cause. There is evidence to suggest that pressure from within this somewhat shadowy body contributed to softening Moscow's position on NATO enlargement in the lead-up to the 1997 Russia-NATO Founding Act, to Yeltsin's responsiveness to a possible territorial accommodation with Japan in 1997-8, and to the toning-down of anti-Western official rhetoric during the Kosovo crisis.[15] At times, the power of the *apparat* was seen to threaten the authority of the Foreign Minister himself, not least when presidential press secretary Sergei Yastrzhembsky, and not Foreign Minister Primakov, attended the 1997 Krasnoyarsk 'no ties' summit between Yeltsin and Japanese Prime Minister Hashimoto.[16]

Under Putin, there has been similar speculation about the role of the President's immediate 'court', in part because of the influence that such figures have historically wielded in Russia, and in part because several Yeltsin-era officials have survived the transition to a new president. Alexander Voloshin, head of the Presidential Administration, Yastrzhembsky himself, and Sergei Prikhodko, the President's foreign policy adviser, are all hold-overs from an earlier period, and there is an implicit assumption that they have therefore retained much of their former policy-making importance.

As elsewhere, the picture is obscure. We are not privy to the inner workings of the Putin administration, so we can often only speculate about who said what to whom, when, and with what effect. However, as with the security services, one can arrive at some reasonable conclusions. The first is that the influence of people such as Yastrzhembsky and Prikhodko who advise the president on foreign policy is limited by several factors: the tiny size of the foreign policy office in the administration,[17] the absence of a sizeable autonomous information base on international affairs, and very little personal and institutional knowledge of international economic issues.[18] In other words, the presidential *apparat* is stretched too thinly to be able to contribute in a *substantive* way to the development of foreign policy positions across the board; it must be selective if it is to make any impact at all.

Moreover, the function of a presidential office is traditionally one of 'gate-keeping', manipulating who sees the supreme power and who does not. Its leading lights are 'facilitators' who point the president in a particular direction by suggesting people he might consult, rather than advisers who provide detailed opinion on specific issues. Their function in this respect compares most closely to that of a principal private secretary to the president/ prime minister in Western democracies: coordinating and filtering advice from various sources, e.g., the MFA, or confirming the president in the course he has already chosen. The exception to the rule is Andrei Illarionov, Putin's economic advisor. As one of the leading commentators on economic policy during the Yeltsin years, Illarionov possesses the specialist credentials to be a credible independent source of advice on the management of Russia's external economic agenda.

Certain figures in the presidential *apparat* serve also an important presentational purpose. It is not coincidental that Yastrzhembsky, in parti-cular, is regularly produced when the Putin administration is looking to put a gloss on Russian policy for a Western audience, as for example over Chechnya. He adds a sophisticated persona to the authoritativeness normally associated with the President's immediate entourage.

Finally, and most crucially, Putin is much less dependent than Yeltsin on his 'court' staff, in general and in foreign affairs specifically. Whereas Voloshin and Yastrzhembsky were members of the so-called 'Family' – the intimate circle of Yeltsin's personal confidants[19] – it is doubtful whether they remain so in relation to Putin given the latter's reliance on his St Petersburg security and economic connections. It is likely, therefore, that their retention reflects the President's desire to make use of people with vital institutional memory and useful bureaucratic skills rather than any particular trust or affection. They are, lest we forget, Yeltsin's people and not his. So their standing and influence, although still high, are less than they were.

Big business

Of all the non-government players, big business exerts by far the greatest influence on Russian foreign policy. And much of the reason for this is that, in a very real sense, it is inseparable from government. The post-Soviet period has been notorious for the incestuous relationship between the two, to the extent that the term 'private sector' is something of a misnomer for a group whose power and profitability derives overwhelmingly from their political access. Big business, represented most visibly in the natural monopolies (oil, gas, mineral resources), is the major player in the sphere of foreign economic policy, where its impact is felt at two levels. The first is in relation to individual priorities, such as maximizing volume production for the world oil market, the development of Caspian Sea energy resources, and the delivery of gas to European customers. If it is no longer so automatic that what is good for Gazprom is good for Russia, then Russia's gas monopoly and Lukoil, the country's leading oil company, nevertheless remain the central determinants of policy in their areas of immediate concern. The clout of sectoral interests is similarly evident in other branches of foreign economic activity, such as large-scale arms transfers and ongoing programmes of nuclear cooperation with China, India and Iran. It is testament to the power of such interests that in these instances the profit motive more often than not outweighs other factors such as concerns over the changing military balance with China or political friction with the United States. Indeed, Putin's controversial decision to jettison the 1995 Gore–Chernomyrdin ban on new arms contracts with Iran[20] suggests that the input of large economic interests in certain areas of foreign policy is even greater than it was under Yeltsin.

But if big business can make its presence felt on specific issues, then the issue is less clear-cut on the broader question of economic integration with the West. Here the course of Russia's WTO accession negotiations will be an interesting barometer of the ability of vested interests to shape macro-economic policy. With many fiercely committed to maintaining a relatively closed, heavily corporatized and monopolized economy, in opposition to the liberalizing reforms of the Gref-Kudrin team, the next few years will tell us much about the balance of power between contending parties, as well as the extent to which economic considerations inform the conduct of Russia's foreign relations as a whole. For ultimately the WTO accession process – as well as other banner issues such as economic partnership with an expanding European Union – may be viewed as a microcosm of the struggle between an expansive Westernizing integrationism and a more introspective world-view that seeks the profits of capitalism but clings to the protectionism and paternalism of the (Communist) past. In this contest much will hinge on the state of the Russian economy, and on whether the Gref-Kudrin reform team is able to demonstrate concrete benefits from its policy of engagement with the West.

The legislature

The legislature, and specifically the lower house (Duma), has been the greatest casualty of Putin's rise to power. For all its setbacks and frustrations during the Yeltsin years, it was nevertheless able to play a prominent role in political life. Today, its ability to influence proceedings is much reduced – and nowhere more so than in foreign policy. Putin's public popularity and his working majority in the Duma have effectively neutered Russian politics,[21] and few 'people's deputies' are now inclined to fight over issues in which they have little direct political or personal interest. As a result, the role of the legislature in foreign policy has undergone a transformation. Whereas under Yeltsin the Duma constituted a constraining influence that undermined effective policy-making,[22] these days it performs more as a 'loyal opposition' at the service of the President. Instrumental considerations continue to prevail, but they have been divested of nearly all their party political content. Instead, the Duma has become a mouthpiece for views which Putin would like the outside world to ponder, but which he would prefer not to express himself. In its most literal guise, this means using senior figures in the legislature to convey specific messages.[23] For the most part, however, Putin's approach has been of a more strategic character. Thus, after 11 September he was able to fulfil the role of unconditional ally of the United States in the fight against international terrorism, emphasizing Russia's civilizational affinity with the West, while Duma members did the dirty work in communicating a lengthy list of quid pro quo: accelerated and preferential accession to the WTO, removal of the Jackson-Vanik amendment and 'discriminatory' anti-dumping legislation,[24] and an enhanced Russia–NATO formal relationship.

This dualism is not new; former Foreign Minister Kozyrev did something similar at the 1992 Stockholm Summit of the Conference on Security and Cooperation in Europe (CSCE).[25] The tactic is not so much one of direct manipulation, but of allowing the extent of the very real anti-Westernism in Russia to reveal itself naturally, as it were. This course has its risks, not the least being that a growing discrepancy between President Putin's advocacy of integration with the West and the latter's alleged failure to 'reward' Russia appropriately could discredit him. But for the time being he calculates that the legislature will continue to be pliant on foreign policy as long as his political authority remains secure – and this rests not on the 'rightness' or otherwise of his approach to international relations but on the course of domestic developments. Putin's foreign policy may not be the same as that of the political elite,[26] but few are disposed to pursue these differences to their logical conclusion. It is notable, in this connection, that Russian politicians have been reluctant to publicly contradict the President once he has committed himself definitively to a particular course of action – an indication that foreign policy issues rarely matter enough to incur the risks of active defiance.

The rest

Several members of the supporting cast merit brief comment. *The academic and think-tank community* retain a modest role, although not as a community as such, but at the level of individuals. It is important, also, to distinguish between members of the traditional academic institutions from the Soviet period, and the Western-style think-tanks of recent vintage. The former are, almost without exception, irrelevant, while some figures in the latter group have a marginal influence as sources of predominantly Westernizing advice.

The media, print and especially electronic, has contributed to Putin's preeminence. But in the realm of foreign policy they have been much more an instrument of the President than an influence on him. Putin's determined campaign to suppress independent outlets – such as Gusinsky's Media-Most group and Berezovsky's TV6 channel[27] – has ensured that the media serves principally as a cheerleader or as a source of 'loyal opposition' (see above), either way operating within fairly strict confines.

With the restoration of central authority and the loss of powers by the Federation Council (the upper house of parliament), the influence of *the regions* on foreign policy – small in the first place – has declined to nil. Well might, say, the governor of Sakhalin province rail against the possibility of territorial concessions to the Japanese over the disputed South Kurile Islands/ Northern Territories,[28] but the Kremlin will make its decision regardless of local sentiment.

Notwithstanding their continuing public profile, *eminent persons* – notably former Presidents Yeltsin and Gorbachev – exert minimal influence. Putin meets them, and accords them every mark of respect. But there is no basis for concluding that they shape his foreign policy thinking in any way. Both are yesterday's heroes (or rather anti-heroes), and it would be counter-productive for Putin to be too closely associated with them and their perceived record of failure. After all, one of his most attractive traits to public and elite alike is that he is *not them*.[29] Here, the retention of Yeltsin-era figures in the Putin administration does not reflect the President's dependence on his predecessor, but rather the usefulness (although not indispensability) of the courtiers who served him.

The role of *the Orthodox Church* is an interesting illustration of two features of the current foreign policy-making environment: the existence of powerful single-issue constituencies, and the use of these constituencies for a broader purpose. There appears to be a tacit accommodation whereby the state supports the established Church in preserving its virtual monopoly of religion in Russia, while in return the Church legitimizes (or 'sanctifies') the administration. Thus Pope John Paul II is still no nearer visiting Moscow, while Patriarch Alexi II says little these days about pan-Slavism and similar themes that might embarrass the Kremlin in its pro-Westernism.[30]

As in the Soviet and Yeltsin years, *the wider public* has had neither the interest nor the means to involve itself seriously in international affairs. Much has been made of the rise of anti-Western popular sentiment over the past year, yet despite that Putin has pursued a consistent course of rapprochement with the West. Displays of indignation over the alleged injustices perpetrated against Russian athletes at the 2002 Salt Lake City Winter Olympics proved, in the end, to be just so much hot air.[31]

Finally, there is little indication that advice from *foreign governments* has played a material role in Russian foreign policy development. While Putin cannot help but be influenced by the *actions* of other countries, his views are essentially home-grown, born of direct experience or borrowed from those around him (in both the past and present). Although he has built an excellent personal rapport with several of his counterparts abroad, there is no particularly 'special' relationship of the type that Yeltsin enjoyed with former German Chancellor Helmut Kohl.[32]

The primacy of the individual and the making (and breaking) of policy

It is ironic that in a society so imbued with collectivist notions (sincere and otherwise) policy-making should have become so dominated by the individual. The latter's primacy has been the basis of government in the post-Soviet period, and nowhere is this more clearly demonstrated than in foreign affairs. We have already referred briefly to the example of Sergei Ivanov in the context of the Security Council and Defence Ministry. But the principle that 'the individual maketh the institution' runs throughout the Russian polity, starting with the President himself.

Putin

One of the political clichés of the past decade has been that Russian foreign policy is 'presidential'.[33] However, whereas under Yeltsin this label was intended to gloss over an anarchic reality, it is an apt description of Putin's management of external relations. As remarked in Chapter 1, to a very large extent Putin *is* Russian foreign policy. Many others play roles of varying importance, but the President is the person who makes things happen – or not. This is partly a function of the disproportionate power of the institution of the presidency, as formalized in the 1993 ('Yeltsin') Constitution. More critically, though, it is the result of Putin's close interest in the detail of foreign policy, which means that decisions made at the top are far more likely to be implemented down the line. And because Putin is a more stable personality than Yeltsin there is also greater consistency in decision-making. Returning to an earlier theme, the privileged class may disagree with the Kremlin on specific issues and even on overall foreign policy orientation, but in the final analysis only one opinion really counts in a political culture as narrowly self-interested as Russia's.

But to affirm that Putin dominates foreign policy is not to pretend that he 'does it all'. The claim by some commentators that, for example, he thought up the post-11 September rapprochement with the West all by himself is implausible, as is the inference that he receives no meaningful advice on foreign policy from domestic sources.[34] Such views smack of an uncritical acceptance of the Putin myth, and appear tacitly to subscribe to a cult of personality that portrays him as omniscient and omnipresent. Like any world leader, Putin absorbs information and takes advice from a range of sources, and the breadth of the foreign policy agenda means there are many issues which, even if he felt so disposed, he could not possibly hope to cover alone. Although he certainly has his own views on a number of frontline issues, these too are hardly the product of original thought but emerge logically out of a particular political and economic context. Thus, in the specific case of the relationship with the West, an improvement was already discernible in the first few weeks of his presidency, mainly because the political class understood, in varying degrees, that something had to be done to arrest its decline after the hiatus of the Kosovo crisis. Rapprochement was fully in accord with the fundamental Westerncentrism of the elite. The West, for all its shortcomings, was still overwhelmingly the source of political, military, economic and technological might in the world; the question, therefore, was not whether Russia should develop a more cooperative relationship with it, but on what basis.

So Putin and the personalization of Russian foreign policy operate in quite a different way than many imagine. Putin is the ultimate controller, he determines the country's strategic direction, and involves himself selectively in the management of high-profile issues. But like any good senior manager, he delegates. What distinguishes him from Western leaders, however, is that he relies principally on individuals instead of institutions, or rather he looks to individuals to ensure institutional compliance and efficiency and, thereby, the implementation of policy. And really it cannot be otherwise. Given the weakness of government instrumentalities and with no solid constituent base to speak of, it is natural that Putin should resort to individual personalities from his past – members of the St Petersburg FSB, liberal economists from the Sobchak days – while giving Yeltsin-era figures a continuing stake in his political prosperity. But if it is true that individuals provide the education, inspiration and advice, who are these people and how do they operate?

Anatolii Chubais

There is nothing about Anatolii Chubais's position as head of the country's electricity monopoly that would indicate his importance in the political firmament, let alone in the sphere of foreign policy. But it is doubtful whether, outside the two presidents of post-Soviet Russia, there has been a more important political figure over the past decade. During the Yeltsin presidency, he fitted the classic stereotype of the *éminence grise*, the subject of widespread opprobrium (including from Yeltsin himself), but nevertheless continuing to run much of the show.[35] His achievements included managing the privatization programme in which state-owned assets were effectively transferred to a new *nomenklatura* of pro-Kremlin entrepreneurs,[36] and obtaining Yeltsin's re-election in the summer of 1996, six months after the President's popularity rating had plummeted to 3 per cent.[37] More generally, Chubais has been the most potent symbol, at least domestically, of the Westernizing tendency in Russian politics since the fall of the USSR.

Chubais is also from St Petersburg, and it is this personal dimension that has helped maintain his influence on the President. At various stages in Putin's political career Chubais has been his patron, ideological inspiration, and eyes and ears. He appeals to the President's instincts for loyalty and ability. Putin may not care for Chubais's involvement in various dubious dealings of the Yeltsin era,[38] but the latter's unparalleled political and administrative skills have so far outweighed this baggage. By virtue of his experience and acumen Chubais is able to point Putin in the direction of certain individuals rather than others. And he has played a critical role in channelling Putin's Westernizing tendencies productively, for example through a greater emphasis on foreign economic priorities and Russia's integration into the global economy. Such is his significance that one can say that as long as Chubais remains close to the Kremlin, Putin will maintain a pro-Western foreign policy line.[39]

Alexei Kudrin/German Gref

Alexei Kudrin's appeal to Putin is threefold. First, they served together as deputy mayors under Anatolii Sobchak in St Petersburg. The shared experience of first political success and then hardship has been instrumental in fostering a close bond between them.[40] Second, Putin knows Kudrin to be the consummate professional, whose lack of glamour is an advantage, not a defect. Kudrin understands market economics and is a good administrator, indispensable qualities in a finance minister and manager of macroeconomic reform. In this connection, he is the ideal counterpart to German Gref, the high-profile Minister of Economic Development and Trade. Gref is the more creative influence, and is particularly important in relation to high-profile issues such as WTO accession, but it is Kudrin who has been instrumental in translating thought into action. Such success as has been achieved in introducing economic reform under Putin is principally thanks to him. Third, with the handling of Russia's Soviet-era debt being one of the most important issues on the foreign policy agenda, Kudrin is among the few people capable of understanding its intricacies while not losing sight of the bigger picture – Russia's integration into the processes of economic globalization.

Sergei Ivanov

Sergei Ivanov is in many ways Kudrin's equivalent in the security dimension of Russia's international relations. He and Putin are almost exact contemporaries by age and profession, and have known each other for over 20 years. Like Kudrin (and Putin himself), Ivanov has an understated personality and a reputation for professional competence. It was consequently natural that the President should choose him, first as Secretary of the Security Council and then later as Defence Minister. In the former capacity he was principally responsible for overall national security policy, while latterly his brief has been to tackle one of the most exacting tasks of all: military reform and the transformation of Russia's armed forces from an ineffectual mass into a force capable of meeting the challenges of the post-Cold War environment.

It is a measure of the trust Putin vests in Sergei Ivanov that the functions of the institutions the latter has headed have been framed with him in mind. Thus, the Security Council's policy ambit expanded and contracted with Ivanov's arrival and departure respectively, while the Defence Ministry has assumed a leading role on the big international security issues such as strategic disarmament and the fight against international terrorism. What is less clear, however, is the extent to which Ivanov's views on such matters shape those of Putin, or whether he is merely a plenipotentiary representative of the President, there to keep an eye on things and report back. Compared to Kudrin, Sergei Ivanov is not an expert on the subjects under his jurisdiction, so his assessments are almost certainly less authoritative – and likely to be viewed as such by the Kremlin. It is probable also that Putin is sensitive to the dangers of Ivanov becoming, however slightly, the creature of his ministry. In this connection, there are already strong indications that it is the Chief of the General Staff, Anatolii Kvashnin, and not Ivanov, who handles the more overtly 'military' or technical issues in the defence portfolio, in particular military reform.[41]

Mikhail Kasyanov

In Soviet times the prime minister was primarily responsible for macro-economic policy,[42] and this remained the case under Yeltsin. Four of the five post-Soviet occupants of the position – Gaidar, Chernomyrdin, Kiriyenko and Primakov – all possessed strong economic credentials and/or came to office in response to particular economic circumstances.[43] Given this tradi-tion, Putin's choice of Finance Minister Mikhail Kasyanov – an expert on debt issues – in May 2000 was no surprise. But if the rationale behind his appointment was clear enough, the exact nature of Kasyanov's role since then has proved difficult to pin down. As Prime Minister, he has been involved in most of the major foreign economic issues – WTO accession, global energy policy, foreign investment, Caspian Sea development, debt, relations with the EU. Yet one cannot readily identify any specific area where his has been the dominant influence on policy development. His approach has been reactive rather than creative, and it is no coincidence that he has frequently been portrayed as a counterbalance to one or other of the economic players (Kudrin/Gref, Illarionov) or, on a more positive note, as the reconciler of policy differences.[44] Either way, his impact on decision-making has been considerably more modest than his official status as Putin's official deputy might have led one to suppose.

All together now?

In Chapter 2 we remarked on the chaotic and fractious character of foreign policy-making during the Yeltsin years. Under Putin, it is evident that a new regime is in place, one more centralized, disciplined and efficient than at any time since before Gorbachev. Internecine conflict has given way to something approximating a team approach. Nevertheless, despite the improvement in bureaucratic culture, the foreign policy-making process remains dysfunc-tional and unstable. Its principal defect is that it is overly dependent on the President, and specifically on his political fortunes, rather than reflecting a consensus vision of the Russian national interest. It is, in the final analysis, a product of political accommodation and calculation, not of shared beliefs. And this means that any diminution of presidential authority could lead to a return, if not to the anarchy of the past, then to an increasingly disconnected, special-interests-driven approach to external relations. Putin's attitude towards

46

policy-making reflects an appreciation of this reality. His reliance on trusted friends (Kudrin, Sergei Ivanov) in strategic areas of foreign policy demonstrates his (correct) view that in present-day Russia having your own people in 'strongpoints' is of prime importance. At the same time, his retention of key figures from the Yeltsin administration – Voloshin, Yastrzhembsky, Igor Ivanov, Kvashnin – amounts to a recognition that his original, St Petersburg FSB/mayor's office constituency was too narrow to operate as the basis for effective policy.

Just as critical as finding an appropriate balance between new and old, however, has been Putin's approach to (i) how these diverse personalities manage their respective area responsibilities; (ii) the way they interact with one another; and (iii) the institutional environment as a whole. The first of these shows that, far from being a micro-managing autocrat, Putin likes to leave the management of individual portfolios to the relevant heads. Igor Ivanov runs the MFA; Sergei Ivanov and Kvashnin between them rule the MOD; and Kudrin and Gref are afforded generous licence on economic policy. Each looks after different parts of the foreign policy jigsaw. In contrast to the Yeltsin administration, there has been no attempt to impose a supra-ministerial structure on individual institutions. Ministers answer directly to Putin. They enjoy excellent access to him, unhindered by any intermediate or rival bureaucratic mechanism such as a Yeltsin-style presidential *apparat*. He may not always agree with them, but they can be guaranteed a good hearing at the very least.

This brings us to the interaction between different foreign policy-related institutions. Because Putin allows them substantial autonomy, they tend not to interfere with each other's responsibilities or engage in turf battles. It is as if they all understand their proper place and function, and that it would be counterproductive to disrupt the façade of government unity – a project very dear to Putin's heart. The consolidation of state authority over the past three years has had a civilizing effect on bureaucratic interaction. Previously, Yeltsin's practice of playing off institutional interests against one another, his worsening health and his indifference to detail had led to many 'empty spots' in the exercise of power, thereby encouraging various foreign policy actors to take matters into their own hands and carve out territory. Today, things are more relaxed and predictable: the President is in charge and taking a close interest in the workings of government, while everyone receives a reasonable amount of the policy pie.

Taken as a whole, foreign policy-making operates along essentially horizontal lines. Although in Russia it has become fashionable to speak about the *vertikal* – the line of command and control from the President down – this operates very differently from the multi-layered hierarchy of the Soviet

47

command-administrative system or even the less rigid arrangements common in Western governments.[45] Perhaps the closest analogy is, ironically enough given recent developments, with the flat cell-like structures of some international terrorist organizations. At the top is the leader who exercises overall strategic control and coordination. Meanwhile, the institutional actors – or 'cells' – fulfil their assigned tasks in accordance with directives from the top, without reference to any third party or mediating mechanisms. Although the different constituent parts must work together, in Putin's Russia they do not do so 'independently', as it were, but back and forth through the common denominator or 'transmission belt'[46] of the President. So while they are autonomous in the sense that they operate with little interference from other 'equals', their autonomy is circumscribed by the need to refer all major decisions and actions back to Putin. The key feature of this arrangement, and one that distinguishes it from government in a Western democracy, is the atomization of the individual foreign policy actors. Its *raison d'être* is the maximization of the leader's authority and image by establishing a pattern of direct dependence on him and, equally crucially, preventing the formation of a bureaucratic caucus that might constitute an alternative source of power or decision-making. In some ways, Putin's underlying motivation does not differ all that much from Yeltsin's divide-and-rule approach to politics. The latter was more antagonistic and crude, as well as less efficient, but common to both is a strong commitment to the notion of control based on the Soviet leadership principle of *edinonachalie* ('single leadership').

Such a personalized system places huge demands on the energy and capacity of the President. Since there is no coordinating structure in place, he is obliged to involve himself in much of the foreign policy detail; the unpalatable alternative is to risk a return to the institutional disorder of the Yeltsin era. However, there is only so much that one person can cover. And this means there are times when aspects of Russian foreign policy are either allowed to run themselves or neglected altogether. This is especially a problem in areas of secondary priority, such as the Middle East and the Balkans. But it also affects the management of primary issues such as Russia's relations with the United States, Western Europe, the EU and NATO. Because Putin must divide his attention among a multitude of policy concerns – domestic and foreign, political, economic and strategic – he cannot always ensure the implementation of a consistent policy line. This is why we see fluctuations even in areas where Putin has pronounced, such as 'strategic cooperation' with Washington post-11 September. And while there is sometimes a tactical element to such inconsistencies – a sort of 'keeping the West on its toes' – more often than not these occur as the result of an information and policy overload.

We should be careful, therefore, not to overstate the extent to which

Putin controls things. When we say that his mastery over foreign policy and its political and institutional context is greater than that of any leader since Stalin (Chapter 1), it is important to remember that the standard by which we are judging is a very low one.[47] For centuries Russian leaders have been notoriously unsuccessful in translating policy intentions into reality. The exceptions to the rule – Peter the Great, Catherine the Great, Lenin, Stalin – have been so few that the theme of the good Tsar let down by his venal subordinates has entered into the folklore of power, transcending regime and ideological change. It is possibly with this history in mind that Putin has pursued a dual-track approach to governance. On the one hand, he has personalized the management of state affairs to an unprecedented degree, in the conviction that in Russia the only way to get things done is to rely on strong friends rather than weak institutions. On the other hand, he is aware that in the long term effective policy-making depends on the development of viable structures and mechanisms. His determined campaign to re-establish the authority of the state by clamping down on centrifugal and/or disruptive forces of various types – regionalism, Chechnya, the excessive independence of big business, disruptions to law and order – indicates that he sees institutionalization as the long-term solution to the problem of government in post-Soviet Russia. Ideally, he would like to see the emergence of properly functioning institutions staffed by competent, educated and above all loyal public servants who serve the will of their political masters. But with realization of this vision some way off, he must in the meantime operate with the context as he finds it, not as he would wish it.[48]

Conclusion

The current policy-making environment is, like many other areas of Russian life, in a state of profound transition. A surface calm masks many contradictions, and the conduct of foreign affairs continues to depend overmuch on the political health and policy commitment of the President. For the time being, the weakness and disunity of the elite provide him with a substantial breathing space in which to promote his external agenda. There is no early prospect of a serious challenge to his policy management, let alone to his pre-eminence of power. Yet despite the vast improvement that has taken place in foreign policy decision-making, its processes remain archaic and inefficient. The excess of institutional and individual players with little binding them except an eye for the main chance; an over-concentration of strategic authority in a single person; the meagre likelihood that a disinterested conception of public service will emerge in the foreseeable future – these are all major negatives militating against a stable and productive institutional framework. In the end, it will be Putin's capacity to address these often elusive challenges that will determine whether he is successful in developing and implementing a fresh vision for Russia's relations with the outside world.

4

The economic agenda

The 'unnaturalness' of economics

Among the things we tend to take for granted in the foreign policy of Western countries is the predominance of economic priorities. While 'old-fashioned' political-strategic themes have their moment, notably in times of war or great crisis (such as 11 September and its aftermath), foreign policy is more often than not an extension of domestic imperatives, an instrument primarily for enhancing national wealth. Since the end of the Cold War, the balance between military-strategic and economic priorities has tilted ever more markedly in favour of the latter, as the threat of direct confrontation between East and West has receded. Although the major powers continue to spend heavily on defence,[1] the fundament of power in the modern world, from which all other trumps follow, is economic. The United States may have thousands of nuclear warheads, but it is its financial and commercial ascendancy that enables it not only to sustain this arsenal, but also to project power and influence throughout the world. Significantly, even nations which in the past pursued a geopolitically and security-driven foreign policy have cast their lot in favour of a pronounced 'economization'. Perhaps more than any other single event, China's recent accession to the World Trade Organization after a 15-year campaign symbolizes the trend and flavour of international affairs in the post-industrial, post-Cold War era.

Russia, however, has long been the exception to the rule. Traditionally, in Soviet and Tsarist times, economic interests had ranked well down the list of foreign policy priorities, very much an ugly stepsister to the 'real' business of security and geopolitics. This mindset survived the fall of the Soviet Union. At a time when every other major power was devoting greater attention to economic priorities, the world-view of the Russian establishment remained unabashedly retrograde, differing only slightly from that prevailing at the height of the Cold War. Although under Gorbachev and then Yeltsin, the Kremlin declared that Russian foreign policy should be directed principally at promoting the wealth of the nation and the well-being of its citizens,[2] this message appeared increasingly formalistic and devoid of meaning. Throughout the 1990s the Yeltsin administration continued to speak the language of zero-sum, balance of power, and spheres of influence, while several very public disagreements with the West – over NATO enlargement, American strategic missile defence, Kosovo – reinforced the geopolitical mindset of the elite. The second-class status of the economic agenda was reflected in the 2000 Foreign Policy Concept – a document finalized under Putin but almost entirely drafted during Yeltsin's final year in power. In the course of an extensive survey of Russia's functional and geographical priorities, the economic aspects of its foreign relations received only a few desultory paragraphs.[3]

Unsurprisingly, Moscow's achievements on the external economic front during this time were few and far between. Membership of a handful of international institutions – G7/G8, the Paris Club,[4] APEC – could not disguise the modesty of Russian participation in the processes of economic globalization. At the regional level, too, the picture was scarcely any brighter, with Russia marginalized from economic integration in the two most dynamically developing areas in the world – Western Europe and the Asia–Pacific. Here, ostensibly economic objectives, such as the development of a 'strategic partnership' with the EU and participation in APEC, became badly skewed by political and security calculations.[5] Even on 'home' territory – the CIS – the trend was negative, with the former Soviet republics seeking, with increasing success, to lessen their economic dependence on Moscow by diversifying sources of external trade, investment and assistance.[6] It was symptomatic of the low priority given to economic considerations in Russian foreign policy that little or no progress was made in promising areas of activity such as the Partnership and Cooperation Agreement (PCA) with the EU,[7] in pursuing membership of the WTO, or in exploiting the oil and gas resources of the Caspian Sea. Meanwhile, traditional economic ties and sources were unable to compensate for this shortfall; indeed, frequently the reverse was true. Arms exports fell sharply from Soviet levels; exports of nuclear and missile technologies led to serious difficulties in Moscow's relationship with Washington; and there were also near-intractable problems in recovering debts from former Soviet client-states and the post-Soviet republics. Overall, the picture was a dismal one, compounded by the leadership's almost total lack of vision or understanding of external economic issues.

Set against this background, the emphasis Putin has assigned to economic priorities has emerged as one of the most distinctive and important features of his foreign policy management over the past three years. Unlike Yeltsin, he has demonstrated the interest and commitment to transform a rhetorical allegiance into a genuine economization of Russian attitudes towards the world. Four key themes, in particular, have dominated this economic dimension: (i) the direct linkage between an active foreign policy and domestic socio-economic transformation and prosperity; (ii) the campaign to integrate Russia into ongoing international economic processes; (iii) the profit motive; and (iv) the interrelationship between geoeconomics and geopolitics, between Moscow's pursuit of economic objectives and its continuing ambitions to project itself as a regional and global power.

In each of these areas, the Putin administration has borrowed substantial elements from its Soviet and post-Soviet predecessors, but also put its own stamp on proceedings. Putin's way of conducting foreign economic policy has been distinctly Russian, reflecting both the relative 'newness' of (and unfamiliarity with) such priorities as well as the lasting influence of Russia's self-perception as a 'great power' and its geopolitical heritage. Far from unquestioningly absorbing Western models, as the Yeltsin administration was accused of doing,[8] Moscow's approach has been at once welcoming and cautious, assertive and defensive, positive and negative. Reflecting the diversity and complexity of the policy-making environment in this area (see Chapter 3), it has been above all multifaceted and contradictory. The outcome of this mix of mindsets, ideas and interests has been a hybrid in a constant state of evolution, a metaphor for Putin's disposition to change the way Russia looks at the world, but also for the considerable practical and ideological obstacles in the way of such an ambitious enterprise.

Foreign policy and economic reform

The idea of using foreign policy to facilitate the realization of domestic goals dates back to Gorbachev's 'new thinking' of the late 1980s. Its original (if largely tacit) premise was that Russia did not have the wherewithal in financial resources and market-oriented expertise to make the transition by itself from a moribund command-administrative system to a profitable economy based on enterprise and competition.[9] Consequently, under Gorbachev and then Yeltsin, it was argued that the West should provide large-scale financial and technical assistance to support the Russian economy in its transition – a project in which it had a direct stake since a prosperous Russia would also mean a stable one for the world.[10] For its part, the Russian government would absorb this aid and advice to undertake far-reaching reforms in the economic system, as well as political democratization and the development of a civil society. Under Yeltsin in particular, the interpretation of the linkage between foreign policy and domestic change was thus overtly liberal and Westernizing.

Unfortunately, a number of factors came together to discredit this nexus. These included a general perception of plummeting living standards;[11] the profound crisis in most branches of the Russian economy; popular disgust at the corruption of those who had enriched themselves from the collapse of the Communist system; disappointment with levels of Western aid, trade and investment; and, finally, the politicization of Western support, which came to be seen as benefiting not Russia so much as the Yeltsin regime. By the time Putin came to power there was an obvious need to 'freshen' up the principle of using foreign policy as an instrument for pursuing domestic goals. On the other hand, the new Kremlin leadership benefited from the fact that a geopolitically driven foreign policy had become equally malodorous. A succession of failures in the military-strategic sphere, culminating in the humiliation of Russia's impotence during the Kosovo crisis, created space for a more balanced foreign policy that would focus on cooperation and integration with the West in place of an aggressive but futile competition. The challenge and opportunity in front of Putin, then, was to find a kind of 'third way' between the Westernizing foreign/domestic policy linkage of the later Gorbachev and early Yeltsin years, and the anachronistic, over-geopoliticized foreign policy of the second half of the 1990s.

Thus far Putin has been remarkably successful in this endeavour. From the outset, in his Open Letter to the Russian Voters during the 2000 presidential campaign, he distanced himself from the failed approach of the most recent past by emphasizing 'the primacy of internal goals over external ones'[12] – a theme he has reiterated on many subsequent occasions. Simultaneously, he has tapped into a broader constituency by repeating the Primakovian line that Russian foreign policy should proceed from its 'national priorities',[13] in effect assuring his audience that there would be no return to the demeaning pro-Westernism of the Yeltsin-Kozyrev type. Significantly, such rhetoric has been accompanied by very real changes in the administration's approach to foreign–domestic policy linkages.

The most obvious difference from the Yeltsin period is that there is now a more independent and sceptical attitude towards foreign advice and models. The IMF, World Bank and the European Bank for Reconstruction and Development (EBRD) continue to visit Moscow, but less frequently and publicly than before. We no longer witness the spectacle of the IMF demanding faster and more radical reforms in the Russian economy as the price of continued credits, or of Moscow bleating about the unreasonableness of international financial institutions. Instead, Putin has rejected the idea of future loans, while Russia has for the first time in the post-Soviet period begun to redeem some of its foreign debt on schedule.[14] The cynic might observe that sky-high oil prices have afforded Putin a luxury that was not at Yeltsin's disposal, but the symbolism of such moves is nonetheless potent; debt resolution is at once legitimizing and empowering, an indicator of Russia's entry into the community of developed nations.

More generally, because Russia has already moved a long way towards a market economy – albeit haphazardly and at considerable political and socio-economic cost – the image of a supplicant nation pawing at the sleeves of the rich countries and institutions of the West is no longer apposite. In place of the hand-out mentality that coloured the economic relationship throughout the 1990s, a more mature and self-reliant approach is evident. The Putin administration has consistently emphasized trade not aid, and opening up opportunities for Russian producers in international markets rather than obtaining outside support for unviable domestic industries. Such thinking has underpinned its campaign for Russia's recognition as a 'full market economy' (as opposed to 'economy in transition')[15] and, more specifically, to increase market access for commodities such as steel which come up against anti-dumping barriers. In similar spirit, although Moscow continues to stress the importance of increased foreign investment, these days it acknowledges that it has a responsibility to create conditions that might facilitate this – improved tax regimes, better legal protection of ownership rights, proper dispute resolution mechanisms – instead of simply expecting the West (and others) to put up capital in return for the vague promise of 'benefits'.[16]

But to acknowledge that Moscow has a more realistic understanding of the relationship between foreign policy and domestic imperatives is not to say that its approach is all pragmatism. On the contrary, Russian attitudes often evince a small 'c' conservatism, centred in a narrowness of vision and an instinctive suspicion of outside involvement and influence. This leads us to perhaps the most important – as against the most prominent – distinction between the Yeltsin and Putin administrations. The former focused above all on the role of foreign policy in promoting domestic political and socio-economic *transformation*. Admittedly, many of its utterances were insincere and self-serving, but the principle remained, if in ragged form. With the current regime, however, the main thrust of foreign policy is less to promote a larger reform agenda at home than it is to achieve other objectives, such as Russia's 'integration' into the global economic community, generating profit for individual industries and for the state, and assisting the projection of Russian influence abroad – all of which will be discussed below.

The importance of this distinction is illustrated by the government's handling of issues such as the WTO accession bid, EU enlargement, and even foreign investment. In theory, it recognizes that the presence of such challenges could act as a useful spur to Russia's economic development. For example, the requirements of WTO accession and the opening up of the economy to increased foreign competition will force whole sectors – particularly in secondary industry and services – to reform or die. Similarly, enlargement of the EU to the Russian frontier will place tremendous pressure on the border regions (in particular Kaliningrad)[17] and on Russia as a whole to adapt or else become marginalized from the expanding European economic space. But in practice the Putin administration has tended to see the requirements for such transforming change more as a threat than an opportunity. It has been especially concerned to insulate backward sectors (notably the car and aviation industries) and regions (Kaliningrad) from external competition, and in important respects appears only too willing to sacrifice the larger goal of a more productive economy for the sake of powerful special interests, such as the aluminium industry and the banking sector. While on the one hand the government makes approving statements about WTO accession and EU enlargement, it qualifies these with provisos regarding the need, respectively, to 'safeguard' Russian industry through extended 'transition' periods (see below),[18] and to preserve Kaliningrad from the 'negative' consequences arising from an expanded EU.[19]

In short, the commitment of the Putin administration to foreign policy as an instrument of domestic change is equivocal at best, a point that raises questions about the limits of the evolution in Russian foreign policy more generally. The President is imbued with a more activist spirit than his predecessor, and has also demonstrated an impressive authoritativeness, both politically and in terms of pushing through policies. But there are serious constraints on what he can or even wants to do. The first is his past experience and upbringing. It is one thing to have observed the widening gap between East and West during Soviet times, quite another to draw the full conclusions from this phenomenon. Although Putin has criticized the rent dependency mentality in post-Soviet Russia,[20] this does not mean he is ready to absorb the Western experience unreservedly – all the more so given the unpleasant connotations of Yeltsinite 'shock therapy' and a historical wariness of Western intentions. As a result, there is a critical tension between a desire to remedy an unsatisfactory and ultimately unsustainable state of affairs, and the 'patriotic' urge to protect often unviable home (*otechestvennaya*) industry. The second major problem arises from Putin's lack of expertise in economics, and the consequent diversification of sources of policy advice and pressure in this area (see Chapter 3). The foreign policy/domestic reform nexus is difficult to grasp properly, involving as it does multiple political and economic interests, and it is unsurprising that the administration's approach towards it should therefore be so uneven. Putin's dominance of politics and policy is not yet such as to give him the confidence to forge ahead regardless. Although he is conscious of the need for far-reaching economic change –

and has achieved much in this direction – he also recognizes the immense difficulties in prosecuting successful reform as well as his own limitations in this regard.

The integration agenda and globalization

Much the same ambivalence can be found in Russia's approach to participation in economic regionalization and globalization. On the face of things, there is nothing the Putin administration wants more. 'Integration' has, in many ways, become the signature tune of contemporary Russian foreign policy – integration into the global community; integration into the wider European political, security and economic space; integration into the 'dynamically developing' Asia-Pacific region (APR); even integration in the context of the former Soviet Union. Putin hardly misses an opportunity to hammer home the point that integration is an intrinsic good and perhaps the most fundamental of foreign policy goals.[21] Its rationale extends well beyond immediate economic considerations, conjuring up all sorts of images of belonging and common civilization as well.

And therein lies the nub of the problem. The symbolism of integration frequently outweighs its directly economic aspects. Granted, the 'club mentality' that was such a feature of the Yeltsin presidency is now less blatant. Whereas before membership of the G7/G8 and APEC was significant above all for its perceived legitimizing effect – on Russia as a newly 'civilized' country and, more specifically, on the Yeltsin regime – WTO accession and recognition as a 'full market economy' are important for practical as well as honorific reasons. And whereas once upon a time Moscow adopted a cavalier attitude towards its obligations as a member of the Paris Club, these days the Putin administration is conscientious in repaying Russia's debts on time. Nevertheless, despite this evolution in attitudes there continues to be a serious disjunction between the hybrid (semi-idealized, semi-concrete) conceptions of economic integration that currently inform much of Russian thinking, and the expectations these international institutions and their key member states have of Moscow.

Nowhere is this better illustrated than in the debate and negotiations over Russia's accession to the WTO, a painstaking process that highlights a number of political, psychological and economic issues. The first, and oldest, is the notion of a 'divine right of membership'. A holdover from the Yeltsin period, this is embodied in the assumption that Russia is simply 'too important' to be excluded from any major international organization and that, accordingly, the entry criteria should be loosened in order to facilitate its early membership. Although prominent Western officials, such as the EU

Trade Commissioner Pascal Lamy, have insisted that 'politics cannot short-circuit economics',[22] the belief persists among many in Russia that the Western powers (the USA, UK, France and Germany) will find a way to accelerate its admission – particularly given the overall rapprochement between Moscow and Washington post-11 September. A precedent for such 'flexibility' already exists in the example of Russian accession to APEC, where a lack of economic credentials and the opposition of a number of member economies proved to be less important than the support of the larger powers in the grouping, notably the USA and China. The second, related, issue is the question of primary motivation – why does Moscow want to join? Is it because it seeks full integration into a global economic community, or is the real reason a more general yen for inclusion? As an editorial in *The Economist* remarked, 'Joining a health club can reflect a genuine interest in fitness – or just a desire to keep up with the neighbours'.[23] Such considerations acquire an added edge in the light of China's accession, a development that leaves Russia as the last major country still to join an organization that already has 140 members and rising.

What transforms these relatively abstract points into concrete problems is that the WTO, unlike the G7/G8, APEC and a host of political-type organizations (UN, OSCE), imposes specific obligations on its members and candidate-members. Although these may possibly be finessed to some extent, they cannot be avoided. It is significant and far from coincidental that, as the prospect of Russia's entry has loomed closer, doubts within the elite have become more numerous and vocal. Far from imagining WTO membership as the source of all riches, the Russian government finds itself having to assess carefully the pros and cons of accession. Do the economic, political and psychological benefits of membership outweigh the costs to individual sectors of the economy, not to mention the more general requirement for Russia to submit to rules-based regimes established by others? In this latter connection, it is all very fine for Western representatives to argue that membership would allow Russia to play a role in developing a framework for the future management of global trade, but this is likely to be of cold comfort to a country that has long been used to dictating its own set of rules – in trade and economics as well as in political-strategic affairs.[24] Moscow's hostile reaction to suggestions that it might usefully submit draft legislation for scrutiny by the WTO highlights the sensitivities over issues of jurisdiction and sovereignty.[25]

WTO accession presents the Putin administration with a stark choice. On the one hand, it offers the prospect of critical benefits in relation to market access and attracting greater outside investment,[26] as well as the inestimable psychological boost of inclusion into the world's foremost trade grouping. On the other hand, the liberalization of the trading environment cuts both ways. Export-based industries such as steel are likely to do well, but many sectors that rely on a monopoly or near-monopoly of the domestic market – the automobile, aviation and metallurgical industries, agriculture, pharmaceuticals, chemical products, banking and insurance services – will struggle to remain competitive, leading to concerns about large-scale closures and mass unemployment.

The government is attempting to balance these conflicting priorities by negotiating extended 'transition periods', whereby currently inefficient industries would be given time to restructure their operations, free from the early threat of foreign competition and insulated by customs duties and export subsidies. Russia would thus enjoy the fruits of membership without incurring – for a while at least – too many of the costs. All very logical. The difficulty, however, centres on the length of the transition periods and the implications this has for socio-economic reform in Russia. The issue of WTO accession is not merely about reconciling liberalizing and protectionist tendencies, but is a microcosm of a debate that has been going on for some 10–15 years since Gorbachev introduced *perestroika* in the mid-1980s, namely, concerning the appropriate pace and nature of economic change. Critics of accelerated reforms argue that these lead to the destruction of vital national industries and cause the population enormous hardship. Proponents of rapid transformation, on the other hand, are mindful of countless examples from the Soviet past in which momentum for much-needed reforms was undermined and then destroyed in stages by bureaucratic foot-dragging and an institutionalized reluctance to forsake old habits of enterprise management.[27] From the WTO's perspective, too, there is the additional spectre that admitting Russia into the organization under overly generous terms could mean that, once in, Moscow becomes complacent and backslides on the obligations of membership.

Perhaps more than any other foreign policy issue, WTO accession puts the question of what type of country Russia wants to be in the 21st century: part of a broader, increasingly interconnected global community in more than just name, or a 'special case' operating on the margins of that community and according to its own set of rules. And it is here where the 'sectionalization' of foreign economic policy-making identified in Chapter 3 becomes critical. Because of the highly technical nature of many of the issues, and Putin's own lack of expertise in such a specialized area, different policy lines and attitudes came into play, with none able to impose itself above the others. The consequence is that the Russian position on WTO accession, and on its involvement in larger processes of economic globalization, is in flux. The presence of multiple and acute contradictions, ranging from the purely technical to the more abstract, points not only to the failure to develop a coherent vision of 'integration', but also to the limitations of the personalized, 'presidential' system of decision-making in foreign policy.

These same problems – a lack of understanding about what true integration involves, and insufficient definition and commitment in decision-making – are apparent in other areas of the external economic agenda, such as the relationship with the EU, and Russia's commercial involvement in the Asia-Pacific region. In the former case, the record reveals an inability to distinguish between integration and cooperation. There is an assumption that increasing levels of trade signify, *ipso facto*, an inexorable integration. Thus, the fact that after the next wave of its enlargement the EU will account for well over 50 per cent of Russia's total trade 'proves' to many that the latter is increasingly part of a 'common economic space' in Europe.[28] Equally, Moscow's attempts to increase gas exports to its Western European customers are motivated not only by a profit agenda (see below), but also by the belief that the greater Europe's dependence on Russian gas the more Russia will be accepted as an 'integral' part of the continent, and not simply as an external supplier of its energy needs.[29] It is much the same story in the East. During the 1990s, when Moscow was making the case for accession to APEC, it did so largely on the basis that expanding economic ties with individual countries, especially China, equated to a *de facto* membership of the region.[30]

At the root of this confusion is a reluctance to accept that integration necessarily entails a certain loss of national sovereignty and freedom of action. The Russian, previously Soviet, experience with international multilateral institutions has been partial and highly selective, with notions of 'uniqueness' and 'special-ness' taking pride of place. In the UN Security Council, for example, a nominal allegiance to consensus decision-making has been more than counterbalanced by the use of veto powers in the event of perceived need. Part of the difficulty here is that Russia has seen itself as a great power for the best part of three centuries, and at no time more so than in the relatively recent past. There has never been any disposition to subordinate national identity to a larger persona, be it European or Asian. Moscow desires the name, cachet and material dividends of economic integration, but not at the cost of being 'just another member' of a larger community, subject to group dictates. If Russia is to be 'integrated' then this must be on its own terms, an attitude that of course is incompatible with the very idea of integration itself.

For economic integration – with Europe, Asia or the world as a whole – to become a reality for Russia requires, therefore, a huge shift in psyche from this overpowering sense of 'great power-ness' to one that places primary value on Russia's 'normal-ness', on its developing a new identity as a nation-state *like the others*. However, while there are some in the elite who acknow-ledge the need for just such an attitudinal transformation, they are in a tiny minority. The problematic course of WTO accession negotiations, the very modest achievements of the Russia–EU PCA and Russia's unimpressive performance in APEC suggest that Moscow continues to believe at heart that others need it more than the other way round. As long as this exclusivist mindset remains, then Russia's economic relations with the outside world will be distinguished not by integration in the proper meaning of the word but by cooperation, in varying degrees, with different countries and institutions.

The profit motive

Although Russian foreign policy has some way to travel before it can be described as well-balanced, there is no doubt that under Putin Moscow's management of external economic priorities has become more practical. Notwithstanding an awareness of symbolic and geopolitical by-products, the bottom line remains income and profit – both to individual sectors and to the state as a whole. Indeed, such has been the power of money that, at times, Moscow has been prepared for its sake to incur serious risks in its relations with the West, in particular the United States.

The course of late Soviet and post-Soviet economic development has ensured that the Putin administration has continued to rely on Russia's traditional strengths as the core of an assertive foreign trade strategy: oil, gas, pipelines, the arms trade and nuclear cooperation.[31] These are the sectors where, by virtue of production capacity, strategic location or comparative price advantage, Russia is competitive in global terms and can realistically hope to maintain or even expand market share. Putin might wish that Russia's economy were more diversified, but it is unlikely that he cares over much as long as the world continues to need and buy its products. The distinguishing characteristic of his administration's export strategy – if one can really call it that – is to capitalize on existing trumps now, while the demand for them remains high, without worrying too much about the medium- or long-term future.

This attitude to business is especially evident in Moscow's approach to the oil industry. Here, there is no inclination to exploit existing wells at a rate that might lead to their offering a better yield in the long term; rather, the state and the major Russian oil companies, such as Lukoil and Yukos, are committed to pumping out the product as quickly as possible. Part of the explanation is directly price- and market-related. There is an irresistible temptation to optimize returns while world prices are at a several-year high due to ongoing instability in the Middle East.[32] This is the main, although not the only, reason why Moscow has been so reluctant to accede to OPEC demands for cuts in production.[33] Such a pecuniary mentality is reinforced by the fact that oil accounts for about a quarter of Russian government revenues,[34] providing the means for Moscow to meet its debt obligations and abstain from borrowing from international financial institutions like the IMF and World Bank. Since debt and potential insolvency are problems that demand immediate (as well as permanent) attention, arguments regarding the long-term benefits of slower energy development become only tangentially relevant.

At the same time, Moscow is seeking to take advantage of the situation in the Middle East to increase Russia's share of the global oil market. Although its stand-offish treatment of OPEC has been portrayed as a civilizational choice in favour of the West, the reality is more prosaic. The Putin administration hopes that the West will increasingly see the organization and its member states as a bad risk, and in their place look to Russia as both more politically sympathetic and economically reliable.

Finally, we should note the influence of a generalized post-Soviet mindset that places little or no faith in any vision of long-term stability, either in Russia or internationally. The turbulence of the last 10–15 years has, in a manner of speaking, 'taught' the elite to make profits while the going is good, in the not improbable event that some disaster – political crisis, a financial crash, slumping energy prices – may be just around the corner.

All that said, in a society so oriented towards short-term gain, the government is nevertheless taking steps to enhance Russia's longer-term production and export possibilities in the oil sector. In the first place, it has sought – albeit with only mixed success – to create a better regime for foreign investment in the exploration and exploitation of resources on the Sakhalin shelf in Russia's Far East. Today one can discern a more committed approach to establishing attractive conditions for participation by foreign companies, although attitudes towards external involvement in the economy remain naïve and paranoid in many respects.[35]

More emblematically, there has been a shift in the Russian position on the development of Caspian Sea energy resources. During the Yeltsin period, this had been one of the most sectionalized and contested areas of foreign policy, in which the MFA's legalist (and business-unfriendly) line had clashed with the commercial perspective of Lukoil supported by then Prime Minister Chernomyrdin. The outcome of this split was predictably unsatisfactory. Russia was unable to prevent other Caspian Sea littoral states, in particular Kazakhstan and Azerbaijan, from moving ahead on large-scale projects, while Lukoil was confined to a modest stake in these ventures.[36] Under Putin Russian policy has become much more coordinated and pragmatic. Moscow has dropped its former insistence that the Caspian be considered an 'inland sea' whose resources must be developed with the agreement of all parties or not at all. Although it is still working to resolve some of the outstanding legal issues, these are now subordinate to the imperative of ensuring that Russia does not miss out on lucrative commercial arrangements. The involvement of Lukoil and Gazprom – partly state-owned companies – in the Caspian Oil Company, a new consortium to develop resources in the Russian sector, indicates how economic considerations are becoming increasingly influential not just in the Caspian, but in Russian foreign policy as a whole.

In a dramatic departure from past practice, Moscow has also softened its opposition to the Baku–Tbilisi–Ceyhan pipeline that will transport oil from the Caspian to the Black Sea via Georgia (sidestepping Russia altogether).[37] Previously, it had strongly opposed this US-sponsored project whose development was seen as the cornerstone of Washington's strategy to displace Russia from the region. These days, however, it views the issue through less overtly geopolitical eyes. While some senior officials, such as Deputy Foreign Minister and Special Representative for Caspian Affairs Viktor Kalyuzhny, continue to pronounce against construction of the pipeline on the grounds that it runs contrary to the national interest, there are some indications that major Russian companies (Lukoil and Yukos) may be preparing to engage themselves in the foreign consortium managing the project.[38]

Most recently, the Putin administration has adopted a flexible stance on behalf of Russian oil interests in Iraq. On the one hand, it has sought to protect short-term returns from the on-sale of Iraqi oil under the UN's oil-for-food programme,[39] while warning of the dangers to regional stability of an American/British military intervention. On the other hand, it has distanced itself progressively from Saddam Hussein so that, in the event of regime change in Iraq, Russian economic interests are not prejudiced for political (or indeed any other) reasons.[40]

The primacy of the profit motive is apparent, too, in the reorientation of Russia's other great commodity export – natural gas. Whereas once the vast majority of exports were directed to Eastern Europe and, after the fall of the Soviet Union, to the CIS, Western Europe currently accounts for nearly two-thirds of the total[41] – a share that is likely to grow as the major European customers look to Russia to supply an increasing proportion of their energy requirements. From Moscow's perspective, a Western Europe flush with funds represents a far more attractive option than Gazprom's customers in the former Soviet Union, such as Ukraine and Georgia, which are constantly late on their payments.[42] Such considerations acquire added significance because gas, even more than oil, is Russia's greatest source of export earnings while Gazprom is the largest contributor to internal tax revenue.[43] The maximization of gas resources is useful also in enhancing Russia's image as an economically developed and powerful nation. Consequently, as with the oil sector, an aggressive strategy of expanding existing markets and opening up new ones typifies Moscow's approach. It is looking to increase its stake not only in Western Europe, but also in Turkey once the Blue Stream pipeline commences operation,[44] as well as in the East where several projects designed to tap into rapidly rising Asian demand – in China, Japan, and Southeast Asia – are in various stages of preparation.

This mentality, at once expansionist and opportunistic, informs the administration's management of other areas of foreign economic activity such as arms sales and nuclear cooperation. In most respects, policy under Putin differs little from that of the Yeltsin period. Then, although there was an element of 'tweaking the West's nose' in Moscow's behaviour, the prime motivation in selling high-tech weapons and sharing nuclear technology with 'countries of concern' to Washington was financial. After the collapse of the USSR Russian arms sales fell to a fraction of Soviet levels, with the lion's share of the market going to the United States (in particular), the United Kingdom and France.[45] The simultaneous collapse of domestic demand – due to the rapid decline of the Armed Forces – virtually crippled the military-industrial complex. Faced with the dual requirement of generating income and keeping the arms industry afloat, the government attempted to regain Russia's lost market share by selling to customers both willing to buy *and* able to pay in hard cash. But this proved highly problematic; former Soviet-era clients demanded special credit and barter arrangements, while some potential new customers, such as the Republic of Korea, were warned off by Washington.[46] In the meantime, the Yeltsin administration's obsession with geopolitics exacerbated an already unhelpful atmosphere in which arms sales to certain customers – such as Iran – were inevitably seen through a strategic prism, in balance-of-power terms rather than as the commercial arrangements they essentially were.

Under Putin the underlying motivation has remained the same, but the approach is considerably more businesslike. When the President revoked the 1995 Chernomyrdin undertaking not to conclude new arms contracts with Iran,[47] he gave notice of a new commercial intensity in Moscow's handling of arms sales. In this context, one of the biggest differences between the Yeltsin and Putin periods is that today the Kremlin is anxious to depoliticize foreign economic policy as much as possible; the implicit message being that the business of money-making – whether in relation to Caspian Sea energy development, pipelines, or arms sales – is too important to be muddied by the baggage of geopolitical pretensions. This is not to suggest that such factors do not play an important role (see below), but that commercial criteria have assumed an unmistakable primacy at a time when Putin is looking to develop Russia as a modern great power on solid economic foundations. And although political and economic considerations cannot always be separated so conveniently, Putin has managed, despite occasional upsets, to improve Russia's relations with the West *while* achieving unprecedented success in promoting the nation's commercial interests (as, for example, witnessed by a post-Soviet record level of US$4.4 billion in arms sales in 2001).[48]

Geoeconomics and geopolitics

One of the most common – and mistaken – assumptions regarding the economization of Russian foreign policy under Putin has been to equate the new emphasis on commercial objectives with the emergence of a fundamentally different world-view in the Kremlin. Specifically, there is a natural temptation to see Moscow's interest in WTO accession, the economic and technical aspects of the relationship with the EU and flexibility over the division of Caspian Sea resources as proof that Russia is renouncing its 'great power' ambitions in order to become a 'normal' nation-state like the others.

This misconception derives in the first place from a confusion between means and ends. Far from implying a modesty of ambition, the administration's choice of economic instruments actually reflects the opposite: an understanding that it is only on the basis of a strong economy that Russia can hope to regain its position as a global power. The great lesson of the late Soviet and Yeltsin periods is that economic weakness has a devastating impact not just on living standards but also on a country's international standing and influence. Conversely, the United States' dominance of the post-Cold War environment highlights the truth that real power comes first from financial and commercial might.

The nexus between economic capabilities and strategic ends has influenced Putin's thinking since even before his accession. In his Open Letter to the Russian Voters, he emphasized that Russia's place in the world was contingent on its economic prosperity: 'There can be no superpower where weakness and poverty reign.' His reference to the primacy of internal over external goals (see above) did not herald Russia's retreat into an inward-looking mindset, but rather recognized that a successful foreign policy depended on a more practical approach to international affairs. The admonition 'Let us not recollect our national interests on those occasions when we have to make some loud statement' constituted a rejection of the virtual foreign policy methods of the Yeltsin regime,[49] but not of the latter's underlying view of Russia as a great regional and global force. Crucially, at no stage

65

has the Putin administration's somewhat narrow brand of realism translated into acceptance of the proposition that Russia should limit its horizons to that of a 'normal' nation-state like Britain, France, Germany or Japan. Such a shift would necessitate a revolutionary departure from centuries of Russian political-strategic tradition – a step which, for reasons that will be explained in Chapter 5, Putin is far from ready to take.

What has emerged as well is a heightened awareness that the rigorous pursuit of economic interests serves more than one purpose. The drive for profit may be the primary motivation impelling foreign economic policy, but the geostrategic spin-offs are also welcome. Indeed, given the decline in Russia's political-military capabilities and the diminishing influence of such assets in international politics more generally, it is frequently the case that economic instruments are all Russia has to project itself as a major power. Their utility is apparent in several areas, most particularly in the energy sector. Although the Putin administration's maximalist approach towards oil and gas exploitation has been overwhelmingly finance-driven, the pivotal position of Russia in international energy flows has critical implications for its credentials as a global actor. As the world's largest exporter of gas and second largest exporter of oil, it is now receiving a measure of attention and consideration unprecedented since the end of the Cold War. Furthermore, whereas for much of the post-Soviet period foreign perceptions of Russia's significance revolved around ideas of damage limitation – avoiding the emergence of a 'mad and bad' regime there, containing nuclear and other WMD (weapons of mass destruction) proliferation – under Putin this importance has become increasingly seen in a positive light: Russia as a trustworthy energy supplier, ready to take up the slack left by an unstable Middle East.[50]

Much of Moscow's success in reaping political and strategic dividends from the pursuit of economic priorities has come from its discreet management of the linkage between geoeconomics and geopolitics. The Kremlin works hard to depoliticize international economic issues as far as possible, even when there is an obvious geopolitical angle. For example, Russia has handled relations with OPEC and Western customers skilfully, managing to appear useful and (at times) cooperative to both while benefiting from the former's negative image to increase market share. Paradoxically, by refraining from crude (and alienating) balance-of-power games it has managed to become the fulcrum in the geoeconomic energy balance between North and South to an extent unimaginable under Yeltsin.

The effectiveness of a softly-softly approach is visible too in other areas too, such as arms transfers and nuclear energy. Putin's success in expanding cooperation with countries such as Iran while maintaining good relations with the West is due largely to the fact that contemporary Russian foreign policy is directed much more towards the concrete business of 'multipolarity' – building influence and projecting power through deeds – than it is to pursuing ideologized but abstract conceptions like the Yeltsin-Primakov vision of a 'global multipolar order'.[51] But for all that, the geopolitical outcome is nevertheless one that should gladden the heart of the most committed *derzhavnik*: Russia's gradual resurgence as a great power, this time on a much more solid footing than before. In an important sense, geoeconomics has become for Moscow the geopolitics of the new millennium, giving fresh impetus to thinking about strategic space, balance of power, and spheres of influence by introducing a hard edge of practicality.

The connection between geoeconomics and geopolitics emerges most clearly at the regional level, where economic factors are increasingly shaping the conduct of foreign policy and its outcomes. Of first importance in this context is Moscow's relationship with Europe. The continent's dependence on Russian energy – gas principally but also other sources like electricity – strengthens the case for Russia's 'membership' of Europe (see above). Because energy is such a strategic good, complementarities in this area are not limited simply to economics but carry political, security and civilizational consequences as well. The more the Europeans come to rely on Russia for natural gas, the more disposed they may be to admit it into other spheres of cooperation – whatever their misgivings about its European credentials. In this way, natural gas, even more than plausible channels such as the formal Russia–NATO and Russia–EU relationships, becomes the spearhead of Moscow's campaign for 'integration' and acceptance.

Possession of energy resources and control over their distribution are likely to be significant also in reinforcing Russia's presence in the Asia–Pacific region. The extended lead times for many planned projects,[52] not to mention various historical, cultural and demographic obstacles (see Chapter 6), make it premature to speak of 'integration' here. But in the long run the growing energy requirements of a rapidly modernizing China and the desire of other Asian economies (notably Japan and the Republic of Korea) to diversify their sources of supply create opportunities for Russia to become an important strategic player in the region. Already, the expansion of arms sales to China and India, close nuclear cooperation with those countries and the potential opening-up of new markets in Southeast Asia in the wake of the Asian economic recovery[53] point to a more developed appreciation of the geoeconomic (and geopolitical) possibilities of an activist approach towards the region.

But it is closer to home, in the former Soviet Union, that the Putin administration has most successfully pursued what might be termed the 'geopoliticization' of foreign economic policy – that is, the conversion of economic trumps into political-strategic capital. And in no other area has its approach differed so much from its predecessor's. As noted in Chapter 2, Russian policy towards the FSU in the 1990s was a hotchpotch, reflecting the sectionalization of elite interests and attitudes, and the disorderly nature of decision-making. It mixed a 'patrimonial mentality'[54] with an actual neglect of Russia's interests in the newly independent republics.

Under Putin, there has been a transformation – in motives, methods and results – in which the dominant elements have been the greatly increased importance of the economic agenda and its central role in the protection and promotion of Russia's geopolitical interests in the region. The clearest example of this is Moscow's exploitation of the economic vulnerability of certain CIS member-states, notably Ukraine and Georgia, to ensure that they take greater account of Russian foreign and security policy interests. By and large, Putin has eschewed the ineffectual geopolitical rhetoric of the past and put the squeeze on where it most hurts – the two republics' dependence on Russian energy and their indebtedness to Moscow. Instead of speaking in the archaic language of 'spheres of influence', he has resorted to very Western arguments of economic rationalism, namely, the debtor's moral and financial responsibility to pay the creditor and the latter's right to turn off supply unless paid.[55] Yet if the means and much of the motivation have been economic, the dividends have been principally strategic. Moscow continues to supply Ukrainian and Georgian energy needs on flexible credit terms. But the quid pro quo is that both – in particular Ukraine – have become more sensitive to Russian geopolitical priorities. Talk of the CIS being a Russian 'sphere of influence' may have been consigned to the lexicon dustbin, but the key if unspoken reality is that Russia remains the regional hegemon, a position it has no intention of relinquishing anytime soon.

The same combination of economic means and geopolitical objectives characterizes Moscow's handling of pipeline issues. From the outset, Putin has realized that there is no mileage in standover tactics. The experience of the Yeltsin years demonstrated that attempting to dictate to the former Soviet republics had doubly negative consequences: it persuaded them to dig their heels in and court outside (Western) parties ever more enthusiastically, while encouraging the United States to 'defend' the recently acquired sovereignty of those states.[56] Tellingly, official pressure from Moscow failed to prevent progress on the major regional energy projects of the 1990s, such as the 'Contract of the Century' for the exploitation of Caspian Sea oil resources[57] or the 1999 agreement to build the Baku–Ceyhan pipeline.

These days, by contrast, Moscow's attitude is understated but increasingly influential. In emphasizing the commercial advantages of Russian participation and pipelines, it has not lost sight of the strategic agenda. But it recognizes that realization of this requires more subtle, economically oriented methods. Better to show that, for example, the main Russian-controlled pipeline between Tengiz and Novorossiisk is more profitable for everyone than the more expensive and logistically awkward Baku–Ceyhan option.[58] Failing that, then better to engage economically in the latter than to exclude oneself altogether – an attitude highlighted by the possibility of Lukoil and Yukos participation in the project.

Generally speaking, the Putin administration's strategy can be defined as one that seeks to achieve traditional objectives by modern means. This dualism arises partly from a consciousness that primitive attempts to exercise geopolitical influence are not in the spirit of contemporary international politics; if Russia wishes to be seen as progressive and part of the 'civilized world', then it needs to behave accordingly. More important than such niceties, however, is that Moscow has little alternative. Russia's nuclear arsenal is no longer relevant as a tool of power projection; its conventional military capacity has degraded to the point that it cannot even win a war on its own territory; and its global standing, although improved, remains modest. That leaves only economic instruments: a strong economy as the foundation of a renewed political and military capability; a pivotal position as one of the world's leading energy suppliers; and the selective application of economic instruments to achieve specific policy aims. The irony is that it is Russia's economy, so long dismissed as a basket-case, that allows it to continue to act as a regional superpower[59] and, increasingly, as a significant international player. In the circumstances, it is hardly surprising that Putin should have assigned such priority to economic policy at home and abroad.

Economization and a 'balanced' foreign policy

Putin has managed, in a very brief space of time, to leaven the oppressive bias towards military-strategic priorities in Russian foreign policy. Management of the economic agenda in its diverse guises is now clearly a central component of Moscow's relations with the international community and in its outlook on the world. But in our enthusiasm and/or relief that the Kremlin's approach these days seems so much more 'reasonable' as a consequence, we should sound some cautionary notes.

The first relates to the distinction between means and ends, and between tactics and strategy. The choice of economic instruments does not equate in itself to an economically oriented world-view. As emphasized earlier, the Putin administration sees nothing incompatible between using the former to achieve long-standing political and strategic objectives. We are a long way from reaching the stage of 'Russia, Inc.'; geoeconomics and geopolitics are interrelated, not separate, entities. It is therefore premature to interpret the economization of Russian foreign policy as signifying its normalization in the Western nation-state sense. It may be that what we are witnessing instead is a process of 'modernization' rather than Westernization, in which the development of a market-oriented economy does not imply acceptance of Western political and social values (cf. the case of China).

Second, there is a normative tendency in the West to view an emphasis on economic means and ends as intrinsically 'good' and 'progressive' as against the 'bad' or 'retrograde' nature of a geopolitically centred foreign policy – indeed, perhaps this book is guilty of adding to this stereotype. We should reiterate, then, the point that the pursuit of an economic agenda is frequently motivated by selfish and unprogressive instincts. There is little that is 'balanced' or enlightened in, for example, many official attitudes towards foreign investment and participation in the Russian economy,[60] or in the attempts to protect backward industries and regions from the winds of structural change. Likewise, the growing influence of many sectional interests is strongly conservative and defensive, seeking to preserve a corporatized and illiberal economic model.

Third, notwithstanding the raised profile of economic priorities, most of the big foreign policy issues continue to be security and geopolitical, as we will see in the next chapter. It is relevant to note here that the pursuit of external economic priorities derives considerable impetus from what Russians call 'conjunctural' factors, such as political and strategic developments. Thus, Russia's WTO accession campaign has gained momentum as much from the fact of China's entry and the fortuitous (for Moscow) events of 11 September 2001 as from any considered evaluation of the advantages and responsibilities of membership. Similarly, the heightened interest in relations with the EU is only partially driven by economic considerations. While there is now a more professional approach to giving life to the provisions of the PCA, the Putin administration continues to view the EU principally through a political prism. It is indicative of this mentality that the main agenda item in the relationship should be visa-free access for inhabitants of Kaliningrad (and other Russian citizens) transiting Lithuania, and not how Russia can benefit economically from EU enlargement.[61] In both cases, WTO accession and Russia–EU relations, the politicization of key issues is likely to impact adversely on the effective implementation of core economic provisions, in the process calling into question how far things have really changed.

Consequently, when we speak about 'economization' and 'normalization' it is important to see the issue in relative terms. We should rid ourselves of any illusions that Putin looks at economic priorities and interests in the same way as his Western European counterparts. Given his background, as well as the elite's unfamiliarity with this agenda – the 'unnaturalness' of economics referred to at the beginning of the chapter – such hopes are wishful in the extreme. It is inevitable that Russian conceptions should reflect the influence of particular historical, cultural and economic features from a Soviet and post-Soviet past. Equally, that they should exclude certain notions that are integral to Western understandings, such as the interdependence between economic growth, democratization and the development of a civil society (see Chapter 6). On the other hand, it is important to recognize the extent to which things have evolved over the past three years. Compared with the almost openly neglectful approach of the Yeltsin administration towards foreign economic policy, the Kremlin today evinces a very different mentality as well as the capacity to give practical effect to general propositions. There is some way to go before Putin, or a successor, is able to realize his vision of the primacy of economic goals in Russian foreign policy – where security still matters more than money – but there is no doubt that the balance between the two is changing rapidly and will continue to do so for years to come.

5

Security and geopolitics

The geopolitical mindset

In a foreign policy notorious for its changeability and uncertainties, one constant has stood the test of time. The geopolitical mindset in Russia has ancient origins, dating back at least to the Mongol invasion in the 13th century, but has continued through the ages to define the conduct of external relations and the world-view of the governing class. In Russia, military power, territorial issues, threat perceptions, and notions of strategic balance have assumed a prominence unmatched anywhere else on the planet. In fact, so entrenched is the geopolitical mentality that the end of the Cold War, in most of the developed world a watershed in the transition to a new global politics, has had little positive impact on the Russian elite. During the first post-Soviet decade, the latter continued to think and act within the conceptual framework of a well-understood geopolitical triad: zero-sum games, notions of balance of power, and spheres of influence.[1] Notwithstanding declarations about an exciting era of cooperation in place of the confrontation of the past, the Yeltsin administration's foreign policy remained firmly centred in the primacy of the security and geopolitical agenda.

With the benefit of hindsight, this outcome should have come as no great surprise. In the first place, a holistic or 'balanced' foreign policy tends to be the luxury of nations that have enjoyed a less turbulent history. More than any other European country, Russia has suffered from invasions and physical aggression – not only from the east, but also from the north, south and, most critically, from the west. In the last case, the bitter experience of a 50-year Cold War, two extraordinarily bloody World Wars, and the Napoleonic invasion in the early 19th century created a virtually inexhaustible well of suspicion and insecurity *vis-à-vis* the outside world. Even in the most optimistic of post-Cold War scenarios, it would have been unrealistic to expect that such an accumulation of negative sentiment could have evaporated quickly; the project of attitudinal change was one of decades, not years.

Unfortunately, the course of events – both inside Russia and in its inter-action with the international community – turned out to be worse than anyone anticipated. Far from a new, if necessarily imperfect, era of inter-national cooperation becoming a reality, the 1990s saw a steady deterioration in relations between Moscow and the West, as well as the consolidation of a siege mentality within the Russian establishment.[2] The perception of an increasing divergence between a flourishing West and beleaguered Russia fostered a culture of blame, while much of the elite sought solace in the country's traditional strengths, namely its political-strategic trumps.

When Putin was designated Yeltsin's heir-apparent in September 1999, the prospects for a transformation of this mindset looked unpromising. Putin had spent a lifetime in the security apparatus, a constituency more than usually partial to geopolitical stereotypes,[3] while the recentness of the Kosovo conflict had widened the divide between Russia and the West, appearing to confirm the 'truth' that ultimate power was military and geopolitical, not economic. *The Economist*'s sobriquet of Putin as a 'Post Cold-Warrior'[4] reflected a generalized anxiety in the West about the likely resurgence of 'great power' ambitions in Russia and a further worsening in relations. And, indeed, some of the early signs were not good. The 2000 versions of the two main foreign policy statements – the Foreign Policy Concept and the Concept of National Security – were heavily weighted in favour of security and geo-political priorities, and expanded on many ideas developed by former Foreign Minister Primakov, very much the symbol of the geopolitical tendency in Russian foreign policy.[5] Meanwhile, in Putin's first few months in power, his visits to China, North Korea and Cuba seemed to suggest an intention to implement a multipolar foreign policy founded in continuing strategic rivalry with the United States.[6]

Three years on, it is clear these fears and expectations were exaggerated. Just as Russia's President has presided over a definite economization in foreign policy, so there has also been a considerable evolution in concepts of security and geopolitics. Many previously popular ideas have become unfashionable, while others have been substantially recast. At the same time, the overall importance of political-strategic issues has, if anything, increased. By revising long-held understandings of security, Putin has given new life to a sphere of policy that had lost much of its vitality and credibility. Well before the events of 11 September 2001, the Kremlin had eschewed the com-petitive approach towards such issues under Yeltsin and embraced in its stead notions about common threat perceptions and joint solutions to inter-national security problems.

As with the administration's emphasis on economic priorities, it is important to distinguish between means and ends, and between presentation

73

and substance. While many of the changes that have occurred are evidently much more than cosmetic, it is unclear whether they signal a quantum leap in Russian security and geopolitical thinking or represent merely an improved, more sophisticated version of the same model. This question is not only of academic interest. Because security-related issues have always occupied a central place in Moscow's outlook on the world, the government's approach here is perhaps the most reliable indicator of the extent to which Russian foreign policy as a whole is changing under Putin. In this connection, two aspects are of particular importance. The first is the evolution of strategic thinking in relation to core geopolitical constructs such as zero-sum calculus, the balance of power in its various dimensions, and spheres of influence. The second, more specific aspect is concerned with concrete threat perceptions and interests – the 'struggle against international terrorism', conflict management and WMD non-proliferation – as well as traditional priorities such as the preservation of Russia's territorial integrity, issues of geopolitical disadvantage, and the maintenance of strategic stability. These two very broad themes, covering respectively the ideology and praxis of geopolitics, are the subject of the coming pages.

Change and continuity in Russian strategic thinking

The evolution of the zero-sum mindset

Three basic concepts dominated Russian strategic thinking in the Soviet and Yeltsin periods. The first, and for a long time most important, was that of the zero-sum game. A product of the bipolar Cold War climate, this was grounded in the basic premise that success for one superpower *ipso facto* equated to a setback for the other, and vice versa. Even following the nominal end of the Cold War in the late Gorbachev period, the inertial power of this idea proved highly resilient. Although it soon became apparent that Moscow could no longer compete effectively with Washington, the political class was slow to grasp the full implications of this reality. Paradoxically, Russia's declining strategic fortunes stimulated rather than constrained the elite's 'great power' mentality. To the rivalry of the past was added a 'national humiliation' complex;[7] the spectacle of one superpower going from strength to strength while the other was down on its uppers imparted a bitter personal edge to the process. For the Yeltsin administration and most of the political class, a series of landmark developments – NATO enlargement, Washington's plans to develop strategic missile defence, the military interventions of the Western powers in Iraq and, most spectacularly, over Kosovo – pointed to one conclusion: the success of the West implied, if not the defeat of Russia as such, then certainly the frustration of many of its foreign and security policy objectives. It was indicative that during the 1990s commentators were apt to lament that Russian interests would have been better served had the West's various successes – such as over Kosovo – been less complete.[8]

Putin's approach to the problem of the zero-sum complex has been twofold. His main tactic has been to avoid any mention, or even suggestion, of political-strategic competition with the West. He has reset the foreign policy agenda in essentially positive terms: Moscow pursues this or that priority because it is in its best interests to do so and not, as in the past, because it wishes to frustrate Western policy intentions. One salient illustration of this new approach is in the CIS, where the administration is prosecuting a number of political, security and economic objectives with a consistency and determination absent during the Yeltsin years, when the Kremlin's approach was almost purely reactive – to developments on the ground and to Western involvement in the region. Another sign of the declining relevance of zero-sum notions is the different emphasis in the government's attitude towards issues such as 'strategic stability'. Whereas previously Moscow focused on the direct impact on Russia – the weakening of its strategic position *vis-à-vis* America – under Putin it has graduated towards a more 'selfless' approach, highlighting instead the security implications for the international community as a whole. Thus Putin called Washington's decision to abrogate the 1972 ABM Treaty a 'mistake' because it undermined global arms control, not because it threatened Russia's ability to defend itself.[9] On a broader level, Putin has been supportive of, or at worst non-committal about, American foreign policy initiatives around the world, e.g., in the Middle East, while also remaining modest about Russian foreign policy successes. The petulance and grandstanding that previously characterized Russian behaviour have gone.

But if the zero-sum complex is less overt these days, it would be premature to claim that it has disappeared altogether. We are witnessing a transformation of the zero-sum mentality into a more positive-sum mindset. But this is very much a work in progress, an evolution rather than a revolution. The second part of Putin's approach to zero-sum, therefore, is the residual, if tacit, assumption that at least some of international politics is still about 'winners' and 'losers'. While there are more opportunities for positive-sum cooperation in which the outcomes benefit nearly everyone – for example, in the fight against international terrorism – there remain areas where the picture is much more ambiguous. A case in point is NATO enlargement. Although the Kremlin's position has softened considerably since Putin came to power, it nevertheless continues to be based in the conviction that enlargement is largely directed against Russia and not, as Brussels insists, to promoting stability and democracy on the European continent. On the one hand, the Putin administration states that it no longer regards

NATO as an 'enemy' organization, and has committed itself to a more substantive and cooperative relationship with it via the Russia–NATO Council.[10] On the other hand, it regards the alliance's move eastwards as an unfriendly act, as its continuing criticisms of impending Baltic accession indicate. In short, although the terms of Russian opposition are milder, being couched in the positive-sum desire for wider European security, the zero-sum mentality lives on nonetheless.

What this contradiction illustrates also is that one person's idea of positive-sum outcomes is sometimes another person's zero-sum game, and that there is still a long way to travel before Russian security perceptions approximate those of Western governments. In this context, a potential complicating factor is that Putin's move away from the crude zero-sum calculus of the past has yet to take root within the Russian establishment. The latter, to a much greater extent than the President, subscribes to stereotypical images of NATO and American geopolitical imperialism. For the time being it is too weak and timid to arrest the evolution of the zero-sum mindset, but over the longer term it may be able to create a sufficient groundswell of negative opinion to undermine Putin's resolve. That is why it is important for the West to engage Moscow as closely as possible, in practical ways and not simply rhetorically. Failure to do so will not bring about Putin's demise, let alone lead to a reorientation of Russian foreign policy, but it would unnecessarily prolong the influence of zero-sum ideas on the administration's thinking.

The balance of power – back to the future?

As long as the Soviet Union remained in existence, the notion of balance of power was relatively straightforward. The overwhelming nuclear capabilities of the two superpowers, together with the longevity of the Cold War, meant that for Moscow the only really important balance of power was the strategic, predominantly nuclear, relationship with Washington. The fall of the Soviet Union and the continuing decline of the post-Soviet Russian state, however, introduced an entirely different set of realities. Instead of the one all-encompassing rivalry there emerged a profusion of balance-of-power notions – strategic and conventional, global and regional, multilateral and bilateral. The question became much more complicated and multidimensional, a fact that only increased its pertinence for the Russian elite. At the same time, with the loss of superpower status the Yeltsin administration was trapped in a critical contradiction between a continuing allegiance to traditional (that is, Soviet) balance-of-power thinking and the requirement to adapt to the changed circumstances of international power. The Kremlin's response, unsatisfactory and inconsistently applied, was to make the balance of power the cornerstone of a geopolitically oriented foreign policy, devoting greater attention to its various forms in inverse proportion to the decline in Russian military and strategic capabilities.

First among these balance-of-power concepts was the ideology of multipolarity developed by then Foreign Minister Primakov in the second half of the 1990s, and formally articulated at the Sino-Russian summit in Beijing in April 1997. The intention behind the creation of a 'multipolar world order for the 21st century'[11] was to substitute a revised bipolarity for the defunct Cold War strategic equilibrium. If Russia could no longer 'counter-balance' the United States on its own, then it would seek to constrain Washington's freedom of action by enlisting the help of others – China, the United Nations, the Islamic world, even Western Europe in some instances. This would not and could never assume the guise of a formal anti-American alliance, but the accumulation of like-minded attitudes on a range of issues might act as a *de facto* check on American 'hegemonistic' tendencies and 'unipolarity'. It was characteristic of ideas of revised bipolarity that they moved away from the old attachment to exact nuclear parity and other strict numerical criteria – such as force and equipment limits under the Conventional Forces in Europe (CFE) Treaty – to embracing a new obsession that interpreted 'strategic stability' in the abstract sense of a rough equality in international decision-making and geopolitical reach. But the motivation and mindset remained much the same, if the Yeltsin administration realized that the obsolescence of Russia's nuclear arsenal made military equivalence unattainable,[12] then this in no way lessened its desire to 'match' the United States wherever and however possible – and all the better for doing so behind the respectable façade of an allegiance to post-Cold War multilateral values.

The 1990s also saw the reappearance of more 'classical', less directly adversarial, conceptions of the balance of power. The 19th-century idea of the 'Concert' of great powers, which originated at the 1815 Congress of Vienna,[13] offered the model of a few major powers – the United States, Russia, Britain, Germany, France, China, Japan – making all the important international decisions. Because within such a framework these powers would balance one another and share certain strategic 'values', they might be more willing to work together for common purposes while refraining from actions that ignored the interests of other 'club members'. The *raison d'être* here was more flexible and less personal than in the case of revised bipolarity. The objective was not so much to constrain Washington as such, but to obtain a broader status quo in which more or less 'equal' players moderated one another and restrained the assertiveness of the regional superpower, *whoever that might be*. In Europe, this was the United States, but in Asia the potential hegemon was China. It was typical of the Yeltsin administration's thinking that it should seek in this latter context to improve bilateral relations with Beijing *and* Tokyo simultaneously, as well as involve itself more closely with Asia-Pacific multilateral security mechanisms. Central to conceptions both of revised bipolarity and the revival of the Concert of great powers was the assumption that it was unhealthy for any one nation to dominate the others, whether globally or in a regional context. Such beliefs arose out of a zero-sum psychology that equated 'excessive' success for the hegemon with insufficient respect for the legitimate interests of other parties – in particular Russia.

It was a natural function of Russia's strategic decline in the post-Soviet period that the balance of power should assume ever more diverse guises in the eyes of a worried elite. Whereas once the United States had been virtually the sole subject of grave concern, the number of potential rivals and threats to national security had now multiplied. In addition to such historical 'suspects' as a resurgent China and newly assertive Japan, there were also regional powers – Turkey, Iran – for which the USSR's dismemberment into 15 independent nations appeared to open up abundant opportunities for maximizing influence at Russian expense. Furthermore, the instability of many of the newly independent republics dramatized the shift from the 'orderliness' of the former superpower nuclear rivalry to a volatile security environment in which maintaining the balance was both more immediately critical and highly problematic.

Given this basket of strategic insecurities, one of the most singular features of Putin's handling of security and geopolitical priorities has been the near anonymity of balance-of-power concepts. The most notable casualty of the government's changed approach has been the competitive multi-polarity associated with Primakov.[14] Significantly, Putin made almost no reference to such ideas during his presidential campaign in the spring of 2000, a discretion that has been maintained since. Although the Foreign Policy Concept published in June that year reiterated multipolarity as the basis of Russia's understanding of (and approach towards) the world, in retrospect this turned out to be the swansong for a construct that had been definitively discredited by Moscow's failed response to the Kosovo crisis. The single most important lesson for Russia from that unfortunate episode was that, for all the disagreements between transatlantic allies or China's rise to a more influential position in global affairs, the vision of a 'multipolar world order' remained a chimera. The United States' political-strategic dominance was beyond challenge, then and in the foreseeable future. Attempting to 'balance' this power by competitive means, multilateral or bilateral, was therefore futile and counterproductive. Far from having any impact on American behaviour, Russia would doom itself to a debilitating marginalization, falling ever further behind the developed world.[15]

In recognizing what had been apparent for some time, Putin moved instead to embrace ideas of cooperative balance similar to those embodied in the Concert of great powers. At one level, he engaged early on in an intensive programme of reciprocal high-level visits around the world – Europe, the CIS, Asia, Latin America – that indicated a continuing commitment to a globalist foreign policy. Part of his motivation here was a need to familiarize himself in an area of government – international relations – where he had relatively little background, as well as to make himself known to others. But more important still was the desire to expand Moscow's foreign policy options. Although some Russian and Western commentators saw the high-level exchanges with 'rogue states' – Iran, Cuba, North Korea – as evidence of an enduring competitive streak in the Kremlin, Putin's approach on these occasions belied this simplistic interpretation. While he attached public importance to ties with such 'partners', he was also careful to avoid negative, anti-American, references or entanglements that might be misinterpreted as part of a global balancing game. On the contrary, it was Putin who, even before becoming president, took the initiative to revive the Russia–NATO relationship that had been in abeyance since Kosovo.

For much of his presidency, Putin has pursued a consciously eclectic and open-ended approach; the message has been that Russia is 'everyone's friend', opposing only the truly egregious and seeking to play a constructive role in the world. And, however one judges the sincerity of such intentions, it is undeniable that the administration has tried very hard to depoliticize the conduct of external relations. In the previous chapter, we mentioned this in connection with its management of international economic issues. But it is also true of the security agenda, which Moscow has gone out of its way to internationalize. Whereas previously the talk was all about the geopolitical threat posed to Russia by NATO 'expansion', Western 'encroachment' in the former Soviet Union, and American 'hegemonism' and 'diktat', today's themes are collective: 'the struggle against international terrorism', WMD non-proliferation, and continental (rather than national) security in Europe, the FSU and the Asia-Pacific. Such a makeover of security priorities, reflecting the switch from a principally adversarial to a cooperative mindset, has effectively invalidated the key premise underpinning the zero-sum mindset and traditional balance-of-power ideas – the existence of an enemy or enemies.[16]

But, as with the zero-sum mindset, the decreased significance of balance-of-power notions does not mean that they no longer feature in Moscow's understanding of international affairs. First, the nuclear balance remains a critical component of national security policy – as demonstrated by the Kremlin's (successful) insistence on a 'binding' strategic arms reductions agreement with the United States in May 2002.[17] What is at stake here is not security in the narrow sense of deterrence, but preserving Russia's highly particularized status as a world power – perhaps no longer the match of America, but certainly a cut above other, predominantly regional powers such as Britain, France, Germany, Japan, and even China. Second, it would be a mistake to interpret comprehension of the changing nature of balances of power as necessarily signifying acceptance, let alone approval. Although there are instances, such as NATO enlargement, where no adequate balance-of-power response is available, there are others where the Russian leadership is very much cognizant of the importance *and* feasibility of maintaining a rough parity. For example, the question of mitigating the security consequences of the demographic imbalance in the Far East[18] is assuming its highest profile for some time – as evidenced by the consolidation and expansion of the original 'Shanghai Five' arrangements on border confidence-building measures.[19] Meanwhile, in Europe the CFE Treaty continues to play an important, if no longer primary, role in Russian conceptions of continental security.

Finally, to return to the theme of means and ends, it is not so much that Putin and members of his administration believe that the principle of the balance of power has become anachronistic, but that balance *in practice* is more likely to be achieved through collective efforts than by a severely weakened Russia on its own. It is a sign that Moscow is attaching more, not less, importance to such ideas that it is pursuing closer cooperation with 'hard' security structures (NATO) instead of, as in Yeltsin's time, attempting to counterpose weak organizations and mechanisms like the Organization for Security and Cooperation in Europe (OSCE) and the Western European Union (WEU) in virtual balance-of-power games with the United States.

This last point suggests that there is sometimes a fine line between modernized balance-of-power principles and collective security in the genuine positive-sum sense. One can envisage a scenario in which, over time, the means are perceived to be so efficient that they become the ends, introducing in the process a new set of 'truths' into security thinking. Putin's Russia, however, is not yet at this stage. The recentness and intensity of the superpower rivalry with America, on top of a turbulent history, have inculcated in its political class, Putin included, deep-seated vulnerabilities that cannot be so easily dispelled. It will take considerable time, as well as a largely trouble-free run in Russia's relations with West and East alike, before its elite ceases to think in the negative terms of balancing power, and moves definitively towards more generous conceptions of security based on shared values.

Spheres of influence — from neo-imperialism to post-imperialism

During the Yeltsin period, spheres of influence — also known as 'spheres of vital interests' — fell into two broad categories. The first and most overt concerned the immediate periphery around the new Russia — the former Soviet republics. The second, more prophylactic in character, covered the former Warsaw Pact nations of Central and Eastern Europe. In both cases, the idea itself of a 'sphere of influence' remained elusive and contradictory. For example, it was clear from the beginning that there would be no territorial reconstitution, however partial, of the Soviet state, just as it was recognized that the rapid Westernization of Central and Eastern Europe was irreversible. The Yeltsin regime was apt to insist that the international community should take Russia's interests in these regions into account, but there was no precise sense of what this meant in practice. Given the lack of consensus within the political class on the general question of Russian 'national interests', it was hardly surprising that there should also be no clear idea of the implications arising from 'possession' of a sphere of influence — a difficulty exacerbated by Moscow's declining ability and will to project power in its former imperial pale. Thus, from time to time Russian forces ('peacekeepers') stationed in various parts of the CIS — Transdniestria, Abkhazia, South Ossetia — would meddle in local conflicts, but largely on their own initiative and without official sanction from the authorities back in Moscow.

The result of this confusion was the worst of both worlds. Russia gained an unsavoury reputation for a patrimonial mentality and imperial syndrome[20] without, however, managing to reinforce its geopolitical interests in the FSU or Eastern Europe. The Yeltsin administration succeeded only in looking at once imperialistic *and* feeble. In Chapter 2, we noted the catalogue of failures in its relations with the FSU: severely reduced political, security and economic interaction; mounting tensions on a number of issues, such as treatment of the Russian diaspora; and the continuation of intra-FSU conflicts, frequently aggravated by the activities of local Russian military contingents. And it was a similarly unhappy tale in Central and Eastern Europe, where Moscow's increasingly desperate responses to NATO enlargement offered a curious counterpoint to its minimal interest in developing relations with the post-communist leaderships of the region.

At the heart of this contradiction was a fundamentally passive-reactive approach towards the notion of spheres of influence. Partly from lack of interest, partly from awareness of the limitations of Russian influence, and partly because of a mindset that tended to believe that the only international issues worth pursuing were the ones involving the other 'great powers', the Yeltsin administration's interest in FSU-related affairs and Central and Eastern Europe remained overwhelmingly derivative. Lacking the consistent desire and energy to make good on its claims of 'zones of special interests', it restricted itself to occasional bursts of activity in response to allegedly hostile Western actions. Typically, the post-Soviet periphery acquired its highest profile whenever NATO conducted joint exercises with CIS member states (Georgia, Ukraine, Azerbaijan, Uzbekistan), or in connection with American participation in Caspian oil exploitation ('Contract of the Century') and pipeline projects (Baku–Ceyhan). Similarly, the countries of Central and Eastern Europe were important to Moscow not on their own merits, but as subjects of growing Western interest as reflected in NATO enlargement and, later, the alliance's intervention over Kosovo.

Putin's approach to spheres of influence is the inverse of his predecessor's. On the one hand, there is very little mention of the concept itself in government statements, except to deny and disparage it.[21] The Kremlin understands that the imperialistic connotations of the term both offend the former Soviet republics and send the wrong signals to influential players in the international community, namely the United States and Western Europe. On the other hand, the passive-reactive approach of the past has given way to a new activism on the ground. Ties with the former Soviet Union are more substantive and multifaceted than at any time since the break-up of the USSR, while Putin has worked hard to re-establish Russia's relations with former Warsaw Pact states like Poland on a qualitatively different basis.[22] Engagement is now valued for its own sake, rather than as an instrument to counter Western strategic advances. To this purpose, the emphasis is on demonstrating the benefits Russia can bring to the interests of those countries, in place of the mixture of threats and complaints that characterized Moscow's behaviour in the 1990s. The paradoxical outcome of this understated approach, however, is that Russian influence in these regions has reached levels unsurpassed in over a decade. Previously obstreperous countries, for example Ukraine, have been far more accommodating towards Moscow's interests than they were during the Yeltsin period.[23]

Implicit in the Kremlin's handling of spheres of influence is a cold-blooded pragmatism. Putin has decided that, as with zero-sum and the balance of power, there is no point in fighting unwinnable battles, or in declaiming about 'spheres of influence' when you are unable to prove your case. In this context, a much underestimated factor in Putin's decision to support the American military deployment in Central Asia post-11 September was that he could not have prevented this in any event.[24] He understood that Russian influence on the Central Asian states, though considerable, was not so great as to forestall an action that was manifestly in their best security interests. Better, therefore, to accept the inevitable with good grace, especially as Russia too benefited from the elimination of a long-standing menace in the form of the Taliban regime. More generally, by revising strategic expectations Putin has set achievable targets. Russia has very real levers of influence on Eastern Europe (as an energy supplier) and the FSU (across the board), but the key to their effectiveness is not to overstrain them. Ultimately, then, it is not that he has thrown out the idea of spheres of influence, but that he has reworked (or 'modernized') it taking into account Russia's capabilities and the changed regional and global environment in which it operates.

The evolution of threat perceptions

The revamping of traditional geopolitical concepts has had a powerful effect on Russian threat perceptions. In Soviet times, and subsequently under Yeltsin, the salience of zero-sum, the balance of power, and spheres of influence in strategic thinking determined a certain set and ranking of priorities. It was consistent with the psychological climate of the Cold War and its aftermath that, for example, defence against nuclear attack by the United States and the dogma of strategic stability should assume pride of place. Likewise, it was logical that against this backdrop Moscow should attach disproportionate importance to issues of geopolitical 'disadvantage', such as NATO enlargement, Western involvement in the CIS, and international conflict resolution in the Middle East (Iraq) and the Balkans. On the other hand, the identification of the United States as prime adversary ensured a relative lack of interest in areas – WMD non-proliferation, international terrorism, and internal political and socio-economic instability – where the importance of such rivalry was secondary or non-existent.

It would be wrong to see the advent of Putin as marking an overnight transformation in Russian security thinking. Since the fall of the USSR, this had been evolving slowly from its Soviet and Cold War bases to a more variegated view of the world that combined conservative stereotypes with a more flexible and expansive interpretation of security. The outcome was something of an oddity, dysfunctional and contradictory. Official statements of Russian defence and security policy – the 1993, 1997 and 2000 Concepts of National Security, and the 1993 and 2000 versions of the Military Doctrine – consistently underplayed the possibility of a state-based (i.e., Western) military attack on Russia,[25] yet defence planning continued to operate from just such a premise. The opposition of a large part of the military leadership to the downsizing of Russia's strategic missile forces;[26] the insistence on maintaining a large conscript-based army; scenario planning for military exercises[27] – all these pointed to a *de facto* conviction that the West remained the enemy. The same unevenness of policy was apparent in relation to 'soft' security. The 1997 National Security Concept was notable for its emphasis on internal instead of external sources of insecurity; the main threats to Russia, it claimed, came from political uncertainty, economic crisis and social deprivation.[28] Yet three years later the updated version was amended in the light of the Kosovo crisis to highlight instead the menace posed by Western, and particularly American, hegemonistic tendencies.[29]

The haphazard development of threat perceptions under Yeltsin was a function of the generalized directionlessness in post-Soviet society and absence of consensus on issues of identity. Since there was no agreement on what sort of nation Russia was or where it was going, it followed that there could be no unity of perception on the threats confronting it, let alone on their respective priority. In these circumstances, what Putin has done is not so much to revolutionize Russian thinking as to introduce a measure of concordance between existing ideas as well as consistency in their application. He has adopted a capacious approach that incorporates traditional notions of 'hard' security (nuclear and conventional deterrence, geopolitical calculus), while ridding them of their more unsustainable aspects. Simultaneously, there has been a renewed stress on 'non-traditional' security problems such as terrorism. The outcome of this combination of old and new is a more consolidated and comprehensive set of threat perceptions, domestic and international. Rather than commit Russia to a particular security world-view, Putin has preferred to borrow from all constituencies in a sort of 'consensus by inclusion'. And while beneath the surface threat perceptions among the elite continue to differ in important respects, this is less significant than the fact that the President is committed to a uniformity of attitudes in this most high-profile area of Russian foreign policy.

International terrorism

There is no doubt that for Putin the number one threat facing Russia is terrorism. From the time of his appointment as Prime Minister in the autumn of 1999, he has rigorously – some might say, fanatically – pursued this theme. Initial doubts that his stance was something of a cynical ruse to capitalize on public reaction to the Moscow apartment bombings[30] and enhance his electability have given way to acknowledgment that this is one issue where he is emotionally as well as intellectually engaged. His hypersensitive responses to Western media questioning of Moscow's conduct of the Chechen war point to a sincerity of conviction and purpose that goes well beyond the call of political pragmatism.[31]

What is less clear is the extent to which Putin really believes that *international* as opposed to domestic terrorism is the major threat confronting Russia and the world. For much of his presidency Moscow has sought to internationalize the Chechen war in order to 'legitimize' Russian military operations in the republic. Unable to justify by 'normal' reasons an all-too-routine brutality and violation of human rights, the government has resorted to the well-worn tactic of rationalizing extreme actions on the grounds of extreme threat. In this connection, the events of 11 September 2001 were a boon to Russia, 'proof' that Moscow and not the Western world had been right all along about Chechnya and the wider terrorist menace lurking behind it. Previously accused of acting in a barbaric manner, the Putin administration has promoted itself as having been ahead of the game, divining the true nature of the threat long before anyone else.[32]

In doing so, it has revived the idea, popular in the 19th century, of Russia as the barrier protecting the civilized West from the hordes of barbarism.[33] The emergence of international terrorism as a worldwide priority is seen as a bridge linking Russia with the West spiritually and civilizationally, and as the principal means of accelerating its political and security integration following the isolation of the Yeltsin period.[34] That is why Putin was so quick to offer his support to the Americans following 11 September, despite the Russian elite's preference for a neutral stance.[35] The events of that day and their aftermath have allowed him to combine sincerity of belief with foreign policy opportunism. Rejecting an outdated strategic logic that advocated taking advantage of American discomfiture, he has understood that there is much more to gain from an enthusiastically cooperative approach. Not only are Western official attitudes to the Kremlin's conduct of the Chechen war much milder these days but, more critically still, Russia has assumed a prominent role as a constructive international player. Its actual influence on proceedings remains modest, but its very geographical proximity to past and present theatres of international terrorism – Central Asia, the Transcaucasus, even the Middle East – has afforded it lasting and privileged participation rights.

All this begs the question of whether international terrorism is likely to retain its position at the head of Russian threat perceptions. Here, the principal determinant will be the course of the Chechen war rather than the success (or otherwise) of American efforts in destroying al-Qaeda and other terrorist organizations. As long as Moscow fails to suppress effective armed resistance in the rebel province, Putin will continue to internationalize the problem for the purposes of legitimization. Although it will take much more than Chechnya to undermine his political position, he nevertheless has a vested interest in maintaining a broadly based rationale for his current approach, one that appeals across the domestic political spectrum and to Western governments alike. The linkage between Chechnya and the global fight against international terrorism is directed to achieving precisely this by tapping into as many constituencies as possible.

The geopolitical map

Putin's first significant foreign policy action following his appointment as Prime Minister (and President-elect) was to resume Russia's security dialogue with NATO within the framework of the 1997 Founding Act.[36] Since then, he has floated various ideas for improving cooperation, including the notional possibility, at some unspecified time in the future and under certain conditions, of Russian membership in the alliance.[37] Most recently, both sides have agreed on a framework and mechanism for future cooperation, the Russia–NATO Council, whereby Russia plays an active part in NATO decision-making in various areas of mutual interest – including international anti-terrorism, crisis management, WMD non-proliferation, and arms control. The Rome agreement, signed in May 2002, represents a significant step forward compared with the former arrangements under which Moscow was restricted to a purely consultative role.[38]

It is tempting, given the changed atmosphere in Russia–NATO relations and the emphasis on meeting common threats, to suppose that the Putin administration no longer views the alliance in an adversarial light. To some extent, this perception is justified. For instance, few believe that an enlarged NATO, even one incorporating the three Baltic states, poses any kind of military threat to Russia. However, we need to differentiate between the notion of physical threat and the more abstract idea of geopolitical disadvantage. The significance of the first declined steadily during the 1990s, notwithstanding reversals such as the Kosovo crisis, while the second has on the contrary maintained its importance. Under Putin the focus on more concrete foreign policy priorities, security as well as economic, has led to a reduction in regime dogmatism on geopolitics. But it would be premature to interpret the currently favourable dynamics of Russia–NATO ties as signifying approval of the alliance's role in European security or of its expanding cooperation with states in Eastern Europe and the former Soviet Union. The Kremlin understands that NATO is the only serious security organization in Europe, and that Russia must find a way to interact effectively with it. However, the paucity of Russia's options does not mean that it regards this state of affairs as satisfactory. For all the improvement in relations, the Putin administration – and the Russian establishment in general – continues to view NATO's domination of European security as geopolitically unhealthy.

Several examples illustrate this ambivalent thinking. First, Moscow remains firmly opposed to Baltic accession, even though this would, if anything, weaken NATO by placing extra demands on alliance resources while offering virtually nothing in return. The real issues are symbolic and psychological. Baltic accession would underline the trend over the past decade of inexorable growth by one half of the former Cold War divide with the other half in a seemingly permanent state of contraction. Irrespective of the mollifying statements of Western leaders, this is a reality that is emotionally disturbing to an elite long attuned to things being the other way round. On a slightly less primitive plane, many feel that Baltic accession should be resisted because it conveys a message that is anti-Russian at heart: the implicit assumption of a Russian threat, if not today, then at some unspecified point in the future.[39] Particularly in the light of lasting tensions over the status of the Russian-speaking populations in Latvia and Estonia, as well as an awareness of more generalized Baltic suspicions about imperialist inclinations in Moscow, there is a natural tendency to conclude that the only possible reason for NATO's inclusion of the three republics is to guarantee their security against the one enemy that could threaten them.

Moscow's opposition to Baltic membership of NATO is part of a generally negative attitude towards NATO activities in the former Soviet Union. Although the administration's reactions to this kind of military-technical cooperation have been less alarmist than under Yeltsin, its initial opposition to American assistance to Georgian anti-terrorist operations in the Pankisi gorge in March 2002 confirmed that Moscow remains acutely sensitive to Western military involvement in areas that it regards as within its (tacit) sphere of influence. The episode was interesting, too, in that it highlighted a real tension between different threat perceptions and priorities. On the one hand, Moscow admitted there was a problem with armed terrorist groups operating in the area, one that could only be eradicated with outside assistance. On the other hand, it resisted the introduction of the most effective instrument for resolving these difficulties because it involved a non-Russian source, worse still the Americans. In demanding that Russian advisors and troops should carry out the job, the Putin administration appeared to be less concerned about the activities of 'international terrorists' in the region than to keep US forces out of Russia's geopolitical pale.[40]

Implicit in the contrary Russian attitudes towards enlargement and NATO activities in the FSU is a tenacious belief that the alliance cannot change its stripes. It may assume additional responsibilities – meeting 'common threats' such as terrorism and WMD proliferation – but for all that it remains for many 'an instrument of the Cold War'.[41] Although the former dichotomy between a 'bad' NATO and 'good' EU is no longer so unconditional as a result of the latter's enlargement and its implications for Kaliningrad,[42] the alliance's image is still predominantly a negative one. The Russian endgame – albeit remote – is therefore not so much the transformation of NATO from a defence into a 'political' organization, but for EU-based security mechanisms – the European Security and Defence Policy (ESDP) and the Rapid Reaction Force (RRF) – to counterbalance NATO-based structures within an integrated European security architecture.[43] Only in this event, the logic runs, would Russia be guaranteed against the further erosion of its geopolitical position in Europe and beyond.

Strategic stability

It is a transparent reality that the strategic gap between the two Cold War superpowers has grown, almost exponentially, over the past 10–15 years. In the 1980s Soviet strategic planners were already moving away from the rule of strict numerical equality towards a 'rough parity' based on a more flexible interpretation of the principle of strategic stability.[44] By the time Yeltsin came to power, the incipient obsolescence of the Soviet nuclear arsenal made it increasingly urgent for Russia to conclude strategic arms control agreements before the imbalance with the United States assumed truly serious proportions, i.e., altered the strategic balance. It was symptomatic of official anxiety on this score that, from their often very different perspectives, the Foreign Ministry and MOD should consistently advocate ratification of the START-2 agreement, and even agitate for a START-3 agreement involving further drastic reductions.[45] The reasoning was simple: if Russia could not sustain nuclear parity at currently agreed levels, then it was imperative to bring the Americans down to a threshold at which this might be achieved.

At the same time, there was more to the Yeltsin regime's attitude than mere arithmetical assessment of a notional security threat. Nuclear weapons, notwithstanding their obsolescence, were the most potent symbol of Russia's identity as a great power.[46] No matter how far things deteriorated in other areas of domestic and foreign policy, they remained a constant, a trump that, in a manner of speaking, raised Russia above the other (non-American) international actors – the Western Europeans, Japan, China. Given the implausibility of Western nuclear or conventional attack, the formalization of arms control agreements with Washington became important chiefly for its geopolitical resonance. The vociferous opposition to American strategic missile defence plans should be seen in this light. There was never much credence attached to the notion that these might, in time, nullify Russian retaliatory strike capabilities;[47] the real point was that Washington was making a decision of global strategic significance in the knowledge that Moscow no longer had the means to respond effectively. The damage was not to Russia's physical security, but to its geopolitical stature and self-respect.

It is typical of Putin's more practical approach to foreign policy priorities that this symbolism has lost much of its former urgency. His relaxed reaction to the American decision to abrogate the ABM treaty reflected, in the first place, a recognition that attempting to resist the inevitable would hurt Russia more than the United States; the supposed 'counter-measures' recommended by some would have no effect except to isolate Moscow. Equally, there has been a noticeable diminution in references to 'strategic stability' which, under Yeltsin, was almost as much an article of faith as the 'global multipolar order'.

Yet, as with the handling of geopolitical constructs, the understating of such ideas in no way signifies their irrelevance. The administration's insistence that nuclear weapons reductions be formalized in a legally binding agreement with Washington demonstrated a continuing attachment to strategic stability and parity, and to preserving what it could of Russia's geopolitical status. Indeed, so important are such priorities that Moscow was less concerned by the details of the framework document signed by Presidents Bush and Putin in May 2002 than to obtain American compliance to the principle itself of bipolar decision-making – at least as it relates to a small but vital corner of international affairs. This explains why Moscow showed unusual flexibility on such contentious points as the disposal – storage (or stockpiling) instead of destruction – of nuclear warheads to be 'eliminated' under the agreement.

The May 2002 agreement highlights, too, the changing character of strategic stability over the past 20 years – from exact parity to rough equivalence to a fragile and highly conditional regime of joint strategic arms control. In a sense, this steady transformation is emblematic of a larger evolution in understandings of security. As the spectre of direct military attack has receded, so it has been necessary to update threat assessments in order to maintain their validity. And while in the West we have been accustomed to viewing this as a largely positive trend involving an emphasis on 'soft' security interests, in the Russian case it entails the recasting – not jettisoning – of many long-standing security and geopolitical concepts such as strategic stability.

The importance of this distinction becomes clearer if China is brought into the picture. For Moscow strategic stability is currently centred in a bipolar control exercised by the United States and Russia and in preserving the strategic status quo between them to the extent possible. Yet at the same time it cannot ignore the rise of China as a global force, a phenomenon that sooner or later is likely to be expressed in a substantial modernization of Beijing's nuclear force capabilities. Consequently, although it would take many decades for China to become a major nuclear power, Putin is already looking to include it in new security arrangements that would effectively restrain it from ever entertaining such ambitions.[48] In this instance, the notion of strategic stability reacquires some of its original, overtly security rationale; the potential threat would no longer be just to Russia's geopolitical position, but would pertain directly to the shifting balance of power on Russia's eastern frontier.

The defence of territorial integrity

It is axiomatic in Russian conceptions of security to assert the primacy of defending the nation's 'territorial integrity'. During the Yeltsin period this principle was frequently invoked to justify Moscow's stance on various foreign and security policy issues – the territorial dispute with Japan, the conduct of the 1994-96 Chechen war – and also in areas where the Russian interest was secondary at best, such as the 1999 Kosovo conflict. In reality, however, the principle of territorial integrity was more rhetorical than real, something to be reiterated on appropriate occasions for its perceived legitimizing effect.[49] The record of the 1990s shows how tenuous this allegedly inviolable principle was in practice. Moscow let Chechnya govern itself for the best part of three years, before a combination of domestic political imperatives, mounting terrorist activity, and Chechen incursions into Dagestan set off in a second military campaign.[50] Yeltsin, supported by liberal elements in the establishment, attempted to reach a territorial settlement with Japan over the disputed islands. And in Kosovo it was evident that solicitude for the territorial integrity of the Federal Republic of Yugoslavia was the least of the considerations shaping Russian policy.

Putin's combination of pragmatism and nationalism has led him to adopt a similarly dichotomous approach. Territorial integrity remains important *qua* principle, but it is not a priority to which the government has devoted much attention, except in the domestic context of Chechnya where the emphasis is on the reimposition of central control rather than on territorial integrity as such.

The uncertain course of discussions with the Japanese over the Northern Territories/South Kuriles[51] reveals this ambiguity well. On the one hand, the administration understands the advantages in brokering a deal with the Japanese over islands that have lost their former, Cold War, strategic utility[52] but that remain a domestic burden and running foreign policy sore. Also, the fact that Putin's Russia is an altogether more confident international actor makes it easier to be 'generous'; previously, such flexibility was viewed by the political class as yet another sign of the weakness of both Russia and the Kremlin.[53] On the other hand, as an advocate of a strong state it is psychologically and politically awkward for Putin to make territorial concessions without obtaining clear dividends (as opposed to expressions of goodwill and intent) in return. Finding a balance on this issue has been further hampered by the nationalist revival in Japan, where the beleaguered Koizumi government has sought to 'compensate' for economic recession by a more assertive attitude on the islands. In the end, the 'threat' is not so much to Russia's territorial integrity as to its self-esteem. Putin's resort to the 1956 formula (under which the USSR undertook to give two of the four islands back)[54] demonstrated a willingness to find a compromise solution on the basis of an earlier Soviet commitment – thereby finessing the atmospherics of territorial handover. But Tokyo's insistence on prior Russian recognition of Japanese sovereignty over all the islands has put him in an invidious position: to accept a solution on these terms would be humiliating and even politically troublesome, reviving the spectre of zero-sum games in which Russia once again finishes on the wrong side of the ledger.

Generally speaking, the issue of territorial integrity has become peripheral in official threat perceptions because scenarios of external attack are now increasingly improbable, particularly after the fall of the Taliban in Afghanistan removed even the theoretical possibility of a radicalized Islam sweeping up through Central Asia. One issue, however, continues to exercise many observers – the problem of the Russian Far East (RFE) and the prospect of Chinese expansion in the region. The perception is not of any threat to Russian sovereignty in the near future, but derives from the premise that 'nature abhors a vacuum'; as the local population steadily decreases, and that of China grows, so the latter will move into the areas vacated by the former in a 'creeping' (*polzuchii*) expansionism.[55] The fact that these territories were acquired controversially through 'unequal' treaties, such as the 1860 Treaty of Peking,[56] only reinforces the opinion of some commentators that the Chinese will pursue irredentist claims, one way or another, as soon as the chance arises. Thus far, however, these warnings have yet to take firm hold in the Putin administration. Not only is it looking for every opportunity to expand economic relations with China, but it is also selling ever larger quantities of high-tech weapons to Beijing – hardly the action of a govern-ment fearful of its neighbour.

International conflict resolution

In many respects, international conflict resolution was the busiest of Russia's security priorities during the Yeltsin years. Peacekeeping and peace enforcement in the CIS, the fighting in Bosnia, the Middle East Peace Process (MEPP), periodic crises involving Iraq, and most notably the war over Kosovo – these provided an almost endless supply of conflict situations to keep the Kremlin interested. At the same time, the issue went well beyond its literal ambit; what was principally at stake was not so much resolving this or that crisis – often an insuperable task – but defining some sort of role for Russia as an influential or at least prominent actor in the conflict resolution process. Frequently, this priority dictated a *laissez-faire* approach on the ground; in the Balkans in particular, Moscow vigorously opposed Western military action to rein in the Serbs in Bosnia and the Milosevic regime in Belgrade. It also advocated a softer line on the inspection of suspected

WMD facilities in Iraq, and condemned US and UK air-strikes intended to force Saddam Hussein's cooperation with UNSCOM (United Nations Special Commission) activities. And in the CIS, peacekeeping operations were more about projecting Russian power than settling the various conflicts in Nagorno-Karabakh, Abkhazia, South Ossetia, Transdniestria and Tajikistan.[57] Indeed, Moscow often had a vested interest in the continuation of a 'controlled' level of violence: neither so great as to be seriously destabilizing, nor so minor as to obviate the need for a semi-permanent Russian force presence in the conflict zone.

Globally, international conflict resolution was also the main ideological battlefield between American 'hegemonism' and 'diktat' on the one hand, and the quest of the major non-Western powers – Russia and China – to build a 'multipolar world order' on the other. At this level, the Yeltsin administration identified a clear interest in conflict resolution, but not because of the potentially adverse consequences for regional and/or global stability. Its motivation was geopolitical, and grounded in zero-sum and balance-of-power thinking. It was typical of the Russian approach that, for example, in Kosovo its principal concern was not the extent of conflict and associated human suffering, but the fact that NATO had sidestepped the UN, that is, the only mechanism through which Moscow could hope to exercise a modicum of influence on developments.

The Putin administration's approach to international conflict resolution contains, as in many other areas of foreign policy, significant elements of continuity as well as transformation. In one sense, the importance of the priority has scarcely changed. Like any 'good international citizen', Russia routinely reaffirms its commitment to international peace and stability. Specifically, too, it would like to see an end to the violence in the Occupied Territories – particularly given Russia's co-sponsorship of the MEPP – while it also has a quasi-security, quasi-humanitarian interest in conflict prevention with regard to Iraq.

Yet in practice such goals are of secondary importance, being either too abstract (and difficult) or somewhat peripheral. The real importance of conflict resolution is therefore not intrinsic but instrumental – just as it was under Yeltsin. What matters is less the priority itself than the extent to which it assists the realization of other, more urgent or significant objectives. This is notably the case in the FSU where the present leadership has 'improved' on the opportunistic outlook of its predecessor by exploiting tensions in Abkhazia to remind the Georgians of their vulnerability to Russian pressure.

But, for all the similarities with the past, a transformation has occurred nonetheless. Instrumentalism continues to inform Russian attitudes and policies towards international conflict resolution, but this instrumentalism is now predominantly positive. Previously dominated by the negative politics of competitive multipolarity with its 'counterbalancing' idea, under Putin conflict resolution has instead become one of the principal avenues for promoting Russia's broader integration into the (Western-centred) global community. Like international anti-terrorism and WMD non-proliferation, it represents a promising field for joint activity, one where Moscow can claim considerable expertise (peacekeeping in the Balkans, peace enforcement in the CIS). It is no surprise, therefore, that it lies at the forefront of efforts to give substance to the new quality of relations between Russia and the West after 11 September. In the NATO context, for example, conflict resolution is one of the hooks for a more active Russian involvement in alliance decision-making, providing the raw material for converting abstract propositions like the 'format-20' (in relation to the Russia-NATO Council).[58] into concrete cooperation.

Contrary to some suggestions, this 'positive instrumentalism' is apparent even when, as in the prolonged dispute over the fate of Saddam Hussein, the Russian stance differs markedly from that of major Western powers such as the United States and Britain. It is instructive to compare the administration's skilful handling of the current crisis with the failed response of the Yeltsin regime to the Kosovo conflict. First, Putin has been careful not to place Russia in direct opposition to Washington, let alone to insist on any 'rights' as a great power. Russian concerns have been couched in constructive and undemonstrative language, conveying an impression of reasonableness and good sense. Second, Moscow's view on possible American/British military intervention has consistently been softer and more amenable than that of either Paris or Berlin. This has afforded it a kind of 'moral insurance', one that protects it from any threat of international isolation. There can be no imputation of Russia as a 'semi-rogue state' when it keeps company with – indeed, is more accommodating than – the cream of Western civilization. Third, and most crucially, the Russian position is flexible above all things. It is true that the government is anxious to safeguard Russian commercial interests in Iraq; it is also probably sincere in its belief that forced regime change from the outside is both destabilizing to the Middle East and an unwelcome precedent for future such actions elsewhere. But at the same time it has given itself plenty of room for manoeuvre in the event that the Americans and British do decide to attack Iraq (with or without UN endorsement).

In the end, Putin understands that the real dividend of the Iraqi crisis is that, for the first time in years, Russia finds itself at the centre of global decision-making – even if for just a brief moment. In order to reap maximum advantage from this situation, it does not want to 'roll over' in the face of American and British pressure, since this could reinforce the perception of the UN P-5, and Russia specifically, as merely a rubber-stamp for American unilateralism. On the other hand, neither does it want to waste precious political credit in trying to stop the inevitable,[59] since this would repeat the mistake over Kosovo when Moscow's response was generally viewed as both unconstructive and ineffectual. It is a matter of fine judgement as to how flexible or firm Russia should be. The key, however, lies in a sober assessment of the strengths and limitations of its position. And this means never losing sight of the end-goal of international conflict resolution – Russia's re-entry onto the world stage as a major, but also mainstream player.

The future of security and geopolitics – from anachronism to rebirth?

In post-Cold War Western conceptions of international security two features stand out above all others. The first is the greatly reduced importance of geopolitical considerations, and a corresponding rejection of competitive or zero-sum views of security. The second is the broadening of security definitions from their traditional base – 'hard' priorities such as defence against external military attack – to include meanings that until the end of the Cold War were scarcely considered to be covered by the term: democratization, economic prosperity, the emergence of a civil society, respect for human rights, and so on. In Russia, too, these revised understandings entered into the vocabulary. The formal emphasis given to domestic sources of threat in the 1997 Concept of National Security indicated a theoretical absorption of Western ideas, while Russian forces participated in the implementation of new security priorities, most notably through the UN multinational peace-keeping operations in Bosnia and Kosovo.

However, neither lip-service to socio-economic threats nor the occasional qualified success in positive-sum cooperation could disguise the reality that the Yeltsin period saw the consolidation, rather than breaking down, of traditional conceptions of security and geopolitics. In an ever more acrimonious atmosphere, the majority of the elite focused on what they saw as the hypocrisy and duplicity of the West's approach: one that mouthed fine sentiments about a brave new era of cooperation while capitalizing on Russian weakness to make massive geopolitical gains. For many, the Kosovo crisis put the seal on a 'double standard'[60] that had become increasingly apparent over the course of the decade; under cover of a 'humanitarian intervention', the West – and particularly the United States – showed that its real agenda was to impose its diktat on the rest of the world.

Given this depressing history, the transformation in the Russian approach to security and geopolitics under Putin has been astonishing. In the preceding pages, we have identified a number of the most important changes in strategic thinking: the evolution of the zero-sum mindset; the revision of balance-of-power notions; and the sophisticated treatment of spheres of influence. Unsurprisingly, these changes have been significant in shaping the administration's threat perceptions. While one can quibble about the instrumentalism that underpins the primacy of international terrorism as a foreign policy priority, the fact remains that the Kremlin is committed – and was so well before 11 September – to developing more fruitful security relations with the West. We no longer have the unedifying spectacle of Moscow attempting, generally without success, to thwart Western actions and policies 'just for the sake of it', as under Yeltsin. On a technical plane, too, the management of security and geopolitical priorities is, in keeping with other areas of Russian foreign policy, much more professional. For the most part the administration is able to identify what it wants, right or wrong, and go about its business accordingly. It is far from always successful – as shown by the difficulties in finalizing strategic arms reductions or establishing favourable arrangements for joint decision-making with NATO – but there is no doubt that today's Russia is taken more seriously as a security 'partner' and, most crucially, is able to achieve at least some of its objectives.

But impressive though their evolution has been, regime attitudes towards security and geopolitics continue to bear the stamp of their Soviet (and Yeltsinite) past. As noted earlier, frequently it is the means, rather than the ends, that have become more modern. For all the changes that have taken place, Moscow continues to be exercised by traditional geopolitical ideas and priorities, although it has learnt enough to package these appropriately. Meanwhile, many conceptions of security in vogue in the West have struggled to find a firm footing. 'Soft' security issues such as international conflict resolution and WMD non-proliferation resonate more positively these days, but Russian participation in the first is modest (and likely to remain so), while its commitment to the second is constantly at odds with a compelling economic interest in exporting arms, missile and nuclear technology to an expanding clientele. As for the broader conceptions of European security that have become the new *raison d'être* of NATO and EU security structures, the uncertain – to put it mildly – course of democratization and civil rights in Putin's Russia calls into serious question his commitment to such ideals.

What we are seeing, therefore, is not so much a revolution as an evolution, in which many elements of old security thinking survive and even flourish. Perhaps the best analogy one can make is with Russia's uneven progress towards a full market economy. In the same way that the post-Soviet economic system is an often dysfunctional hybrid of command-administrative and market principles, so the post-Yeltsin security world-view brings together the idealist with the cynical and instrumental, the progressive and enlightened with the retrograde. Although its outcomes are sometimes unpalatable and even downright ugly, the most important thing is that the overall trend is largely positive – and for that Russia and the West alike should be grateful.

6

Identity, values and civilization

Of the many foreign policy challenges Putin has faced during his presidency, the normative dimension – the sphere of identity, values and civilization – has proved the most intractable. The elusiveness of the issues involved, the gulf in moral and cultural perceptions between Russia and the West, the accumulation of atavistic prejudices on both sides, the instability of post-Soviet life – all these factors have come together to perpetuate an image of Russia as the 'great other' that, notwithstanding recent developments, continues to think and act in ways that set it apart from everyone else.

It may seem odd to highlight philosophical and somewhat abstract considerations at a time when, the world over, tangible goals like physical security, economic prosperity and social efficiency have acquired an unprecedented profile. Yet the paradoxical fact is that the normative dimension, in relative decline everywhere, has nevertheless come to represent the last frontier in the 'normalization' of Russian foreign policy. Putin has restored professionalism to decision-making, achieved a substantial economization in external priorities, and changed Moscow's approach to the security and geopolitical agenda. But this evolution, impressive as it is, has still to make real inroads in counteracting the widespread notion abroad of Russia as an alien country, strange, unfathomable, even at times barbarous. Although there has been growing talk in Moscow and the West about Russia's integration – in Europe, with Western structures and institutions, in the global community – the uncomfortable truth is that this has yet to occur in a meaningful sense, and will not do so until there is a much greater concordance of identity, values and civilization than exists at present.

This chapter considers three closely interrelated aspects of the normative dimension. The first is the ancient question of Russia's international identity and geographical orientation. We saw in Chapter 2 that Putin has managed to take much of the contentiousness out of the domestic debate on this by adopting a multifaceted and capacious approach. Viewed in that particular context, his purpose has been essentially instrumental: to use identity as a force unifying instead of dividing society and as a means of consolidating his political authority in the process. Here, the theme is more literal, focusing on how Putin and the governing class actually view Russia's position in the contemporary world, as opposed to how they have portrayed it. To what extent does the Kremlin seek integration with the West and what does it understand by the notion of integration itself? How genuine is the much discussed phenomenon of Eurocentrism, and what is its impact on the management of concrete foreign policy priorities?

The second aspect concerns the specifics of the normative dimension: the Putin administration's handling of issues such as democratization, the construction of a civil society, and human rights issues. It is an easy thing to speak about sharing moral perceptions and values, but it is a far tougher task to demonstrate this in practice *and* convince others that one is doing so. The continuing gulf between Russian and Western perceptions of Moscow's conduct of the Chechen war is a notable case in point.

The final question arises from the dynamic between the previous two sets of issues. Does a formal commitment to integration with the West plus progress with democratization and a civil society add up to an identifiably different Russian world-view (*mirovozzrenie*) – one that reflects an inexorable if incomplete process of transition from empire to nation-state? And, relatedly, is it the case that we are finally witnessing the beginnings of a civilizational convergence between Russia and the West?

The burden of the past

History has afforded Putin few favours in providing him with the building blocks of a revised national identity and accompanying sense of purpose. Although Russia's cultural and intellectual heritage is very rich, it is also one that has rarely harmonized with Western political and civilizational traditions. For much of its existence, Russia's identity in Europe has consistently been that of an outsider – whether at the time of the Renaissance, during the Enlightenment, or in the modern industrial age. Although there have been periods when it has been closely involved in continental politics, such as during the reigns of Catherine the Great (second half of the 18th century), Alexander I (Napoleonic and post-Napoleonic eras) and Nicholas II (pre-Revolution), for the most part distance, physical size, linguistic and cultural differences have conspired to consign it to the periphery.[1] The predominant view of Russia in the West has been as a backward and uncivilized nation, a stereotype reinforced in Communist times by the additional layer of an all-embracing ideological and strategic confrontation.

The arrival of Gorbachev and then Yeltsin appeared to offer the promise of a different era. The former appealed to a Western audience for his human face and as the embodiment of *glasnost, perestroika* and 'new thinking' in foreign policy, while the latter conjured up a compelling image of a man of the people courageously taking on and overcoming a tyrannical system. Unfortunately, the 15 years between the advent of Gorbachev and the abdication of Yeltsin were notable above all as a period of extraordinary and sustained chaos. Very real achievements were overshadowed by more immediate and spectacular developments – the collapse of one state and chronic instability in its successor, accelerating economic decline and abject poverty, endemic crime and corruption, and an increasingly erratic foreign policy. The new state was obviously more democratic and progressive than its predecessor, but it was also much more unpredictable. While it had assumed some of the trappings of Western civilization and political culture – more or less democratic elections, market reforms, some elements of a civil society – Russia seemed to have almost nothing in common with the West. The nature and forms of its 'other-ness' might have changed, but it remained a deeply alien nation nonetheless. Indeed, in some respects, the situation was arguably worse than before. Whereas the old Soviet Union had been able to command a certain international respect, along with the more habitual fear and loathing, its post-Soviet successor appeared to fail on all fronts: having jettisoned the intimidating persona of old, it had been unable to replace it with a fresh identity as a properly functioning nation-state. A culture of disappointment and resignation – 'Russia-fatigue' – became embedded in the consciousness of Western governments, even as they continued to utter ritualistic noises about Russia's importance as a constructive international actor.

Putin's primary task has been to overturn these accumulated prejudices and convince the West (and the rest of the international community) that Russia has emerged as a qualitatively different country, strong and independent, but above all like-minded. It is clear that this process will be prolonged and difficult. The challenge is not only to implement Russia's 'normalization' through deeds, but also to convince a deeply sceptical external audience that it holds dear many of the same values and beliefs. Moreover, whereas Gorbachev and Yeltsin enjoyed considerable leeway in meeting Western standards of political democratization and a civil society, the failures of the 1990s have narrowed the limits of outside tolerance. Today, more than ever, the onus is on Moscow to demonstrate incontrovertibly that the backwardness of Tsarism, confrontation of the Soviet period and the 'failed state' of the Gorbachev/Yeltsin years are indeed relics of history.

The gulf in values

Moving on from the past in any emerging nation is no easy matter. For Russia, however, the task has acquired a particular complexity arising out of its historical exclusion from the European (or indeed any other) moral-civilizational mainstream.[2] Notwithstanding the liberal inclinations of a minority within the elite, there has always been a gulf between many of the political and social beliefs Russians understand and/or cherish and those taken for granted in Western countries. Although the latter have endured anarchy and oppression at various times in their history, they have also been well exposed to democratic and civil traditions. Russia's experience of such values, on the other hand, is practically nil.[3] The law of power has always been stronger than the power of law; authority, not equity, is the abiding principle of rule. What citizens have expected of, and respected in, their rulers is the ability to govern strongly, even when this involves – as has often been the case – a brutal hand. 'Order' (*poryadok*) and 'strength' (*sila*) are more important than sensitivity towards rights and freedoms, individual or collective – and this is especially so during times of great instability, as in the late Soviet and post-Soviet periods. In this connection, the very different perceptions of Gorbachev in Russia and the West are a microcosm of a more general polarization in mindsets. The latter admired him for his 'humanism', while Russians came to despise him principally because of his weakness and diminishing ability to exercise authority. The new freedoms were all very well, but they did not compensate for political turmoil, economic crisis, and the disintegration of the Soviet Union. Indeed, just the contrary; a natural association grew between perceptions of anarchy on the one hand and Westernizing liberalization on the other.

The Yeltsin years provided further grist to this conservative, semi-authoritarian mill. Communist and nationalist successes in the 1993 and 1995 Duma elections were a rejection, not of the West as such, but of Western political, economic and social values – at least as they had been filtered and managed by the Yeltsin administration. Democratization appeared a sham to many, in no way altering the basic realities of power politics;[4] economic liberalization became tainted by overweening corruption and almost obscene income inequalities; while the notion of a civil society seemed either academic or laughable given rampant crime, diminishing life expectancy and a crumbling social infrastructure. Many people saw Western conceptions of human rights, media freedoms, and other elements of a civil society as benefiting only a tiny minority of the already privileged, all the more irrelevant (and offensive) when there was so much other, more urgent business. It was inevitable, too, that they should seek refuge from the uncertainties of modern life by recalling a bygone (if non-existent) golden age of order, predictability and security in which citizens had confidence in their future[5] and a powerful and self-confident Russia bowed to no nation. By the time Putin moved into the Kremlin, the dominant mood within elite and society was one strongly in favour of conservative change, as embodied in the restoration of law and order, societal and economic discipline, and state authority. It was no coincidence that figures such as Margaret Thatcher and Augusto Pinochet should feature prominently in opinion polls on the ideal of a national leader, or that at a more direct level Putin derived much of his public appeal as the spiritual and institutional successor of Yurii Andropov – the archetypal Soviet conservative reformer.[6]

None of this is to argue that the recent democratization and civic gains of Russian society can be easily reversed. But it is clear that the resonance of such priorities has declined steadily over the past decade. One of the ironies of the post-Cold War period is that Russians, long notorious for favouring the philosophical over the practical,[7] are in many respects more materially focused than citizens in the West. With the latter, government and people have to some extent learnt to take material comforts for granted, thereby freeing them – so to speak – to aspire to more intellectual and spiritual goals. In post-Soviet Russia, by contrast, the material struggle has been all-consuming; in such an atmosphere few are particular about political shenanigans, lack of transparency or violations of individual human rights so long as their rulers can assure them a reasonable measure of political stability, economic prosperity and national security. It is worth noting here that one of the reasons why Moscow has never accepted the argument that NATO enlargement is principally about promoting democratic and civil values in Central and Eastern Europe is that this objective seems so secondary, even trivial, to the Russian mind: why would a political-military alliance expend so much effort, and draw so much opposition, for such an abstract purpose?

Integration with the West

'The only game in town'

In spite of the many differences that separate it from the West, Russia has always seen itself as part of Western, that is, European civilization. Unique it might be, but this 'uniqueness' (or *spetsifika*) is conditional, being closely associated in one form or another with the political and cultural traditions of the developed Western countries. Although the Yeltsin administration made half-hearted attempts, through the prism of Primakovian multipolarity, to pretend at a multi-vectored foreign policy, its world-view – and that of the elite – remained overwhelmingly Westerncentric *in practice*.

For all the fissures over whether Russia is principally Slavic, European or Eurasian (see Chapter 2), the fact is that no alternative civilizational orientation has ever received serious consideration. Reduced to its essentials, the debate has centred on the modalities of interaction with the West and the extent to which Russia should seek to 'integrate', not whether it should go east or south. Conventionally, 'civilization' equates with Western civilization, with the East connoting barbarism and external threat.[8] Although the economic resurgence of the Asian powers in the 20th century has modified this primitive view, its fundamental premise – the 'superiority' and emotional/intellectual closeness of the West to Russia – remains basically intact, as true for Slavists and Eurasianists as for Westernizing liberals.

So when Putin came to power, there was no significant conceptual or ideological opposition to his determination to reinforce an already extant Westerncentric emphasis in thought and deed. In many ways, this was consistent with what Yeltsin had tried to do in the early 1990s, or indeed with what Leonid Brezhnev had set out to achieve via the superpower détente of the early 1970s. Moreover, it was evident, even to stringent critics of the West, that the Putin administration needed to salvage relations from the slough of despond of post-NATO enlargement and the Kosovo conflict. If the early Yeltsin/Kozyrev period of Atlanticism was one of 'romantic masochism',[9] then it had become apparent that the later Yeltsin/Primakov era was one of masochism full stop. Russia found itself increasingly isolated, from Europe as well as the United States, while it remained a marginal player (at best) in all other regions of the world with the exception of the former Soviet Union.

Putin's subsequent engagement with the major Western or Western-dominated structures – NATO, the EU, the WTO – needs to be seen in this light. 'Integration', as it came to be known, responded to diverse emotional, intellectual and material imperatives; the West was not only a kind of civilizational home, but it became once again both the metaphor and the means for Russia's future progress as a developed nation. To deny this was, effectively, to resign oneself to an ever more palpable backwardness and irrelevance – a fate feared by everyone from *derzhavniki* to liberals.

Civilization and strategic culture – the myth of Eurocentrism

What is less clear, however, is the nature of this Westerncentrism. The conventional wisdom is that under Putin Russian foreign policy has become Eurocentric. The President, members of his administration, and many commentators have played up this theme, pointing to numerous reciprocal high-level visits as well as to growing bilateral and multilateral cooperation. Meanwhile, Putin has seized every opportunity to emphasize that Russia considers itself to be an inalienable part of Europe,[10] looking to enhance its participation in integrationist processes on the continent. Eurocentrism would seem, furthermore, to tick every box in a pragmatic foreign policy. It resonates positively with the political establishment; it is strategically logical, considering Russia's geographical location and reduced international capabilities;[11] and it is economically sensible, given that the EU accounts for a third of Russia's total trade, a figure that will probably rise to 50–60 per cent after the next round of enlargement.[12]

On closer inspection, however, the picture is much more ambiguous. The first, if obvious, point is that Russia's Westerncentrism is not a holistic phenomenon; it, too, is full of contradictions. And the most important of these is the tension between a civilizational affinity of venerable standing on the one hand, and a strategic culture of relatively recent vintage on the other. Putin's experience in East Germany and St Petersburg may have predisposed him emotionally and intellectually towards Europe. But for nearly his entire professional life he has been personally engaged in an intense struggle against the United States. More broadly, the political and strategic environment in which he and the Russian elite have lived has been one of superpower bipolarity. Although the major Western European powers have played important roles at different times, it is to Washington that Moscow has consistently looked over the past half century.

The end of the Cold War has only accentuated this bias; far from the world becoming more multipolar as myth would have it, today's dominant reality is the emergence of America as global hegemon – strategic, political, economic, technological, and cultural.[13] It plays the leading role in most international issues of consequence and this is even truer in relation to Russia. If we run down the list of the Putin administration's principal foreign policy priorities – international terrorism, the strategic disarmament agenda, geopolitical developments in Europe (e.g., NATO enlargement), WTO accession, CIS affairs, the global financial environment, the international energy market[14] – it is the United States that has consistently been the primary external actor. If indeed Putin is the pragmatist everyone says he is, then he cannot ignore this reality.

And, of course, he has not. While he has worked assiduously to expand political and economic relations with Western Europe, he understands that Washington remains the decisive actor in nearly everything that affects Russian interests. In this connection, there has been much ill-judged comment about Putin's supposedly insouciant attitude towards the United States during his first 12–15 months in office. The fact is that Washington ignored Moscow during this time, not the other way round. The fag-end of the Clinton administration, the lengthy hiatus over the outcome of the 2000 US presidential elections, the settling-in period of the incoming Bush administration, and the latter's deliberate strategy of minimizing Russia's profile in

American foreign policy[15] – all these factors added up to a sustained neglect *by* America, not *of* America. In the circumstances, Western Europe represented the only possible avenue for a Westerncentric Russian foreign policy. Tellingly, once Washington decided to resume substantive dialogue, around the time of the Slovenia summit in June 2001,[16] America once again emerged as the prime focus of policy attention, a reality that 11 September reinforced but did not create.

The thesis about the Europeanization of foreign policy, then, needs to be nuanced more carefully than has been the case up to now. First, for all his awareness of Russia's diminished stature, Putin continues nevertheless to see it as a global as well as regional power. If nothing else, his extensive programme of overseas visits indicates this. He has undoubtedly sought to correct what had been a gross imbalance between regional and supra-regional priorities, but that does not imply that he views the former as being more important than the latter. Second, it is wrong to interpret Putin's handling of foreign policy priorities through a zero-sum prism, whereby an emphasis on, say, Europe automatically means a reduced interest in America, East Asia or the former Soviet Union. The evidence of the past three years suggests strongly that Putin believes he can have it all – become 'integrated' with Europe, improve relations with the United States, reassert Moscow's influence in the CIS, and jump on to the Asia–Pacific economic bandwagon. The critical variable here is that government under Putin is far more activist and efficient than it was under Yeltsin. The resources available to it may not be greater, but they are being put to better use. So while it is true in one sense that Russian foreign policy is now more 'European', it is also simultaneously devoting more attention to America, the Asia-Pacific, the Middle East and the CIS.

'Pragmatism' and the moral agenda – Chechnya and all that

For Russians, and the Putin administration specifically, one of the most disconcerting aspects of the relationship with the West is the latter's apparent obsession with matters that Moscow regards as its internal business and/or where no outside political, security or economic interest is immediately evident. During the Cold War era, the intrusion of such issues was to some extent comprehensible given the wider climate of ideological and strategic confrontation. But these days, at a time of rapprochement on all fronts, the West continues nonetheless to criticize Russia's approach to various normative issues. What exacerbates the situation is that in the majority of cases Moscow believes firmly that it is doing the right thing from a moral-civilizational standpoint, acting to eliminate the sorts of abuses and problems that have long troubled the West. In its view, instead of carping, the West should be grateful for what Russia is doing.

This lack of synchronization emerges most clearly in relation to the conflict in Chechnya. The Putin administration sees the Chechen rebels as a cancer, not only corroding the fabric of state and society, but also seeking to undermine every moral and civilizational norm dear to the West as well as Russia.[17] We have already mentioned (in Chapter 5) Putin's emotional commitment to the war, one that well exceeds a cynical political calculus. He views the issue in Manichaean or Old Testament terms, whereby a very great 'evil' must be destroyed by whatever means at hand; the struggle is unconditional and does not admit shades of rightness. Hence his intolerance of Western critics when they focus on human rights violations or, worse still, insist that he negotiate a political settlement with the rebels on the basis of compromise and respect for Chechen self-determination. To Russian eyes this attitude comes across as especially perverse in its suggestion of a moral equivalence between the warring parties, and quite at odds with how Western governments would deal with a similar situation in their own countries. There is genuine perplexity, too, that the West should be so concerned about the detail of the military operations given the import of the larger picture. Moscow's view is that, yes, perhaps there are sometimes human rights abuses, but even if this were true such happenings are inevitable in war as well as trivial in the greater scheme of things, that is, the enormous terrorist and extremist menace the Chechen clans pose to civilization *as a whole*. In other words, the ends absolutely justify the means – particularly when these means appear to be the only ones available.[18]

The case of Chechnya is interesting also for revealing the limitations of Eurocentrism in Russia. Moscow, with some cause, perceives a dichotomy between American and Western European attitudes towards such issues as human rights, liberation movements/terrorist organizations, and freedom of expression. To put it crudely, it sees *realpolitik* as the driving force behind American foreign policy – albeit with some moral trimmings thrown in from time to time.[19] On the other hand, the military limitations of the Western European powers have meant that they have relied less heavily on traditional instruments of power (i.e., force or the threat of it), resorting instead to economic and moral means of persuasion. Simplistic though the distinction between a 'hard' United States and a 'soft' Europe' may appear, there are a number of examples that reinforce it in the Russian consciousness. Thus, Western Europe has always been more sympathetic than the US to the Palestinians and national liberation movements in general; European states and structures – like the Council of Europe – have been in the vanguard of Western protests about Chechnya; there is the obvious contrast between an American-dominated NATO that focuses on security and defence issues, and a European Union that concentrates on economic, social and political priorities; and, finally, in international conflict resolution – Bosnia, Kosovo, Afghanistan – it is the Americans who appear at the forefront of the fighting, while the Europeans busy themselves with the post-conflict settlement. All this creates an impression of differences not only in capabilities between America and Europe, but also in their moral-civilizational outlook.

Particularly since George W. Bush succeeded Bill Clinton in the White House, the Russian elite has seen American foreign policy as increasingly 'realist' – in every sense of the term – and therefore more sympathetic than the Europeans. Just as the West is not a monolithic entity so there is a perception of different moral emphases in the foreign policy of Western nations: on the one hand, a conservative American tradition that emphasizes order and stability; on the other, a more liberal European spirit that gives primacy to self-determination and to political and social rights. This division is far from perfect, and of course there are many exceptions to the 'rule'. Nevertheless, the fact remains that, in this particular aspect of the normative dimension, the Putin administration is more Americacentric than Eurocentric. Right or wrong, the United States presents as more 'pragmatic', less inclined to allow discomfort over moral 'side-issues' to interfere with the main – security and economic – business at hand.

The domestic reform programme – interests and values

During the post-Soviet period, the ultimate test of Russia's emergence as a modern, post-industrial nation has been the extent to which it has been able to fulfil an ambitious domestic reform agenda. This program may be categorized in terms of three strategic objectives: political democratization, the development of a full market economy and the construction of a civil society. The quest here is not only about meeting the technical requirements of political, economic and social reform, but carries a fundamental moral-civilizational premise as well: if Russia is to become integrated into the global, Western-dominated, community then it must subscribe to Western values in their various dimensions, moral and political as well as economic. Thus, market liberalization is more than about, say, providing a better investment climate for foreign capital; it becomes a symbol of a civilized modern state. Democratization and civil reform are important not merely for their own sake, but because they confirm Russia's break from a primitive and oppressive past.

So much for theory. In practice, fulfilment of the domestic reform programme has proved extremely problematic – so much so that during the Yeltsin years the many failures in this sphere reinforced, rather than counteracted, the historical perception of Russia as a backward nation, doomed to subsist in a kind of civilizational half-light. Few in Russia or the West were fooled into believing that the holding of presidential and parliamentary elections made Russia democratic, while the vision of a civil society based on law and values remained nascent at best. As for economic reform, the changes they wrought achieved a certain marketization. But it was evident that there was little in common between the 'market economy' as it developed in Russia and the economies of the developed Western nations.

In these circumstances, one of Putin's biggest challenges has been to achieve substantive progress on the specifics of the domestic reform agenda while at the same time convincing the West of Russia's essential like-mindedness. And it is here where a real divide has opened up between concepts of shared interests and shared values. On the one hand, the Putin administration has presided over unprecedented legislative activity, especially in the economic sphere, with literally thousands of new laws and normative acts being passed. Furthermore, the gap between policy formulation and implementation has begun to narrow; some of the new laws, for example in relation to taxation, are taking practical effect and leading to a more receptive environment for foreign investors.[20] On the other hand, the administration's activism has manifested itself in a conservative as well as liberal direction. Thus, in its determination to reimpose government authority in the regions the Kremlin has resorted to highly questionable political manipulation.[21] Equally, in ridding society of the most prominent Yeltsin-era oligarchs – Boris Berezovsky and Vladimir Gusinsky – and the corruption and graft they personified it has adopted methods that would have no place in a functioning civil society. So while the West welcomes the fact that Russia has become a more orderly and efficient partner, it cares little for the way in which much of this has been done. If the West's political, security, and economic interests are now better served under a Putin administration, the same cannot necessarily be said about many of its political and civil values.

This disjunction between interests and values is an unending source of frustration to the Russian leadership. As with the disagreements over Chechnya, there is puzzlement as to why the West should concern itself over the way Moscow manages its affairs when the outcomes appear to favour Western interests. From the Kremlin's perspective, it should be enough that, finally, there is a regime in place that is committed to expanded and improved relations, is taking steps to deal with crime and corruption, and is fostering a better business environment. When Western politicians concentrate instead on individual human rights abuses, the curtailment of media freedoms, and restrictions on religious activity, Moscow's natural reaction is to accuse the West not only of 'interference in Russia's internal affairs',[22] but also of hypocrisy and double standards. This divergence of view feeds an ingrained suspicion that there is a kind of glass ceiling, whereby Russia is allowed to look at and occasionally taste the fruits of the West, but in a partial and conditional way only.

In fact, the problem comes down to a sincere difference of opinion over the linkage between means and ends, and between the notion of values as intrinsic goods as opposed to values as instruments for realizing more material objectives. In the first instance, there is little understanding in Russia of the liberal humanist notion that the means are often as important as the ends. To take one example, the Putin administration has shown that it is not prepared to allow due democratic process to run its course if the likely end-result is the victory of a corrupt (but electable) regional governor, such as Alexander Rutskoi in Kursk *oblast* (see note 22, chapter 2). In a Western democracy, such 'pragmatism' would be regarded as self-defeating, on the basis that if you corrupt the process then the outcome becomes corrupted and therefore worthless. Similarly, it was consistent with the Kremlin's power-based mindset that it should look to suppress the so-called 'political' oligarchs,[23] Gusinsky and Berezovsky, by adopting dubious means to close down their media outlets.[24] In this case, the result – ejecting the least politically cooperative and most publicly unpopular of the oligarchs – was what counted, not the propriety of the methods.

On the whole, the Kremlin views democracy and a civil society chiefly in instrumental terms. Democracy, or at least the image of it, serves above all as a great legitimizer; with his public rating holding consistently around the 70 per cent mark it is logical that Putin should play up its importance. But the reality is that today's Russia is a less pluralist polity than it was three years ago, owing mainly to Putin's emasculation (although not open suppression) of alternative sources of political power in the centre and the regions.

Such instrumentalism emerges especially clearly in Moscow's conception of a civil society. Whereas in the West a civil society is an end in itself, in Russia it serves a window-dressing function for an international audience and as a means of enhancing economic efficiency and social order. The much publicized issue of civilian control over the military illustrates this distinction well. In the West this is above all a question of democratic accountability, part of building an open, liberal society; in Russia, however, it is principally about reinforcing executive and state control – both in broad terms (management of the military) and on specifics, such as restraining defence expenditure and downsizing the armed forces. Significantly, whenever Putin has spoken of a civil society he has emphasized laws rather than freedoms – the restoration of collective order in place of anarchy, and the proper functioning of the judiciary and bureaucracy rather than individual civil rights and liberties.[25]

This is not simply a matter of differences between conservative and liberal perspectives on the nature of a civil society, but goes to the heart of what a civil society entails. In the West, irrespective of whether a conservative or liberal administration is in office, the emphasis is overwhelmingly on the individual citizen's right to live and work in a free society. Of course, that citizen has responsibilities too, and even the most radically progressive government will devote considerable energy and resources to maintaining law and order, protecting private property, and so on. But the differences are essentially of degree, not in overall perspective. In Russia, the situation has long been the reverse; the first priority (and expectation) – for rulers and ruled alike – is law and order. Once again, various regimes throughout history have exhibited greater or less benevolence, enlightenment, tolerance, etc. But the balance of priority is quite different compared to the West. This is perhaps the main reason why the post-Soviet road to political democratization and a civil society has been so rocky. There is no natural constituency that understands, let alone supports, the attainment of a civil society in the fullest, Western humanist sense.[26]

So while Putin grasps that Russia needs to move towards the West in terms of political and civil values if it is to become 'integrated' in the community of 'civilized' nations, there continues to be a discrepancy between what he thinks will achieve this aim, and the level of Western expectations. Moscow believes, for the most part, that it should be enough that Russia shares common interests with the West – such as meeting the threat of international terrorism, improving trading and investment regimes, and ceasing geopolitical competition – and that, further, such commonalities will in time lead inevitably to a confluence of values. For a substantial body of opinion in the West, however, it is the other way round: values generate a common approach to interests (hence the popular wisdom that developed democracies do not fight wars against one another). Consistent with this view, Russia will not be properly integrated until it subscribes fully to the moral-philosophical code of the West.

Identification with the West and the evolution of the Russian world-view

These cardinal differences of interpretations lead us naturally to assess the sincerity of Putin's attempts to identify Russia with Europe and the Western world more generally. To what extent does he believe his own rhetoric, and how well does he understand the implications of integration and identification? As there is no straightforward answer to this puzzle, it makes sense to break it down into two parts. The first relates to the innate Westerncentrism of the Russian elite. There is little doubt that Putin is banking on the West, and has done so from the beginning of his administration – notwithstanding his commitment to developing other areas of Moscow's external relations.

The bottom line is that the United States and Western Europe are richer and more powerful than anyone else; they are also more cohesive than any other group of nations, members of by far the most effective and influential multi-lateral structures – NATO and the EU – operating in the contemporary world. Consequently, a cooperative, friendly relationship with Western nation-states and institutions lies at the heart of any pragmatic approach to foreign policy. And if this can be wrapped up with at least the symbolism of integration – as represented in membership of, or association with, Western structures – then so much the better.

At the same time, Putin is aware that such 'integration' comes at a cost. Too close an identification brings with it restrictions on freedom of man-oeuvre, notably in the exercise of sovereignty. In the particular case of Russia, such problems are exacerbated by its historical burden. As an outsider with a clouded past, it needs to do more than those already in the circle or other applicant nations such as the Central and Eastern Europeans. Moscow can-not just fend off criticisms of its domestic policies by claiming that these are no one else's business; it has actually to convince the critics and the doubters that it is doing the right thing, and in a way that conforms to Western values as well as interests. Refusal to play by these rules is to maintain the glass ceiling that has been the bane of Russian policy-makers. So there is a delicate balance to be reached between maintaining policy control and doing enough to meet external standards of domestic and international behaviour.

The record of his presidency suggests that Putin believes he can do both, albeit with some presentational adjustments along the way. First, as noted earlier, the Russian view is that there is no unanimity in Western moral-civilizational perceptions, a factor that Moscow can turn to its advantage. In this connection, it has eased Putin's task that it is the weaker Western European powers, rather than the United States, which have pressed him hardest on Chechnya and human rights abuses.[27] Had it been the other way round, or had the West been speaking with one voice, the Russian govern-ment's position would have been much more uncomfortable. Second, and relatedly, there is a sense – particularly with a Republican administration in the White House – that something of a civilizational convergence is taking place between post-Soviet attitudes in Russia and a post-liberal (i.e., conser-vative) mindset in the West. In other words, we are witnessing a two-way process: Russia is evolving into a modern nation with some of the style of a democratic and civil society, while conservative political and social philo-sophies are becoming more popular in America and a number of Western European countries. It may be premature to speak of like-mindedness, but the two, formerly ideologically opposed, camps are within touching distance. Third, Putin has acted during his presidency as if time is on his side. Not in the economic sphere, where the pressure has constantly been on Russia to catch up, but in the normative dimension. Eventually, the argument runs, the increasing confluence of political, economic and social interests between Russia and the West will translate into a perception of common values (see above). As long as Moscow continues to demonstrate tangible achievements in the key areas, namely security and economic, and pass enough appropriate signposts elsewhere, then there should be no reason why convergence should not occur – and sooner rather than later. In this way, instead of Russia unconditionally identifying or integrating with the West, both sides would identify with one another over a middle ground.

In reality, of course, the picture is much more complex and less harmonious than this thinking would suppose. Several problems, in particular, could either arrest or reverse the process of rapprochement in attitudes. The most important concerns the end-vision of Russia's place in the world. There is nothing to suggest that the political elite, or Putin himself, would be content with a long-term outcome whereby Russia becomes just another major, predominantly regional, power along the lines of the UK, France, Germany or Japan.[28] Putin is canny enough to know that reverting to Yeltsinite great-power-speak would be counterproductive; now, more than ever, is the time to play the integration game and to retain a modest aspect. But that is no reason to exclude the possibility forever, particularly if Russia can modernize its economy and society as Putin envisages.

Here, one can draw a rough parallel with China, in which modernization becomes the magic key that transforms a regional into a global power. The China analogy also points to the likelihood that the development of greater national capabilities could be seen as threatening by others, notably the United States. Given the legacy of the Cold War and the inadequacies of democratic and civil development in Russia, there is ample potential for renewed tensions between the former superpower rivals. For the time being, the Americans (and others) prefer to emphasize the commonality of interests, but it would be foolish to assume that they therefore think of Russia as like-minded in the fullest sense of the word. For all the apparent conservatism – by European standards – of contemporary American society, it nevertheless remains infinitely more liberal than either the vision or actuality of Putin's Russia. And as long as such a gulf in values exists, then it may not take much for a divergence in vital interests to assert itself once again.[29]

The second problem relates to the glass ceiling and contrasting expectations of partnership and cooperation. A modernizing and more predictable Russia may be welcome to sit at the table of Western structures and institutions – NATO, EU, the WTO – but that does not mean Moscow is PLU ('people like us'). For many in the West, there remains a worrying discrepancy

111

between the attitudes of Putin himself and those of the elite, one that hints at a lack of solidity in Russian foreign policy. The experience of the past 10–15 years has exposed the fragility of a cooperative approach in the Kremlin. Even allowing for the fact that Putin is a more stable personality than Yeltsin, there is no guarantee that Russia's approach to the world might not lurch back, if not into confrontation, then at least into another phase of reluctant and conditional 'cooperation'. It is noteworthy here that much of the political class is still insisting on American 'concessions' (*ustupki*) in return for Russian assistance, instead of viewing cooperation and like-mindedness as ends in themselves. Typically, such people look at the present relationship less as a strategic partnership than as a bargaining process between two less than wholly trusting parties.

There is from the Russian perspective a sense that the West 'uses and abuses' it for specific purposes, but is fundamentally disinclined to consider it as entirely 'civilized'; as soon as Moscow meets one requirement or standard, than another, more problematic, test is put forward – and so the process repeats itself *ad infinitum*. Hence, the continuing attachment to 'concessions' since these are seen as concrete as opposed to values, which are often intangible (and therefore seemingly illusory). As long as Russian and Western interests coincide, this divergence of perception is not such a big problem. But as soon as conflicts and disagreements arise – as they do even in the closest of relationships – then they could acquire an added, and complicating, normative dimension. In this event, a difference of view would not remain simply that, but become symbolic of a larger civilizational cleavage.[30] We can already see a hint of this in relation to Moscow's conduct of the Chechen war which, for many in the West, has become less an aberration arising from extreme circumstances than a metaphor for Russia's continuing 'other-ness'.

Finally, there is the issue of Russia's 'independence' in an increasingly interdependent and globalized world. It is psychologically very hard for a nation that has been a major continental power and then superpower for 300 years to accept outside constraints on its governance. Consequently, the Putin administration is looking for a best-of-both-worlds outcome: obtaining the benefits of political and economic integration with the West while retaining a special 'separate' status within that integration. Its attitude towards the newly created Russia–NATO Council illustrates this dualism very well. Moscow seeks direct participation in alliance decision-making processes on the basis of 'equality', but interprets this equality in idiosyncratic fashion: Russia is equal, not to individual NATO members, but to the totality of NATO member states.[31] Part of the motivation here is ego, but part of it is also the wish to have the option of using this 'equality' to frustrate the implementation of NATO policies in cases of perceived need – similar to the veto option in the UN Security Council.[32] As long as such particularist attitudes persist, Russia's 'integration' in the West will always be selective and conditional. Both sides will speak of integration, common threat perceptions, shared interests and values, but meanwhile both will continue to think very differently – about each other, and about the world in general.

Conclusion

Few countries have undergone such a painful normative transition as post-Soviet Russia. It was one thing to discard the ideological carcass of a Communist system whose tenets had become almost entirely formalistic; it was quite another to develop fresh values, a qualitatively different foundation on which the new state might prosper. The Yeltsin years witnessed many attempts to delineate a national idea that could serve both as a moral-spiritual basis for society and a guide to interaction with the outside world. But the multiplicity of identities in a volatile political and economic environment meant that, in a very real sense, Russia became a state without an identity – except as an increasingly embittered nation on the edge of continents. The major international trends of the post-Cold War period – the magnifying of the United States' global dominance, the emergence of a 'single Europe' through NATO and EU enlargement, the rise of China, economic globalization – appeared to pass it by. By the time Boris Yeltsin announced his retirement, it seemed Russia had in many respects devolved rather than evolved, further away from discovering a sense of self than at any time since the collapse of Communism. To an extent scarcely imaginable, it had become the ultimate atheistic and even nihilistic state, with beliefs and mores stripped of all but their instrumental content.

Viewed against this background, the Putin presidency has seen a substantial evolution in notions of identity, values and civilization. For the first time in years, there is a genuine belief that a resurgent Russia is capable of playing an important *and* constructive role in international affairs. Emerging from the disorientation of the Yeltsin period, it is belatedly enjoying the respect and sense of 'belonging' it has long craved but had found impossibly elusive since the fall of the Soviet Union. No longer dismissed as a 'failed state' or as a quasi-rogue state, Russia is playing a real part in the post-Cold War world. It is no longer the case, as it was during the 1990s, that its participation is largely nominal, a fig-leaf to cover an actual lack of interest and inability to contribute. Putin has dragged Russia away from many of the stereotypes – historical, geopolitical, civilizational – that had marooned it in a sterile and unwinnable rivalry with the West, and instead pushed it firmly along the path of integration and commonality of interest and perception.

Given these considerable achievements, it may seem churlish to conclude that Putin's performance in this aspect of foreign policy-making has been notable as much for its shortfalls as for its successes. He has had to juggle contradictory sets of priorities and propositions, many of them profoundly alien, and not surprisingly he has sometimes failed. For all the development in Russia's normative mindset, there are many areas and aspects where its attitudes remain mired in traditional perceptions and thinking. While Putin's record is impressive when stacked up against that of his predecessors, it would not do to exaggerate the extent of the attitudinal changes he has stimulated. As in other aspects of his foreign policy, we are talking about evolution, not revolution. When we ask ourselves the key questions – is Russia politically and economically integrated with Europe/the West, is it part of a common civilization with shared values, has it discarded the imperial and 'great-power' legacies in favour of becoming a 'normal' nation-state – then it becomes apparent that Moscow has just set out on what promises to be a very long, arduous and unpredictable journey.

7

11 September and after

Western views of 11 September and its implications tend to divide naturally into two schools of thought. The first, popular in Washington and London, argues that the terrorist attacks on the Twin Towers and the Pentagon were transforming events, not just for America, but for the entire planet. We now live in a very different world, one that faces altogether new challenges. As a consequence, the character of international politics, too, has altered radically. It is no longer meaningful to speak in terms of strategic competition and traditional security priorities, but rather of developing common responses to the fresh dangers that threaten civilization as a whole. In the post-11 September environment, positive–sum notions of cooperative security and economic partnership have displaced the negative, competitive politics of a Cold War hangover. Such cooperation will not be without its difficulties, yet it is centred in, and derives strength from, an essential unity of perception and purpose among its principal actors.

The alternative interpretation, increasingly common in the non-Anglo-Saxon world, regards much of this as humbug. Very little has changed – at least in a positive sense. Far from international politics becoming more inclusive and integrated, the shock of 11 September has pushed the United States, the sole superpower, to act in ever more hegemonistic and unilateral fashion. It is as though the last restraints on its behaviour have been removed. Certainly, Washington seeks to enlist others in support of its foreign policy objectives, but it has shown that it is prepared to go it alone and, worse still, ride roughshod over the interests and concerns of others, even close allies. According to this view, the ongoing dispute over what to do about Saddam Hussein is only the latest illustration of a new and overweening arrogance of power in American foreign policy.

Russian attitudes towards 11 September likewise fall into two categories. There is the official line that coincides closely with that of Washington and London. The world has truly changed, a fact that provides Russia with a unique opportunity to put past difficulties and conflicts behind it and become fully integrated with the developed West – not just in the everyday business of political, security and economic affairs – but also culturally and civilizationally. 11 September is the wand that transforms Russia from its former ugly duckling condition into, if not a swan, then at least a fully-fledged member of the community of civilized nations. At the other end of the analytical spectrum, however, a sizeable portion of the Moscow political establishment maintains that 11 September has been more damaging than beneficial to Russian foreign policy interests. It is not only a question of America looking to establish a unipolar world order – a popular refrain from the Yeltsin years – but of actively asserting its presence in the one area where Russia has been the dominant power, the space of the former Soviet Union.

A binary division is apparent, also, in contrasting summations of the impact of 11 September on the Putin administration's management of foreign policy. Some observers speak of the Kremlin as having made a 'strategic choice' in favour of the West,[1] away from the politics of competitive multi-polarity that defined much of the conduct of external relations under Yeltsin. Implicit in this view is the premise that Russian foreign policy post-11 September differs fundamentally in philosophy, orientation and execution from its previous incarnation in the first 18 months of the Putin presidency. While the 'new' version is by no means the finished article, a process of far-reaching transformation has been launched – a reality that will become increasingly evident with time and as opportunities arise for Moscow to demonstrate its cooperative disposition. On the other hand, however, there is a growing body of opinion that argues that the real impact of 11 September was to catalyse existing trends in Russian foreign policy, rather than to revolutionize its basic principles or *modus operandi*. According to this interpretation, the pro-Westernist approach of the Putin administration that emerged so publicly after 11 September had already been in place some time before.

It is of course very early to be making conclusive judgments about the latest trends in Russian foreign policy given the recentness of 11 September and its continuing reverberations. The haphazard course of Moscow's approach to international affairs in the post-Soviet period warns us to be careful about over-extrapolating from at the time momentous, but ultimately transitory, phenomena. It is worth recalling that ten years ago, in the first flush of the Yeltsin regime, many were talking in very similar terms about a new era of international cooperation. Yet it was not long before the President himself began to speak of a 'cold peace' (a milder variant of the Cold War) and condemn Washington for seeking to impose its diktat through a unipolar world order.[2] Conversely, at various times over the past decade – during the first wave of NATO enlargement, the Kosovo crisis, and American preparations for strategic missile defence – talk has centred on geopolitical conflict and the irretrievable deterioration of relations between Russia and the West. However, the advent of Putin proved that negative trends, as well as positive, could quickly be arrested and reversed given the requisite political will. Taking into account the fickleness of circumstances and mentality, we need to ask whether this latest trend might not turn out to be a fizzer, good for a limited period perhaps, but vulnerable to adverse developments such as a sudden international crisis or 'misunderstandings' over specific issues.[3]

The purpose of this final chapter is not so much to substantiate claims of a revolution in Russian foreign policy, or to dismiss the significance of the actions taken by the Putin administration since 11 September, but to compare Moscow's approach to various aspects of external relations, 'before' and 'after'. The preceding chapters have focused on the policy-making process, the economization of foreign policy, the management of security and geopolitical priorities, issues of identity, values and civilization, in large part because they have been the primary spheres of foreign policy activity under Putin. By considering what changes, if any, have occurred in these areas over the past year we can get a better sense of longer-term trends – even if definitive conclusions are likely to elude us for some time yet.

The last section is by way of a prognosis, looking to answer what in many ways is *the* key question: how does the basket of changes and continuity add up in terms of shaping Russia's relationship with the world in the new century? While we may be able to make fairly accurate predictions about Moscow's attitude towards a specific issue or set of issues, it is a much more difficult enterprise to grasp the undercurrents and mentality that lie at the root of all policy. Yet the challenge must be accepted if we in the West are to develop a proper understanding of, and functional relationship with, a country whose rising importance is one of the very few certainties left in international politics.

Policy-making – image and reality

Putin's response to the events of 11 September and their aftermath has cemented his almost legendary reputation for running Russian foreign policy virtually single-handed. His initial reaction – the quickest among world leaders – showed an agility that would have been inconceivable in the Yeltsin, or indeed any other, era. By offering instantaneous and unconditional moral support, he ensured that the atmospherics of Moscow's interaction with Washington would be overwhelmingly positive. Significantly, Putin made this commitment contrary to prevailing political and institutional advice which advocated a position of neutrality.[4] Subsequently, he was to assert his personal stamp even more clearly. When the Bush administration first broached the possibility of using bases in the Central Asian republics as jumping-off points for the military operation in Afghanistan, Moscow's response was strongly negative. Defence Minister Ivanov and Chief-of-Staff Kvashnin indicated that Russia would view such moves as intruding on its natural sphere of influence. This position, grounded in traditional Soviet- and Yeltsin-era geopolitical logic, remained in place for the first week or so. But following a meeting of security heads in Sochi on 22 September, and subsequent telephone conversations with the five Central Asian leaders, Putin turned this thinking on its head by giving his blessing to the latter's burgeoning military cooperation with the United States.[5]

Putin's decision represented a victory for pragmatism over a stereotyped and anachronistic strategic mindset; he understood there was nothing he could do, even had he wished, to prevent the basing of American soldiers in Central Asia, and that he was best off making a virtue out of necessity.[6] But the most interesting aspect of the whole affair was that Putin, by taking policy by the scruff of the neck, as it were, highlighted the degree to which the foreign policy decision-making process had become personalized under his rule. In this particular case, what mattered was his voice; the fact that he was greatly outnumbered mattered not a whit. The axiom that he *is* consensus, or rather that his consensus is the only one that counts (*'le consensus, c'est moi'* – Chapter 1), was never more convincingly proven.[7] And because he decided that Russian interests were best served by an openly and consistently cooperative approach with America, then this was what eventuated. More than anything, 11 September provided the perfect setting and opportunity to highlight the 'presidential' character of Russian foreign policy. It is no concidence that since that time Putin has become increasingly synonymous with Moscow's external face, to such an extent that it is almost as if everyone else is just making up the numbers, performing only limited functions under the close direction of the Kremlin.

Almost, but not quite. Tempting though it is to see Putin as the sole font and executor of pro-Westernism in Russia, the truth is rather more prosaic. In the first place, as noted before, from the outset of his presidency there has been a general consensus in favour of restoring functional relations with the West after the débâcle of Kosovo and Russia's consequent isolation. Although elite and public opinion may have harboured uncharitable thoughts towards the United States in particular, such sentiments were less significant than recognition of the need to find a better way of managing the interaction with Washington and major Western European capitals.

Second, there have always been influential pro-Western elements in and around the Putin administration. Chubais, Kudrin, Illarionov, Gref, as well as other public figures including Nemtsov, Kiriyenko and Gaidar, make up a powerful Westernizing constituency at the highest levels of power. They have helped determine the positive tone and much of the content of Russian policy towards Western Europe and, from around the time of the Slovenia summit in June 2001, with America. Suggestions that Putin was more or less on his own in conceiving of, and then prosecuting, a cooperative line with Washington after 11 September effectively overlook the role of this active group of advisors.

Third, it is worth asking how another Russian leader, say Yeltsin, would have responded had he been in Putin's shoes. Given the wave of sympathy flowing towards the United States in the immediate wake of the terrorist attacks, it would have been strange indeed if Putin had adopted a more neutral position in defiance of majority opinion in the developed world. Any leader of a nation aspiring to be called 'civilized' would have acted as he did. Granted, he did so with an alacrity unusual in Russian leaders, but in reality he had little alternative, especially given his prior strategic commitment to Russia's 'normalization' and integration with the West. Equally, too much has been made of his public role in articulating and representing Moscow's position. It is difficult to imagine any world leader not doing the same in response to arguably the most spectacular event in international politics since the fall of the Soviet Union. After all, during the 1990s even an ailing (and much less active) Yeltsin took the lead on selected foreign policy issues, such as the rapprochement with Japan, and in moderating the Russian position on the Kosovo crisis.[8]

It is important, therefore, to distinguish fact and reason from legend and image-making. Putin did face political and institutional opposition to his overtly pro-American stance, but this was never either serious or influential enough to deflect him from what was the only practical course of action. One should differentiate here between the habitual but ineffectual grumbling of the Russian elite – a regular feature of the post-Soviet foreign policy land-scape – and determined and effective opposition based on fundamental disagreements over substance. Far from being an aberration, Putin's actions post-11 September flowed logically from an ever more Westerncentric attitude in Moscow. He was more alive than many of his contemporaries to the possibilities the new situation offered to Russian interests, but this is not to say that others were unaware of these. Ultimately, where Putin made a difference was in his positive handling of the modalities of interaction in a changed international climate, *not* in introducing a conceptual revolution. He showed impressive leadership and a superior understanding of revised global realities, but it is fanciful to depict him as some kind of Horatio struggling manfully to turn back the forces of anti-Western reaction in Russia.[9]

All this raises the issue of whether 11 September has altered the balance of power among the various foreign policy actors and the way they interact with one another. On the former question, it is hard to discern any major changes. The same players – the Presidential Administration, the security apparatus, the Foreign Ministry, the Defence Ministry – appear to have retained their functions. One interesting development, the significance of which is difficult to gauge as yet, is that the increased salience of international security issues has enhanced the MOD's public profile in foreign policy-making.[10] The accelerated pace of rapprochement between Russia and the West post-11 September has also underlined the importance of economic actors. At the same time, the sectionalization of foreign economic policy continues to be as much in evidence after 11 September as it was before. On the one hand, the more vigorous pursuit of Russia's WTO accession bid points to the increased sway of advocates of liberalization such as Illarionov, Gref and Kudrin; on the other hand, Putin's insistence that accession take place 'on conditions acceptable to Russia'[11] suggests that the more conservative (i.e., protectionist) players retain considerable clout as a 'braking mechanism'. Although it seems that the liberalization constituency is in the ascendancy, its advantage looks far from decisive at this point; there is clearly a lot of play left in the policy debate. Big business continues to have a powerful say in the formulation and execution of policy in areas of direct concern to it, such as the energy sector and WTO accession. At the lower end of the scale, there is minimal movement. The marginal players – the Duma, the academic community, regional leaders, the public – remain marginal, while claims that foreign leaders are responsible for Putin's pro-Westernism are unproven and unlikely. The Russian President may be on first-name terms with his American counterpart, but it would be naïve to assume from this that the new 'George and Vladimir' dynamic influences Russian decision-making any more than did its predecessor, the 'Bill and Boris' show.

As long as international terrorism remains at the head of Moscow's external priorities then personalities, not institutions, will continue to make and break policy. For all sorts of substantive, emotional and presentational reasons, Putin is taking a very close interest in this issue – an intimate involvement that carries over to other areas of the security agenda as well as colouring Russia's overall approach to international relations post-11 September. An already heavily personalized system is becoming more so rather than less. As Putin's criticisms of the bureaucracy in his 2002 address to the Federal Assembly indicate,[12] it will be a long time before government institutions develop to the point where they displace individuals as the principal policy actors in either the domestic or the external arena. Meanwhile, the horizontal 'cell-like' structure of foreign policy decision-making stays much as it was.

Individual ministers manage their respective portfolios, with interdepartmental coordination taking place via the medium of President Putin. However, while his day-to-day involvement in the detail of policy has increased since 11 September, it is unclear whether this heightened interest is translating into more effective control. It remains true that one man, no matter how capable and dedicated, cannot control everything.

Taken as a whole, the '11 September effect' on the policy-making environment has been to accentuate existing trends, rather than dramatically change the way Russia's external relations are managed. This outcome is to be expected. The events of that day (and after) asked no searching questions about the policy process that were not already being considered. Russian foreign policy is a little more personalized, more 'presidential', more closely coordinated, than before. But since these were its principal characteristics in any event, the impact of 11 September has been underwhelming. Putin's image as master of all he surveys has received a powerful boost, but the underlying realities remain much as they were.

The economic agenda – Westernization with qualifications

It is somewhat paradoxical that the sequence of global developments since 11 September, centred in the primacy of international security issues, should have had the effect of accelerating the economization of Russian foreign policy. Ordinary logic might have dictated that economic priorities, while not being neglected altogether, would nevertheless have been relegated to the policy margins for the time being. That the opposite has occurred raises a number of interesting questions, not only about the balance between security and economic objectives, but also about the evolving yet contradictory character of the administration's attitude towards the outside world.

The most visible consequence of 11 September on the external economic agenda has been a more single-minded pursuit of economic integration as a strategic objective. Although WTO accession was a major administration priority from the beginning, the Russian campaign has stepped up markedly. It was indicative that Putin's 2002 address to the Federal Assembly should focus heavily on the accession bid and the need for Russia to adapt to the demands of economic globalization.[13] This did not signify some 'road to Damascus' conversion or the primacy of economic over security objectives; rather, it reflected the liberal belief that in the post-11 September international climate Russia had a unique opportunity to achieve strategic benefits that, under normal circumstances, would have taken decades to materialize. In other words, a convergence of international security perceptions opened up the possibility of a softer, more 'flexible' Western stance in other areas of relations with Russia, including its direct participation in Western and Western-dominated trade and economic structures. Not in the crass horse-trading sense of holding security cooperation hostage in exchange for 'concessions' – as many in the political establishment were advocating – but through a seamless conflation of political, security and economic interests between Russia and the West. The United States would be suitably grateful for Moscow's assistance in the fight against international terrorism, but more importantly it would conclude that the unconditional nature of this support indicated that Russia was committed to a long-term vision of like-mindedness, and was not simply looking to capitalize tactically on the misfortune of others. However, in order to communicate this message persuasively the Putin administration needed to demonstrate a comprehensive approach that extended well beyond a purely security agenda. Hence the redoubled emphasis on WTO accession, at once the most practical and emblematic representation of economic cooperation and 'integration' with the West.

This kind of instrumentalism has also influenced Moscow's handling of other areas of foreign economic policy. The previously unalloyed pursuit of the profit motive has been moderated. For example, while the Putin administration remains committed to fulfilling lucrative nuclear and military contracts with, for example, Iran, these days it is more cognizant of American concerns. Although it is not yet prepared to abandon such cooperation, it is looking for ways to reconcile the conflict between a continuing desire to exploit its comparative advantage in certain spheres of commercial activity – arms transfers, nuclear cooperation – with the larger objective of economic (and other) integration with the West. For the time being at least, Moscow seems to think that it can manage this delicate balance,[14] but it would not be surprising if in the not so distant future it decided that sustaining the economic relationship with Tehran was no longer worth the trouble, particularly taking into account growing differences over the division of the Caspian Sea and its resources.[15]

A more nuanced approach is likewise discernible in Moscow's handling of the connection between geoeconomics and geopolitics. The basic proposition that Russia's revival as a world power depends above all on a strong economic foundation remains as valid as ever. But at a more 'micro' level, the use of economic instruments to project geopolitical influence has undergone some change in the light of the American military presence in the former Soviet Union. Although the rationale for this presence is security-based, in practice it is not always easy to separate it from a wider political and economic interaction between Washington and the independent states in the region. In this context, it has not escaped notice that Moscow's capacity to pressure Tbilisi and Kyiv is less than it was before 11 September. As in the case of cooperation with Iran, the Kremlin has increasingly to balance its priorities: on the one hand, the pursuit of a traditional, proto-imperial agenda,[16] albeit in an economic guise; on the other, closer integration with the West, with the attendant need to control (or at least sanitize) patrimonial inclinations *vis-à-vis* the CIS.[17]

These trends – the intensification of the WTO accession bid, a more careful approach to the pursuit of profit, a similar caution with regard to the geo-economics/geopolitics nexus – would seem to suggest that 11 September has pushed Moscow further in the direction of a Western economic mindset and system. In fact, appearances can be deceiving. If we mean by this that the Putin administration accepts that Russia must manage its economy and trade with other countries according to rules commonly accepted in Western market economies, then the outlook is mixed, to say the least. First, 11 September has had no major impact on the introduction and implementation of relevant legislation. The government has been aware for some time – since the Putin succession – that the time for words is over, and that Russia must deliver concrete outcomes in the form of an improved business climate, a more transparent economy, and so on. In appearing as a window of opportunity 11 September may have underlined this lesson, but since the pace of legislative activity was frenetic anyway it is hard to discern a tangible 'added value'.

More significantly still, many of the economic problems and misunderstandings between Russia and the West in the period before 11 September have continued to dog relations. The Russian economy remains heavily corporatized and oligarchic; attitudes to foreign economic participation are ambivalent; the relationship between government and business is as incestuous as ever; competition, except in a strictly circumscribed sense, is a dirty word; and legal and administrative transparency continue to be very partially applied concepts. The continuing difficulties Moscow has in fulfilling the provisions of the 1994 Partnership and Cooperation Agreement with the EU testify to the gulf between very different conceptions of market economics. It is possible that the ongoing rapprochement between Russia and the West will lead in time to a convergence in this as in other areas. But for the moment it is too early to say.

A new conception of security?

The view that 11 September was a transforming event in history is grounded in the premise that a conceptual revolution in the global security agenda has taken place over the past year. In a variant of 'big bang' theory, proponents of this thesis present a stark picture of two contrasting worlds: the pre-11 September security environment characterized by geopolitical competition and differing threat perceptions; and the post-11 September world, in which a chastened global community, suddenly perceiving the larger menace of international terrorism and other 'non-traditional' threats, unites for the greater good. In both thought and deed, the Putin administration has demonstrated its partiality to this interpretation – but with the critical qualifier that the revolutionizing impact of 11 September was on the West rather than on Russia, whose security perceptions had already evolved some time ago. Indeed, in some of its initial reactions Moscow evinced a smug, 'told you so' attitude. Having tried, but failed, to convince others that its conduct of military and 'police' operations in Chechnya was justified as part of humanity's wider struggle against the scourge of international terrorism, the Russian government seized on the attacks of 11 September as proof of its foresight and judgment.[18]

The administration's approach to international security priorities in the following months has reflected this thinking. First, contrary to what one might suppose, there has been no substantial change in Russian security perceptions. The real difference lies in the fact that 11 September afforded Moscow a priceless opportunity to take advantage of America's new-found vulnerability, not in order to score cheap and short-lived geopolitical points, but by showcasing Russia as an indispensable player in developing a new global security regime. Throughout the 1990s, the Yeltsin administration had attempted to achieve just such an aim through various devices and notions – a 'multipolar world order', a 'comprehensive European security architecture' under the aegis of the OSCE, a 'Comprehensive Security Concept for the 21st century', the UN Security Council, the Russia–NATO Founding Act and the Permanent Joint Council (PJC). However, with the Kremlin unable to reconcile itself to the reality of NATO's primacy in European security, such proposals became ever more impractical, a flimsy cover for Russia's increasingly desperate attempts to preserve its status as a 'great power'. When he came to office, Putin dispensed with much of this ideological baggage, and reactivated relations with NATO. But the legacy of the Soviet and post-Soviet past meant that old prejudices and stereotypes – in Russia *and* the West – died hard. There appeared no obvious way in, no transforming event to facilitate a quantum leap in security relations – just a hard slog over a period of years, perhaps longer.

The terrorist attacks on New York and Washington provided the hook the Kremlin was looking for. That is why Putin was so quick to offer his support to the Bush administration and the American people. It was not only a question of retroactively justifying Moscow's actions in Chechnya. From the start, the stakes were much, much higher. Played correctly, the revised security game offered enormous potential dividends: a political, economic, civilizational, as well as security integration in Europe and with the West; Russia's re-entry as an international actor, but this time on a much more solid and positive basis; and a free hand in Chechnya and on domestic politics. Furthermore, such benefits reached out to a wide audience at home: integration for the liberals, great power status for the *derzhavniki*, improved economic opportunities for corporate interests.

The challenge, then, was how to maximize the opportunities arising from 11 September while containing any adverse consequences to Russian security and geopolitical interests. Here Putin has been very successful – as his handling of four sets of issues demonstrates.

The first is the international security agenda itself, and Moscow's role in relation to it. Putin has effected a smooth and rapid transition in the traditional Western image of Russia as a largely obstructive presence to one where it is a major and above all constructive contributor. Second, he has neutralized the importance of old-style geopolitical calculus in Russia and the West. True, there are numerous domestic critics who condemn the increased American presence in Central Asia and the Transcaucasus. But it is obvious to all but the most intransigent that Russia was powerless to prevent this in any event; better therefore to package it as part of a strategic partnership against a greater enemy, and this Putin has done brilliantly.[19] Third, the strategic disarmament agenda, an area where Russian interests appeared to be in a state of public rout, has miraculously metamorphosed into the spearhead of Russia's global resurgence. Putin has managed to recover from a serious setback – Washington's decision to proceed with strategic missile defence and abrogate the ABM Treaty – and persuade the Americans to conclude a 'legally binding' strategic arms reductions treaty. That this treaty binds the United States to nothing[20] is less relevant than the fact that it offers an important, if symbolic, recognition that Russia is not just another European nation-state or minor power, but something much more.[21] The fourth and most recent achievement arising out of 11 September and its aftermath is renegotiation of the relationship with NATO. Again, the substance of the Rome agreement of May 2002 is less significant than the fact of its existence. Contrary to official claims, the newly formed Russia-NATO Council – the so-called *dvadtsatka* (group of twenty) – is unlikely in its present form to give Moscow the clout it seeks in security decision-making on the continent.[22] But even with its limitations the agreement represents a definite step forward, marking a growing acknowledgement in the West of Russian like-mindedness while offering Moscow the prospect of substantive involvement in European security affairs. Compared to the outlook a little over a year ago, let alone during the Yeltsin period, this is perhaps the most impressive of all Putin's achievements in the security sphere.

What is much harder to assess is the longer-term impact of 11 September on Russian security perceptions. Does the sequence of developments sound the death-knell of geopolitics and presage the widening of security concepts to include political and other types of soft security? Although it is difficult to answer this so soon after the event, some observations are apposite.

Exposure to new experiences can be a fine – or a harmful – thing. Inclusion in structures such as the Russia–NATO Council and the development of joint consultative mechanisms with Washington following the strategic arms reductions treaty hold out the prospect of a steady convergence of perceptions, not only in security and defence matters but also in overall political culture. Regular high-level consultations, the growing presence of Russian army officers in Brussels, military exchange visits, joint peacekeeping operations and defence exercises – these could be the building blocks of a new consensus between Russia and the West. Alternatively, however, they may turn out to be the seeds of mutual disenchantment. One of the potential downsides of Putin's many security achievements in recent times is that they have considerably raised expectations on all sides. The West hopes and maybe even trusts that Moscow will continue along the path of political and security rapprochement, while many Russians believe that joint decision-making in, say, the Russia–NATO Council will mean precisely that. In this connection, the example of the 1997 Founding Act and the PJC stands as a salutary lesson. The alliance and the Yeltsin administration (in particular) overestimated the scope and utility of the newly created consultative mechanisms, with the result that inflated expectations soon gave way to mounting disappointment, culminating in a virtual divorce during the Kosovo crisis. With the memory of a warm inner glow still fresh after the Putin–Bush and NATO–Russia summits, there is a danger that Russia and the West may lose perspective and overlook the number and magnitude of the differences that still separate them. If previously the mistake was to focus too much on divisions instead of commonalities, then today the situation threatens to be the reverse.

Next, both sides need to appreciate that the process of political and security rapprochement will be prolonged and difficult, interspersed with the occasional crisis or major disagreement, setbacks of one kind or another, confusion and misunderstanding. It is unrealistic to expect that the slate of half a century of strategic confrontation can be wiped clean in a couple of years or through a few, albeit important, agreements. In the end, the latter are just the tip of the iceberg, masking enormous contradictions that will take considerable time, effort and patience to straighten out.

Finally, geopolitics may seem on the way out in Russia, but it would be a brave person who would forecast its imminent demise. It is not only the inertial force of centuries of strategic tradition; there is also a question mark about what happens if Russia becomes a *bona fide* (as opposed to convalescing/aspiring) world power. In those circumstances, it might not take long for issues of geopolitical projection and competition to recover their former priority. At the risk of sounding cynical, it is worth pointing out that, for a state currently with few other options, making common cause with the West has been the best and perhaps only means of maintaining its position as an international player. The acid test of how far Moscow's security thinking has evolved will come when Russia becomes strong again, not while it is still weak.

The repackaging of identity

It is in the sphere of identity, values and civilization that the notion of 11 September as a turning-point has emerged most forcefully. The convergence of economic and security perceptions between Russia and the West has acquired a wider significance, one extending well beyond a mere coincidence of interests. Today, the talk is about a common civilization with shared values, in which Russia has shed its outsider status and once again entered the mainstream of the West in all its dimensions. The original Yeltsinite vision of an 'indivisible Europe' – a limited but nevertheless unattainable dream – has magically transmuted into an 'indivisible civilized world' whose new-found unity, it is proclaimed, will slowly but surely overcome the great dangers facing it.

For Putin, 11 September provided an extraordinary and entirely unexpected opportunity to accelerate the process of repackaging Russian identity in the contemporary world. As in the case of the security agenda, he had been working for some time to change this image, and with some success. But no amount of skilful public diplomacy could erase the memory of the running sore in Chechnya, nor allay Western concerns about the clampdown on the independent media or other anti-democratic behaviour. Putin the statesman may have presented as rational and businesslike, but for all that it would be a long time indeed before the West considered Russia to be 'normal'.

In this atmosphere of ambivalence the events of 11 September intervened, not in altering the fundamentals, but as a radical catalyst for existing policy trends. The consequences were at once comprehensive and fast-acting. The first was to reinforce the prevailing Westerncentrism in the Kremlin. At one level, Putin's uncompromising identification of Russia with the struggle against international terrorism was unsurprising given his attempts to justify the Chechen war on that basis.[23] However, whereas this had looked (and was) driven by a narrow national self-interest, his association with the fight against terrorism post-11 September came across as motivated by a largeness

127

of civilizational spirit. This, in turn, had the effect of lightening the historical burden and narrowing the gulf in values discussed in Chapter 6. A cooperative Russia 'suddenly' appeared to think in very similar terms to the West on the most urgent global priorities, while the latter's receptiveness to Russian support offered encouragement to the Kremlin in its pro-Western stance, including the prospect of tangible political, economic and security benefits down the line. In short, something of a chain reaction took place, whereby 11 September opened up all sorts of possibilities that did not seem to be there before. Moreover, contrary to the case ten years earlier, when the original vision of post-Cold War cooperation turned out to be illusory, this time changed international circumstances seemed to point to the real thing.

11 September also stripped away the myth of a Eurocentric foreign policy. It was apparent after the June 2001 Bush-Putin summit in Slovenia that Moscow would continue to take America as its principal point of strategic reference, and would therefore seize the first chance available to restore a functional relationship with Washington. But the terrorist attacks of Black Tuesday removed any lingering doubts. With the Bush administration adopting a much more activist approach to world affairs, American global pre-eminence reasserted itself with a vengeance. For Putin, the heightened Americacentric emphasis was therefore not only a matter of shared perceptions regarding the evils of international terrorism; as the executor of a 'pragmatic' foreign policy he needed to make the best out of a global situation in which the US was once again playing a super dominant role. In these conditions, geographical proximity and historical-cultural affinity with Europe were all very well, but the abiding reality was that, more than ever, Russia's most vital interests were bound up with the United States.[24]

The reinvigoration of Americacentrism in Moscow's world-view has been accompanied by a new confidence that it can achieve a civilizational convergence more or less on its terms, in other words, on the basis of shared interests instead of 'alien' liberal humanistic values. At an immediate practical level, the Putin administration sees 11 September as leading to the virtual nullification of outside concerns over its conduct of the Chechen war,[25] restrictions on the independent media, or manipulation of democratic processes. Faced with a 'clear and present danger' in the form of international terrorism, the West has neither the leisure nor the inclination to focus on individual civil liberties or issues of self-determination. More generally, for Moscow the new assertiveness in American foreign policy points to the likelihood that concrete priorities – security, trade and economic cooperation – will increasingly dominate international affairs, with more abstract aspirations being relegated to the margins. In the altered psychological state of the West post-11 September, the ultimate dividend is Russia's meteoric ascent from the status of tolerated outsider or 'constituent other'[26] to constructive and valued international actor.

Strategic opportunism

The common theme defining Moscow's approach to foreign policy priorities after 11 September is one of opportunism. Putin did not so much make a 'strategic choice' in favour of the West, but took advantage of an extraordinary set of circumstances to pursue objectives that were already in place but, for one reason and another, were difficult to realize. If we examine the different spheres of foreign policy management – the policy-making process, the economic agenda, security issues, the normative dimension – then it is hard to make the case for a qualitative shift in Kremlin thinking, let alone in the substance of Russian foreign policy. The real shift was not in Moscow, but in the West and particularly in Washington. The American government, shocked by events it failed to anticipate or else underestimated, took the lead in reshaping the system of international interactions. The result was a greatly enhanced role for Russia, one that no amount of effort on its part could have produced independently.

So in one sense Putin – and Russia – was extremely fortunate in how developments unfolded, not only on 11 September but also in the following months. The liberal politician Boris Nemtsov was quite right in judging that Russia had been afforded a 'fantastic opportunity' (*potryasayushchii shans*) to make a breakthrough in relations with the West and in its overall approach to the world.[27] But if Putin was undoubtedly lucky in the way things turned out, he was also perspicacious enough to grasp the essence of the new global dynamic, and to make the best of the surprising chance he had been given. It was this agility that conveyed the impression that he had made a strategic choice. For while most of the Russian political class was looking to the short term, advocating a tactical opportunism to exploit Washington's shock and temporary disorientation, Putin took the longer view – one of *strategic* opportunism. This involved, in the first instance, not being tempted by irrelevant point-scoring or petty bargaining for 'concessions' – both approaches that would have unravelled much of the good work that had already been done in Moscow's relations with the West. It meant staying faithful to the goals he had set out to achieve from the beginning of his presidency: establishing Russia as a respected international player; mending and then improving the relationship with the West; opening up real – as opposed to illusory – foreign policy options; and restoring national self-respect. In the end, there was nothing inconsistent in Putin's policy towards the West (and the world) after 11 September compared to what had gone before. His 'strategic choice', such as it was, occurred much earlier – it is just that prior to the terrorist attacks in the United States he had very limited scope to implement it.

Towards a sustainable foreign policy

It has become fashionable lately to apply the analogy of Gorbachev to Putin: both men ahead of their time, both men of vision, and both therefore vulnerable to the vagaries of political fate and the machinations of their contemporaries. At the same time there continues to be an ambivalence in the West, thankful for a more cooperative Russia, but fearing that things may be too good to last. Given these concerns, it would useful to conclude by briefly considering three questions: (i) how sustainable is the present foreign policy course; (ii) does Putin have a 'strategic vision' for Russia in the world; and (iii) what sort of place and role is Russia likely to occupy in that world?

By any fair-minded assessment, Putin has been exceptionally successful in his management of foreign policy. This is not to say that mistakes have not been made, or that he has achieved all his aims. However, given the mess he inherited and taking into account the collapse of his country's fortunes over the preceding 10–15 years, he has presided over a remarkable transformation. This overall success is the first guarantee of the sustainability of his foreign policy. As long as Putin or a successor can demonstrate concrete benefits in various areas of external relations – and principally with the West – then it is improbable that the present course of strategic (but constructive) opportunism will be discarded.

If, on the other hand, the setbacks begin to outweigh the achievements, in number and gravity, then the issue of sustainability becomes more complicated. It is not that foreign policy failures would lead to Putin's ejection either by the elite or democratically; in Russia, as in most countries, leaders become unpopular not because of foreign policy defeats but because of their perceived mishandling of domestic priorities, especially socio-economic. A more plausible scenario is therefore that of the beleaguered leader attempting to 'compensate' for domestic troubles through an assertive (read: aggressive) stance abroad, as Yeltsin was wont to do in the 1990s.[28] But although this possibility cannot be discounted, it too is not especially plausible. The hallmark of Putin's management of foreign policy is not so much pro-Westernism *per se*, as pursuit of the most effective means of maximizing Russian national interests. And it so happens that good relations with the West fit the requirements of a pragmatic approach to the world and will do so for many years to come. Consequently, while there may be fluctuations, upsets and minor reversals ahead, the likelihood of a strategic about-turn is small.

That is why, even in the event of something happening to Putin, a change of foreign policy course is not on the cards. As noted earlier, the world-view of the Russian elite and general population is strongly Westerncentric, and will become increasingly so with generational change. The frequent claim that 'Putin's foreign policy is not that of the elite' is only true – sometimes – in relation to the modalities of individual policies and to the overall atmospherics. Such a statement is wholly misleading, however, if it is understood to imply that in Putin's absence Russian foreign policy could become confrontational towards the West, or turn 'Eastern' and rogue-like. For all the elite's misgivings and suspicions about the West, the balance of national interests dictates a Westerncentric and generally cooperative foreign policy as the only way forward. This is a reality that future Russian leaders, of whatever political persuasion and temperament, will understand sooner rather than later – that is, if they have not already absorbed the lesson.

The matter of Putin's 'strategic vision' is harder to answer. It has become almost clichéd to describe him as a 'pragmatist', but this is by and large a fair summation. The operating principle of his conduct of foreign policy appears to be 'whatever works'; he is not fixated on ideology, geopolitics or cultural and civilizational categorizations. He has shown that he is prepared to be whoever and whatever depending on context and timing. Thus, he is European in Europe, transcontinental 'strategic partner' when dealing with the United States, Asian and Eurasian in Asia, and cautiously integrationist in the CIS. At the same time, he does not subscribe to the infantile view that strategic and economic cooperation with the West (or East) must necessarily be at the expense of good relations elsewhere. Although there may be times when uncomfortable choices have to be made – for example, possibly with Iran (see above) – he will continue for the most part to pursue a genuinely multi-vectored foreign policy, if with a strong Westerncentric bias. This not only accords with his strategically opportunistic outlook, but also with the key principle/emotional element in his make-up: namely, the belief that Russia was, is and must always be a world power. In this latter connection, the West should harbour no illusions that Putin envisages a 'normal' Russia as we might understand it. For him, and for the vast majority of his compatriots, Russia's normal state is as a great global actor, *not* as a second-line and essentially regional power like the leading European nations. Irrespective of whether Moscow is able to make good on such grandiose ambitions, this great power mentality will prove highly resilient.

This leads on to the final question regarding the sort of role Russia is likely to play in the world over the next 15–20 years. One can speculate endlessly (and enjoyably) on such a vast and open-ended theme, but unfortunately with very little certainty. It may be, however, that the Russia of today, 'Putin's Russia', is the model of the Russia of tomorrow: a country with a profoundly globalist mentality, conscious of its history and potential as a great power, but also one that understands the value of cooperative international behaviour, of good relations with other states and multilateral institutions, and give-and-take in the pursuit of the national interest. Such a Russia might not turn out as the West would ideally like – a fully integrated member of the international community of democratic nation-states – but for all that it would reflect a truly impressive evolution from the contrary misanthrope of recent history.

Notes

1 The Putin phenomenon

1 Putin's career in the KGB was good but not spectacular. His five-year posting (1985–90) in East Germany indicates that his superiors thought quite highly of him, yet carries the whiff of second class when compared to the placements enjoyed by others, for example, Sergei Ivanov (KGB First Main Directorate; Soviet Embassy in London). It is notable that Putin's career only really took off after he returned to the security services following his stint as Deputy Mayor of St Petersburg.

As General Secretary of the Communist Party's Central Committee, Stalin occupied a position of little glamour, but considerable latent power. In particular, his responsibility for personnel issues (including placements) enabled him to consolidate and then expand his position in the Party hierarchy. Although Stalin was far more of a political careerist than Putin, and unlike him sought power with a single-minded intensity over a period of years, the critical common denominator is that their bureaucratic/administrative background misled their contemporaries into severely underestimating their political capacities.

2 Lilia Shevtsova, 'Mezhdu stabilizatsiei i proryvom: promezhutochnye itogi pravleniya Vladimira Putina', *Brifing Moskovskogo Tsentra Karnegi*, January 2002, p. 2.

3 Given the apparent contentiousness of this conclusion, it is worth listing the criteria used in reaching it. For the record, these are:
   (i)   the extent of the leader's political security (or vulnerability);
   (ii) the presence (or otherwise) of rivals;
   (iii) the nature of the leader's rule – individual or collective;
   (iv) the existence of political checks and balances on the exercise of power;
   (v)   the capacity to ride out opposition to policy formulation and implementation;
   (vi) resilience in the face of political and policy setbacks.

Against these criteria, Putin emerges very favourably in comparison with the other post-Stalin leaders. Konstantin Chernenko and Yurii Andropov were in power for too brief a period (with the latter's potential as a strong General Secretary being undermined by kidney disease), while Georgii Malenkov was overthrown after only two years. Boris Yeltsin's two presidential terms were marked by acute political uncertainty, and he came perilously close to losing power on at least three occasions: the October 1993 stand-off with the Supreme Soviet; the run-up to the

1996 presidential elections; and in 1999 when he came within a few votes of impeachment. Mikhail Gorbachev, in addition to being subject to the (albeit diminishing) constraints of collective leadership, was unseated by the August 1991 putsch, and then more permanently by Yeltsin. More generally, his six-year rule witnessed an ever more anarchic situation in the country, culminating in the disappearance of the Soviet state – surely the ultimate loss of political and policy control.

That leaves only two plausible candidates: Nikita Khrushchev and (the early, pre-1976 stroke) Leonid Brezhnev. Although the former sometimes cut an impressive figure as a leader without apparent limits, appearances were deceptive. First, he was almost overthrown by the Politburo in 1957 (saving himself only by convening an emergency meeting of the Party Central Committee), before being definitively removed in 1964. Second, even at the height of his personal power, the Politburo remained the supreme policy-making body in the Soviet Union; ultimately, the basis of authority was collective rather than individual. Third, his control over policy was often illusory, as exposed spectacularly by such débâcles as the 1962 Cuban missile crisis. Ironically, it is the unimpressive Brezhnev, the butt of countless jokes and all-round contempt, who represents the main 'competition' to Putin. For all his obvious limitations, he was politically secure, with putative rivals like Alexei Kosygin and Mikhail Suslov fading from contention. However, the Brezhnev period also marked the high point of collective decision-making in the shape of the Politburo; there were many more *effective* checks and balances in the system than exist today.

Putin, by contrast, is as secure as any leader in the developed world; has no meaningful rivals; rules in a much more individual fashion than any leader since Stalin; faces far fewer political or institutional checks and balances than his predecessors; has frequently been able to override policy opposition, even in controversial areas such as land reform and the strong pro-American emphasis post-11 September; and has emerged practically unscathed from even very public setbacks such as the Kursk submarine sinking. None of this is to claim that he is omnipotent, either politically or in policy-making. There are clearly whole areas of the latter, in particular, where the presidential writ is little more than nominal. But by the (admittedly very low) standards of the post-Stalin past, Putin stacks up well.

4 In contrast to the Soviet principle of 'collective leadership' – see note 3 above.

5 Although there has been some media criticism of Putin, this has for the most part been sporadic, peripheral and/or muted. In a country whose government professes a strong allegiance to democratic and civil ideals, the overwhelmingly laudatory coverage of the President is striking indeed.

6 Bobo Lo, *Russian Foreign Policy in the Post-Soviet Era: Reality, Illusion and Mythmaking* (Palgrave Macmillan, Basingstoke and New York, 2002), pp. 5–6, 151–4.

7 It has been estimated that Putin visited more countries in the first year of his presidency than Yeltsin did during his two presidential terms.

8 Lo, *Russian Foreign Policy in the Post-Soviet Era ...*, pp. 154–5.

9 Lenin used the phrase *kto kogo* to encapsulate the zero-sum, life-and-death, nature of the political struggle.

10 Dmitri Trenin, '"Osennii marafon" Vladimira Putina: k rozhdeniyu Rossiiskoi vneshnepoliticheskoi strategii', *Briefing Moskovskogo Tsentra Karnegi*, 20 November 2001, p. 6.

11 It has even been claimed by a certain foreign minister, who for the sake of his reputation should remain nameless, that Russia is now as insignificant as it has been at any time since before Peter the Great in the late 17th century.

12 See 'Verkhnyaya Volta s yadernymi raketami, velikimi sportsmenami i bezmozglymi funktsionerami', *Nezavisimaya gazeta*, 26 February 2002, p. 1.

2 The inheritance

1 Viktor Chernomyrdin succeeded Yegor Gaidar in December 1992, surviving (at times miraculously) until March 1998. His successors showed nothing like the same powers of political longevity: Kiriyenko managed four months before being unseated by the August 1998 financial crash; Primakov, appointed in September 1998, was dismissed in May 1999; and Stepashin lasted a derisory three months (May–August 1999).

2 Perhaps the most public of these scandals was the one involving the Swiss construction company, Mabetex, and members of Yeltsin's close family (including Yeltsin himself and his two daughters). The *Washington Post* alleged in September 1999 that Mabetex had paid millions of dollars into the private accounts of the Yeltsin family in return for winning contracts to refurbish the Kremlin.

3 Although the financial crash led to a four-fold devaluation of the rouble, it also resulted in Russian consumer goods becoming much more competitive, both internally and internationally. Virtually overnight, many Western imports became unaffordable, leaving the field open to domestically produced commodities. The crash significantly improved Moscow's already positive total trade balance, and led to a marked increase in trade turnover with the CIS (particularly Belarus).

4 The Army's bombardment of the White House – the seat of the Supreme Soviet – in October 1993 marked the culmination of a prolonged and increasingly bitter struggle for power between the executive and the legislature. For an excellent account of these developments and the issues involved, see Lilia Shevtsova, *Yeltsin's Russia: Myths and Reality* (Carnegie Endowment for International Peace, Washington DC, 1999), pp. 37–90.

5 The most notorious of these was the 1995 'loans-for-shares' arrangement whereby blocks of shares in state-owned blue-chip companies were given to banks in return for generous loans to the government. See Joseph R. Blasi, Maya Kroumova and Douglas Kruse, *Kremlin Capitalism: Privatizing the Russian Economy* (ILR Press/ Cornell, Ithaca and London, 1997), pp. 74–6.

6 It was Primakov who, in the 1990s, did most to popularize the term 'multivectored'. He appears to have first used it in public in 1993 in connection with the creation of an 'integral system of collective security' in Europe ('Opravdano li rasshirenie NATO?', *Nezavisimaya gazeta*, 26 November 1993, p. 3). Subsequently, in his first press conference as Foreign Minister, he applied the term to describe the administration's intended approach to the conduct of Russian foreign policy more generally (see 'Primakov nachinaet s SNG', *Moskovskie novosti*, no. 2, 14–21 January 1996, p. 13).

7 See, for example, Georgi Arbatov, 'A New Cold War', *Foreign Policy*, no. 95, Summer 1994, p. 101.

8 Andrei Kozyrev thus noted: 'Russia, one way or another, remains a great power. For the communists and nationalists, an aggressive and threatening power, for the democrats, a peaceful and prosperous one. But in all cases a great power. And therefore it cannot be a junior partner [with the West], only an equal partner' – *Preobrazhenie* ("Mezhdunarodnye otnosheniya", Moscow, 1995), p. 221.

9 In this context, Kozyrev spoke about the importance of the 'consultation reflex', whereby the West would consult or at least inform Russia prior to undertaking any significant international engagement – 'Rossiya i SShA: Partnerstvo ne prezhdevremenno, a zapazdyvaet', *Izvestiya*, 11 March 1994, p. 3.

10 The proposed 'counter-measures' included non-ratification of the START-2 agreement and the development of the CIS as a counter-bloc to NATO (see Defence Minister Rodionov's comments in Igor Korotchenko, 'Igor Rodionov vystupil za sozdanie oboronnogo soyuza stran SNG', *Nezavisimaya gazeta*, 26 December 1996, p. 1). On a more general note, Primakov foreshadowed early on a 'fundamental rethinking' of Russian security thinking ('Opravdano li rasshirenie NATO?', *Nezavisimaya gazeta*, 26 November 1993, p. 3).

11 See, for example, Primakov's comments in an interview published by *Rossiiskaya gazeta* on 10 January 1997 ('God Evgeniya Primakova'), p. 2.

12 During his short stint in power (14 months, of which the last six were inactive), Andropov initiated some important reforms in enterprise management and to improve labour incentives – see Bobo Lo, *Soviet Labour Ideology and the Collapse of the State* (Macmillan Press and St Martin's Press, Basingstoke and New York, 2000), pp. 37–45. As for his patronage of Gorbachev, the latter acknowledged that '[a]mong the leaders of the country, there was no one else with whom I had such close and old ties, and to whom I owed so much' – *Memoirs* (Doubleday, London, 1996), p. 152.

13 See *Ot pervogo litsa: razgovory s Vladimirom Putinym* (Vagrius, Moscow, 2000), pp. 72–5.

14 A senior Western diplomat in Moscow described to me Russia's selective approach to engagement with the West as 'integration *à la carte*'.

15 *Ot pervogo litsa*, p. 156.

16 A notable exception is the heavy pressure Russia has been exerting on Georgia in relation to the presence of Chechen guerrillas in the Pankisi gorge. Interestingly, domestic liberal criticism of government policy here has been muted, as has that of an international community preoccupied by the early prospect of American military intervention against Saddam Hussein.

17 Television statement by President Putin on 13 December 2001 (*http://www.putin.ru/status.asp*).

18 During the Yeltsin years there were two occasions in particular when Duma ratification of START-2 appeared imminent: the first in December 1998; the second in March 1999. Both times, however, ratification was derailed by extraneous developments – American and British air-strikes on Baghdad, and the NATO military intervention over Kosovo, respectively

19 Sergei Karaganov correctly observed that Primakov's appointment had ensured that there would be virtually no discussion of foreign policy during the six months of the 1996 presidential campaign – 'Diplomatiya: kommunisty ukhodyat bez boya', *Moskovskie novosti*, no. 25, 24–30 June 1996, p. 5.

20 After Lenin's death in 1924, Stalin formed a ruling triumvirate with Lev Kamenev and Grigorii Zinoviev, united against Leon Trotsky who had commanded the Red Army during the Civil War of 1918–21. Subsequently, Kamenev and Zinoviev allied themselves with Trotsky to oppose the growing power of Stalin. By this time, however, the latter had cemented his administrative control over the Party, while making common cause with its right wing led by Nikolai Bukharin, architect of the (relatively) liberal New Economic Policy. Trotsky, Kamenev and Zinoviev were defeated and then expelled from the Party in November 1927. The final act of Stalin's struggle for power was played out at the 16th Party Conference in April 1929, when he engineered the public condemnation of Bukharin and his supporters and emerged definitively as the sole leader of the Soviet Union.

21 Although strictly speaking the Putin government does not enjoy an absolute majority in the Duma, in practice the latter no longer has the capacity or the will to coordinate opposition to the rising power of the executive. The share of seats of the main Communist-Agrarian opposition has fallen from 220 (during the second Yeltsin term) to 130, while the merger in December 2001 between Putin's party, Edinstvo ('Unity') and the Primakov-Luzhkov party, Otechestvo-Vsya Rossiya ('Fatherland-All Russia'), has ensured that the so-called 'centrist' bloc dominates Duma proceedings. The extent of executive control is further reflected in the rapid turnover of legislation through parliament.

22 Gusinsky and Berezovsky were targeted for domestic political reasons. Although the government insisted that it had not influenced either Gazprom's takeover of the Gusinsky Media-Most group (including the NTV channel) in April 2001, or the subsequent closure of Berezovsky's TV6 channel in January 2002, these disclaimers were met with widespread scepticism. Certainly, it was hardly coincidental that the only oligarchs to be subjected to an unprecedented financial rigour were those whose media outlets had been most critical of Putin's policies, especially the conduct of the war in Chechnya.

   The case of Rutskoi is slightly different. He did not so much actively defy Putin as represent a general political embarrassment to the government. As a consequence, he was barred from standing for re-election at the Kursk gubernatorial elections in October 2000, for which he had been the warm favourite. The circumstances of the ban were extremely suspect: a local court order came through, literally hours before the first round of the elections, excluding him from participation on the grounds that he had not supplied an accurate statement of his property holdings.

23 In a famous article in *Foreign Affairs*, Kozyrev called for a 'constructive partnership' between Russia and the United States that would 'influence positively the course of world affairs' ('The Lagging Partnership', *Foreign Affairs*, vol. 73, no. 3, May/June 1994, p. 59). See also Clinton-Yeltsin declaration at the Vancouver summit in April 1993 – *Izvestiya*, 6 April 1993, p. 1.

24 CTR, established by US Senators Sam Nunn and Richard Lugar in 1992, is an ongoing programme for the safe dismantlement and disposal of obsolete Soviet/Russian nuclear missiles and their materials.

25 The main sticking-point here was the question of placing Russian peacekeepers under NATO command. In Kosovo, their 'autonomy' was nominally preserved by putting the Russian contingent under the UN's formal control, without impinging

on NATO's operational management on the ground. Of course, such a compromise has not been without its problems. A senior diplomat from one of the NATO member states observed to me that NATO–Russia interaction within KFOR has frequently been more uncomfortable than either side would care to admit.

26 Kozyrev, *Preobrazhenie*, p. 221 (see note 8 above).

27 For example, at the World Economic Forum in Davos, Switzerland, in February 1997, Anatolii Chubais claimed that a NATO enlargement over Russian objections would be the West's biggest political mistake in 50 years. Later, Grigorii Yavlinsky criticized the alliance's military intervention over Kosovo in very strong terms (*Segodnya*, 25 March 1999, p. 2).

28 This was a fairly common complaint of Western European diplomats in Moscow, especially during Yeltsin's second term.

29 Under the Founding Act, Russia and NATO undertook to 'work together to contribute to the establishment in Europe of common and comprehensive security based on the allegiance to shared values, commitments and norms of behaviour in the interests of all states' (*Founding Act on Mutual Relations, Cooperation and Security between the North Atlantic Treaty Organization and the Russian Federation*, p. 3). On a slightly more concrete level, the Founding Act established a Permanent Joint Council (PJC), a 'mechanism for consultation, coordination and, to the maximum extent possible, where appropriate, for joint decisions and joint action with respect to security issues of common concern' (p. 5).

30 The share of CIS countries in Russia's total trade fell from 75–80 per cent in 1990 to around 20 per cent in 1995 (see Abraham Becker, 'Russia and Economic Integration in the CIS', *Survival*, vol. 38, no. 4, Winter 1996–97, pp. 118, 126–7). Although the rouble's four-fold devaluation following the August 1998 financial crash partially reversed this decline by radically increasing the cost of non-CIS imports, even in 2000 the CIS (principally Belarus and Ukraine) accounted for 13.4 per cent of Russia's exports and 34.4 per cent of its imports (*Tamozhennaya statistika vneshnei torgovlya Rossiiskoi Federatsii*, 2001, p. 7). With the next wave of EU enlargement these percentages are likely to decline significantly.

31 It has been claimed that in eight years as president Boris Yeltsin failed to meet with any of the Russian diaspora communities in the former Soviet Union (Natalya Airapetova, 'Stranam SNG sleduet ozhidat syurprizov ot Rossii, *Nezavisimaya gazeta*, 25 January 2000, p. 5). On a more substantive level, Anatol Lieven has remarked on Moscow's unwillingness to invest even in such relatively low-cost ventures as Russian-language TV broadcasts to diaspora areas in the CIS ('The Weakness of Russian Nationalism', *Survival*, vol. 41, no.2, Summer 1999, p. 59).

32 In various conversations during the 1990s, Chinese diplomats and journalists suggested to me that Moscow viewed good relations with Beijing principally as a means of managing the geostrategic balance with the United States.

33 The Asians outside the 'big two' (China and Japan) felt this neglect especially keenly.

34 During a visit to Moscow in September 1997, Egyptian President Hosni Mubarak made a very public point of saying that Russia had become largely irrelevant in the MEPP ('Hosni Mubarak: "Rossiya dolzhna vernutsya na blizhnii vostok"', interview in *Nezavisimaya gazeta*, 23 September 1997, p. 1).

35 This was particularly the case over Iraq. Intense Russian mediation efforts in the second half of the 1990s were ineffective in persuading Saddam Hussein to cooper-

ate with UNSCOM inspections or in preventing American and British air-strikes against Iraqi targets (culminating in Operation Desert Fox in December 1998).

36 Vladimir Lukin, then Russian Ambassador to Washington (and later Head of the Duma's International Affairs Committee) wrote that while there would always be 'tensions and disputes' within the democratic community, they were the 'problems of a common civilization with a shared system of values based on the ideas that human life is precious and that the individual comes before the state' – 'Our Security Predicament', *Foreign Policy*, no. 88, Fall 1992, p. 75.

37 The 'climax' (or nadir) came during Yeltsin's last overseas visit, to Beijing in December 1999. On this occasion, he reacted to American criticisms of the war in Chechnya by angrily declaring that Russia and China, not America, 'would dictate to the world' – see Dmitrii Gornostaev, 'Eltsin napomnil Klintonu i miru: Rossiya ostaetsya yadernoi derzhavoi', *Nezavisimaya gazeta*, 10 December 1999, p. 1.

38 See comments by NATO Secretary-General Lord Robertson during a visit to Moscow in November 2001, in 'NATO brings radical offer to Putin', *http:// news.bbc.co.uk/1/hi/world/europe/1671654.stm*.

39 Putin and Bush met for the first time at the Russia–USA summit in Brdo, Slovenia, in June 2001 – a good six months after Bush's victory in the American presidential elections.

40 See Putin's televised remarks at a meeting with government ministers on 8 October 2001 (*http://www.putin.ru/status.asp*).

41 In his latest volume of memoirs written after his retirement, Yeltsin refers to his fears in the second half of 1999 that Primakov's political success would 'lead the country back to the socialism of yesteryear' – *Midnight Diaries* (Phoenix, London, 2001), p. 268.

3 The policy-making environment

1 As Stalin put it, 'the cadres decide everything' – address to graduates of the Red Army Academies, 4 May 1935 (see *http://www.marx2mao.org/Stalin/GRA35.html*).

2 A very senior Foreign Ministry official encapsulated the problem in the following contradictory terms: on the one hand, the MFA now had greater control and influence over foreign policy, while the overall policy-making environment was also more disciplined and functional. On the other hand, the number of foreign policy actors had grown, and with it the problems of foreign policy free-lancing by often unqualified parties. His summation was that the environment was now a better one for the MFA (and Russia) than under Yeltsin, but remained difficult.

3 The most categorical of a raft of dismissive comments about the Foreign Ministry is to be found in *The Economist* which claims that the MFA 'provides little more than a delivery service for other people's messages' – 'The president's ear', 16–22 February 2002, p. 46. This view is fairly representative of much of Russian elite opinion.

4 The term 'braking mechanism' (*mekhanizm tormozheniya*) was originally used by Gorbachev to describe the 'alien' (to socialism) phenomena that had arrested the Soviet Union's socio-economic development in the second half of the 1970s – *Perestroika i novoe myshlenie dlya nashei strany i dlya vsego mira* (Politizdat, Moscow 1987), p. 13.

5 A senior NATO country diplomat in Moscow told me that the MFA – at Deputy Minister level – had led the Russian side in the substantive negotiations prior to the NATO–Russia Rome summit.

6 The most conspicuous example of the heightened profile and influence of the security services in the MFA was the appointment in June 2000 of the then head of the Foreign Intelligence Service, Vyacheslav Trubnikov, as First Deputy Minister of Foreign Affairs.

7 Perhaps the most dramatic illlustration of such freelancing was the seizure by Russian peacekeepers of Slatina (Pristina) airport in June 1999. As Foreign Minister Ivanov's comments at the time revealed ('the mistake will be corrected'), the MOD failed to inform, let alone consult, the Russian Foreign Ministry over this highly controversial action – see Natalya Kalashnikova and Andrei Smirnov, 'Kuzkina mat dlya vnutrennego potrebleniya', *Segodnya*, 14 June 1999, p. 1.

8 As formalized in the joint ministerial Consultative group on strategic security, established at the May 2002 Russian–American summit in Moscow.

9 *http://www.3.itu.int/MISSIONS/Russia/Bull/2001/25–2106B.htm.*

10 According to one story doing the rounds in March 2002, the Security Council had not met for five months. Although one should be cautious about accepting such accounts at face value, they nevertheless serve to highlight the Council's declining policy fortunes following Sergei Ivanov's transfer to the MOD.

11 A related problem here is how to evaluate the introduction of senior security figures into the MFA, such as the appointment of former SVR head Trubnikov as First Deputy Foreign Minister (see note 6 above). Does one interpret this and similar cases as highlighting the influence of the security services, a sort of 'securitization' of the Foreign Ministry, or do they reflect instead the latter's growing stature at the expense of the former?

12 It is rumoured that a delegation of prominent Moscow political figures called on Putin in early 2002 to express their concerns on this score.

13 A well-placed liberal commentator told me that Gaidar and Nemtsov had worked very long hours in preparing Putin's 2002 address to the Federal Assembly. Although it is impossible to confirm this directly, it cannot be coincidental that (i) the speech focused principally on socio-economic reforms and requirements; and (ii) the dominant foreign policy themes were WTO accession and the challenges economic globalization posed for Russia.

14 During the post-Soviet period, the Central Bank, particularly under the leadership of Viktor Gerashchenko, acquired a reputation for conservatism and unreconstructed attitudes towards economic reform and foreign investment. Few in the foreign economic community were sorry to see his eventual dismissal in March 2002.

15 On the Presidential Administration's moderating effect on policy, see (i) re NATO enlargement, *Rossiiskaya gazeta*, 10 January 1997, p. 2; (ii) re Kosovo, Vitalii Marsov and Nikolai Ulyanov, 'Chernomyrdin zaimetsya yugoslavskim krizisom', *Nezavisimaya gazeta*, 15 April 1999, p. 3.

16 A senior MFA official told me at the time of the Krasnoyarsk summit that the Ministry had been very concerned at Primakov's exclusion, as well as by the fact that 'unrealistic' expectations had been raised about possible territorial concessions to Tokyo.

17 The head of the Presidential Administration's foreign policy office, Sergei Prikhodko,

emphasized in an interview shortly after his appointment that the size of the office was far too small even to contemplate supplanting the Foreign Ministry in any way – 'Administratsiya prezidenta – ne apparat TsK KPSS', *Segodnya*, 17 October 1997, p. 3.

18 Yastrzhembsky has spent most of his recent career in public diplomacy – as MFA and then presidential spokesman, as deputy chief-of-staff in the Presidential Administration, and as Moscow Mayor Yurii Luzhkov's deputy with responsibility for international relations. He was also formerly Russian Ambassador in Bratislava. Before becoming Yeltsin's foreign policy advisor, Prikhodko was Deputy Director of the Second European Department, covered relations with the Baltic states, worked on Warsaw Pact and OSCE issues, and served two postings in Prague.

19 See Boris Yeltsin, *Midnight Diaries* (Phoenix, London, 2001), p. 217.

20 Under this informal agreement, the Russian government undertook not to negotiate any new arms deals with Tehran and to wind up existing commitments over the next few years.

21 Putin's public popularity has remained consistently at around 70 per cent. Even after the Kursk submarine disaster (August 2000) and the President's unwise decision not to curtail his holiday in the Crimea, his rating did not dip below 65 per cent (see Galina Kovalskaya, 'Osnovnoi instinct', *Itogi*, 29 August 2000, p. 23). Meanwhile, Putin has enjoyed an effective (if not a technical) majority in the Duma since the December 1999 elections – see note 21, chapter 2.

22 Alex Pravda described the influence of the Duma under Yeltsin as essentially indirect, 'less as a body exercising formal accountability than as a forum articulating and amplifying opinions which affected the political climate in which executive decisions were made' – 'The Public Politics of Foreign Policy', in Neil Malcolm, Alex Pravda, Roy Allison and Margot Light, *Internal Factors in Russian Foreign Policy* (The Royal Institute of International Affairs and Clarendon Press, Oxford, 1996), p. 218.

23 One notable example of the use of parliamentary figures in 'kite-flying' exercises was the refusal of Federation Council speaker Sergei Mironov to meet with Palestinian Authority leader Yasser Arafat during a visit to Israel in March 2002. The non-meeting conveyed a strong message about Russia's changing position towards the MEPP post-11 September, while allowing Moscow to explain away a highly provocative move as merely Mironov's 'personal initiative' (see *http://english. pravda.ru/politics/2002/03/18/27029.html*). It is inconceivable that Mironov, a close personal confidant of Putin from St Petersburg, would have acted in this way without at least a nod and a wink from the President.

Mikhail Margelov (Head of the Federation Council's International Affairs Committee) and Dmitrii Rogozin (Head of the Duma's International Affairs Committee) have also served their president well, if in somewhat more cautious fashion. On the occasion of the Shanghai Cooperation Organization summit in St Petersburg in June 2002, Margelov reiterated the official fiction that Russian foreign policy was geographically balanced between East and West – the purpose being to dilute the reality of an all too transparent Westerncentrism following the Russia–USA and NATO–Russia summits. As for Rogozin, his appointment as the President's special representative on Kaliningrad underlined the increasingly flimsy nature of the separation of powers in today's Russia.

24 Under the 1974 Jackson-Vanik amendment, the provision of American financial and commercial privileges to foreign countries became conditional on changes in the latter's emigration policies. Although the legislation applied globally, the real target was the Soviet Union and its discriminatory treatment of Jews wishing to leave the country.

Anti-dumping rules in the European Union were designed to protect local steel industries from 'unfair' competition from outside (i.e., non-EU) producers, in particular Russia, which benefited from lower production costs and who were therefore able to undercut on price.

25 Kozyrev gave a highly controversial speech at the summit in which, among other things, he described the former Soviet Union as 'post-imperial space' exempt from the full application of CSCE norms. Russia, he stated, would 'insist' that the newly independent republics enter into a new federation or confederation under Moscow's leadership. Kozyrev subsequently defended his inflammatory remarks as a ruse, the only means of highlighting the threat posed by reactionary forces in the Supreme Soviet to Russian democracy and to post-Cold War reconciliation with the West. See Andrei Kozyrev, *Preobrazhenie* ("Mezhdunarodnye otnosheniya", Moscow 1995), pp. 5–7.

26 See comments by Andrei Ryabov in an interview with *Vremya MN* of 19 October 2001 (*www.rferl.com/rpw/2001/10/27-301001.html*).

27 See note 22, chapter 2.

28 See NAPSNet Daily Report of 3 October 2001 (*http://www.nautilus.org/napsnet/dr/0110/OCT03.html#item17*).

29 For interesting survey data on this question, see Julie Corwin, 'Is Putin Popular Because He's Not Yeltsin?' *Radio Free Europe/Radio Liberty, Russian Political Weekly*, vol. 2, no. 9, 18 March 2002, *http://www.rferl.org/rpw/2002/03/9-180302. html.*

30 Although the Patriarch has from time to time inveighed against the effects of Western moral and cultural influence on Russia, he has been careful to avoid any implication of culpability on the part of the Kremlin. It was noteworthy that, in a symbolic display of secular and religious unity, Putin and Alexi II should jointly meet up with the Russian Olympic team before its departure for the 2002 Winter Games in Salt Lake City.

31 Many Russians, both within the elite and among the general public, were especially incensed by controversial judging decisions, and several prominent figures, including the film director Nikita Mikhalkov, called for the early withdrawal of the Russian team. Putin's own reaction was understated. Although expressing some concerns, he avoided the hysterically nationalist *amour-propre* of others. For an example of the latter, see 'Verkhnyaya Volta s yadernymi raketami, velikimi sportsmenami i bezmozglymi funktsionerami', *Nezavisimaya gazeta*, 26 February 2002, pp. 1, 3.

32 Much has been said about the relaxed personal relationship between Putin and George Bush evident at the Slovenia (June 2001), Crawford (November 2001) and Moscow/St Petersburg (May 2002) summits. However, while the two presidents clearly get on very well, it would be incautious and premature to accept the glad-handing and the *bonhomie* completely at face value. At the risk of stating the obvious, the building and projection of such atmospherics are all part of the job of developing more productive relations between countries. The Yeltsin–Kohl

relationship is a different case, not least because it has survived the retirement of both leaders. Neither has a particular reason, other than close personal friendship, to continue seeing the other.

33 The principle of a 'presidential' foreign policy is enshrined in the 1993 Constitution. Article 86 notes that the President shall 'govern the foreign policy of the Russian Federation', as well as hold negotiations, sign international treaties and ratification instruments, and receive diplomatic credentials (*http://www. constitution. ru/en/10003000–05.htm*).

34 According to *The Economist*, Putin 'seems to have thought up his new pro-western policy mainly off his own bat'. It adds, more generally, that Putin 'looks quite lonely on [the foreign policy] front. He may have his best chats on foreign affairs with other world leaders …' – see 'The president's ear', 16–22 February 2002, p. 46.

35 Speaking of grey eminences, certain parallels can be drawn between Chubais's role under Yeltsin, and those of Cardinals Richelieu and Mazarin under Louis XIII and Louis XIV of France.

36 As Anders Åslund has noted, '[p]rivatization was supposed to change not only the economy but the whole society' – see *Building Capitalism: The Transformation of the Former Soviet Bloc* (Cambridge University Press, 2002), p. 295.

37 See Yeltsin, *Midnight Diaries*, p. 16.

38 Subsequent to his involvement in the loans-for-shares arrangement (see note 5, chapter 2), in November 1997 Chubais became embroiled in a very public scandal after he accepted a US$90,000 advance payment for a proposed book on privatization.

39 It is interesting that Chubais consistently ranks fourth in *Nezavisimaya gazeta*'s monthly poll, Russia's '100 leading politicians', behind Putin, Prime Minister Kasyanov, and Head of the Presidential Administration Alexander Voloshin, but ahead of such notables as Sergei Ivanov (fifth), Alexei Kudrin (sixth) and German Gref (tenth).

40 In *Ot pervogo litsa*, Putin refers to Kudrin by the affectionate diminutive, Lyosha (p. 120).

41 Certainly the snail-like pace of military reform and footdragging over alternative civilian service would appear to support this interpretation.

42 In Soviet times, the prime minister's role in relation to economic reform could be progressive or conservative. Thus, Alexei Kosygin spearheaded (ultimately unsuccessful) proposals for devolutionary enterprise reform from 1965, while in the Gorbachev era Nikolai Ryzhkov became increasingly associated with conservative and anti-market forces.

43 Gaidar was a well-known academic economist; Chernomyrdin was the head of Gazprom; Kiriyenko's background was in banking and oil; while Primakov (whose first degree was in economics) was appointed as an anti-crisis response following the August 1998 financial crash. With hindsight, the list of 'economic' prime ministers might also include Stepashin. Although his background is in the security services, he has been the head of the State Audit Chamber since April 2000.

44 See Michael Lelyveld, 'Russia: economc advisors disagree on tariffs for natural monopolies', *Radio Free Europe/Radio Liberty*, 11 December 2002, *http://www. rferl.org/nca/features/2001/12/11122001084347.asp*, also Elena Dukun, 'The President Will Carry Out Three Cabinet Reshuffles', *Prism*, vol. 7, no. 7, 31 July 2001, The Jamestown Foundation, *http://russia.jamestown.org/pubs/view/pri_007_007_004.htm*.

45 For example, Russia has never had a bureaucratic hierarchy in the Weberian sense; there are institutions, but no superstructure that functions as a mechanism for the distribution of power. (I am indebted to Ole Lindeman for this insight.)

46 The term 'transmission belt' was originally used in Soviet times to describe the dual but complementary role of trade unions: representing the workers' interests to the government, while ensuring the efficient implementation of state economic plans by the workforce

47 See note 3, chapter 1.

48 See Putin's criticisms of the bureaucracy in his 2002 address to the Federal Assembly, *Rossiiskaya gazeta*, 19 April 2002, p. 4.

4 The economic agenda

1 According to the Stockholm International Peace Research Institute (SIPRI), global net military expenditure has risen consistently since 1998. The events of 11 September 2001 are only likely to reinforce this trend. See *SIPRI Yearbook 2002 – Armaments, Disarmament and International Security* (Oxford University Press, New York, 2002), p. 232.

2 Certainly, Gorbachev regarded this as a self-evident truth. In his memoirs, he wrote: 'There is probably no need to prove that perestroika and the fundamental reform of both our economic and political systems would have been impossible without corresponding changes in Soviet foreign policy and the creation of propitious international conditions' (*Memoirs*, Doubleday, London and New York, 1996, p. 401). In similar vein, Yeltsin emphasized early in his presidency that the chief priority of Russian foreign policy was to ensure 'favourable external conditions for the success of … political and economic reforms …' ('Chto skazal Eltsin Rossiiskim diplomatam', *Rossiiskie vesti*, 29 October 1992, p. 1).

3 The 2000 Foreign Policy Concept comprises five parts: (I) 'General Propositions'; (II) 'The Contemporary World and the Foreign Policy of the Russian Federation'; (III) 'Priorities of the Russian Federation in Resolving Global Problems'; (IV) 'Regional Priorities'; and (V) Formation and Realization of the Foreign Policy of the Russian Federation'. 'International Economic Relations' rank third in the third section, behind 'The Formation of a New World Order' and 'Strengthening International Security', and ahead only of 'Human Rights and International Relations'. The relevant sub-section pays the briefest of lip-service to economic globalization, but contains no ideas about how Russia might respond to its challenge. There are the usual references to the country's 'economic security', the need to protect Russian exporters against 'discrimination', the importance of attracting foreign investment, and a qualified commitment to pay the Soviet-era debt 'in accordance with the country's real capacities' – see 'Konsteptsiya vneshnei politiki Rossiiskoi Federatsii', *Nezavisimaya gazeta*, 11 July 2000, p. 6.

4 It is worth emphasizing here that Russia's membership of the Paris Club owed much more to the size of its Soviet-era debt to Western creditors, than to its 'integration' in global economic processes or its creditor status *vis-à-vis* former Soviet republics and client states.

5 For example, Deputy Foreign Minister Karasin remarked following APEC's decision to admit Russia that he saw 'nothing objectionable' in the USA, Russia,

China and Japan pursuing 'flexible forms of cooperation aimed at resolving not only economic but also political questions, for example, in the field of strategic security' – '"Zolotogo dozhdya" ne ozhidaetsya', *Moskovkie novosti*, no.48, 30 November-7 December 1997, p. 5.

6 See note 30, chapter 2.

7 The Partnership and Cooperation Agreement (PCA) sets out the basic framework for political, economic, social, cultural, environmental and technological cooperation between Russia and the EU. The agreement was signed in June 1994, but did not enter into force until some three-and-a-half years later, in December 1997.

8 Much of the criticism of 'shock therapy' under Yeltsin has been unfair to say the least. It is possible that the original Gaidar programme of radical market reforms might have failed and revealed itself as inappropriate to Russian conditions. But Gaidar and the other 'young reformers' were never afforded the time to test their vision of the free market. The failure of economic reform in the 1990s was therefore not the failure of shock therapy as such, but rather the inevitable outcome of policy confusion, lack of political will, and entrenched institutional and ideological opposition.

9 See Gorbachev, *Memoirs*, p. 401.

10 Kozyrev, for example, argued that the world needed Russia 'as a strong member of the family of free, law-based, democratic states and not as a "sick man" of Europe and Asia' – 'The Lagging Partnership', *Foreign Affairs*, vol. 73, no. 3, May/June 1994, p. 62.

11 As Anders Åslund has noted, the actual situation regarding living standards in post-Soviet Russia remains unclear. Unreliable statistics and household surveys, the distorting effect of the monetary overhang inherited from the Communist period, widespread falsification of income declarations and tax evasion, the rising share of cash transfers, increased private ownership of cars and TV sets – all these make it very difficult to determine whether living standards have fallen and, if so, by how much. See Åslund, *Building Capitalism*, pp. 305–9.

12 See Putin's Open Letter to the Russian Voters, *http://www.putin2000.ru/07/05.html*.

13 See Putin's annual address to the Federal Assembly, 3 April 2001 – 'Ne budet ni revolyutsii, ni kontrrevolyutsii', *Rossiiskaya gazeta*, 4 April 2001, p. 4.

14 See *The Economist* (print version), 29 November 2001, *www.economist.com*.

15 These efforts were ultimately successful. The EU formally conferred on Russia the status of a 'full market economy' at the Russia–EU summit in Moscow on 30 May 2002, with the United States following suit a week later.

16 It is worth mentioning in this connection that the Putin administration has laid considerable stress on establishing conditions that would attract the return of Russian capital from 'safe havens' abroad (such as Cyprus).

17 Kaliningrad's singular geographical location, as an economically backward exclave within an expanding European Union, makes its situation especially difficult.

18 The whole issue of 'transition periods' is very messy, with time-scales varying according to sector and item. But the lack of realism in some Russian attitudes is reflected in the comment by Andrei Kushnirenko (Head, Department of Tariff Policy and Protection of the Domestic Market, Ministry of Economic Development and Trade) that Russia would need a transition period of at least 10–15 years

in order to safeguard its automobile industry – see interview in *Kommersant vlast*, 6 November 2001, p. 18.

19 See comments by Igor Ivanov – 'Igor Ivanov: Zapadnye subekty Rossii dolzhny ne poteryat, a vyigrat ot rasshirenie ES', 6 March 2002 – *www.strana.ru*.

20 See Putin's 2001 address to the Federal Assembly, *http://www3.itu.int/MISSIONS/Russia/speechs.html*.

21 Economic integration and the specific question of Russia's WTO accession emerged as much the most important foreign policy themes in Putin's annual address to the Federal Assembly on 18 April 2002 (see *http://www.great-britain.mid.ru/GreatBritain/prezident.htm*).

22 'WTO Accession: What's in it for Russia', speech at the Roundtable: 'Russia, the International Economy and the WTO', Moscow, 30 March 2001, *http://europa.eu.int/comm/trade/speeches_articles/spla54_en.htm*.

23 *The Economist* (print version), 22 November 2001, *www.economist.com*.

24 One need only recall the example of COMECON (or Council for Mutual Economic Assistance – CMEA), a body created to reinforce the Soviet Union's grip on its client states. The existence of a strictly nominal community hardly masked the reality that all policy flowed out of Moscow.

25 See 'The Road to the WTO', *Economist Intelligence Unit*, 31 July 2001, *file://C:\Program Files\RBB31\Work\HTML\RB3233.HTM*.

26 It should be emphasized that the main impact of WTO accession on levels of foreign direct investment in Russia is likely to be indirect. The point is not so much that accession itself necessarily generates increased outside investment; rather, that in order to achieve membership the Russian government would need to introduce far-reaching reforms, leading, in time, to a more attractive environment for foreign economic interests and their capital.

27 Such institutionalized opposition was one of the principal reasons behind the failure of economic reforms under Kosygin in the 1960s and Gorbachev in the 1980s.

28 The notion of a common European economic space involving Russia was formalized at the EU–Russia summit in May 2001. Its basic rationale is to establish a closer economic relationship between the two parties, involving greater economic integration and synchronization of laws and regulations – see *http://europa.eu.int/comm/trade/bilateral/russia/rus_memo.htm*.

29 See, for example, Marina Volkova, 'Energeticheskii krizis sblizil Moskvu s Evrosoyuzom', *Nezavisimaya gazeta*, 31 October 2000, p. 1.

30 As an Australian diplomat in Moscow in the latter half of the 1990s, I often encountered this argument in discussions with the MFA's Second Asia Department (responsible for Japan, Oceania, and Asia-Pacific regional issues, including APEC accession).

31 According to a report by the US government's Energy Information Administration in October 2001, energy alone accounted for 40 per cent of Russia's exports (*http://www.eia.doe.gov/emeu/cabs/russia2.html*). The State Customs Committee puts the figure even higher, stating that fuel-energy products comprised 53.5 per cent of total exports in 2000 (see *Tamozhennaya statistika vneshnei torgovlya …*, 2001, p. 15).

32 See 'Poslednii kartel', an interview by Andrei Illarionov in *Itogi*, 12 March 2002, p. 15.

33 The Paris-based International Energy Agency (IEA) claimed that Russia increased

rather than decreased its production of crude oil in January 2002 (see David Buchan and Andrew Jack, 'Oil producers failing to honour output pledges', *The Financial Times*, 9 February 2002). Although Moscow denied this, it is significant that in February 2002 Russia pumped out more oil (7.3 million barrels per day) than Saudi Arabia (7.2 billion barrels), thereby becoming, at least temporarily, the world's largest oil producer (IEA report, cited in Jeremy Branston, 'Russia: Boost in Oil Production Grabs World's Attention, But Can It Be Sustained?', *Radio Free Europe/Radio Liberty*, 26 March 2002, *http://www.rferl. com/nca/features/2002/03/ 26032002095743.asp*).

34 See 'Russia: Oil and Gas Exports', USA Energy Information Administration fact-sheet, October 2001, *www.eia.doe.gov*.

35 A senior Western oil executive described the situation to me as 'improving, but still very difficult'.

36 Lukoil's stake in the Caspian Oil Consortium managing the 'Contract of the Century' was a modest 10 per cent, and this only after belated negotiations – see Georgii Bovt, 'V politike nichya chasto oznachaet pobedu', *Kommersant-Daily*, 10 October 1995, pp. 1, 4.

37 Moscow's basic concern was that construction of a major pipeline bypassing Russia altogether would exclude it from the region, not only economically but also strategically – see Konstantin Varlamov, 'Sammit OBSE – porazhenie Moskvy?', *Nezavisimaya gazeta*, 23 November 1999, p. 5.

38 In early 2002 the president of the Azerbaijan state oil company (SOCAR), Natik Aliev, claimed that Lukoil intended to buy a share of 7.5–8 per cent – see Michael Lelyveld, 'Caucasus: Will Russia's LUKoil Join The Baku-Ceyhan Pipeline Project?', 27 February 2002, *http://www.rferl.org/nca/features/2002/02/27022002092411.asp*.

39 Under UNSC Resolution 986 (April 1995), Baghdad was allowed to sell a limited amount of oil and oil products (initially US$2 billion per annum) in order to buy food, medical and other humanitarian supplies for its population suffering under the burden of the UN sanctions regime. The programme remains in operation, although restrictions on the amount of oil that can be sold have been removed, while the proceeds may now be spent on non-humanitarian items (e.g., pipeline transit fees through Turkey). It is estimated that around 30 per cent of the oil under the oil-for-food programme goes to various Russian companies (see Iraq Country Analysis Brief, USA Energy Information Administration, October 2002, *http://www.eia.doe.gov/emeu/cabs/iraq.html*).

40 An interesting early indicator of Moscow's coolness towards Iraq was Foreign Minister Ivanov's refusal to meet with Iraqi Deputy Prime Minister Tariq Aziz when the latter stopped over in Moscow on 30 January 2002. Significantly, this occurred the day after President Bush's State of the Union address, in which he described Iraq as one of the countries belonging to the 'axis of evil'.

41 See 'Russia: Oil and Gas Exports', *www.eia.doe.gov*.

42 For example, Ukraine's gas debt is estimated to be around US$1.4 billion (*http:// www.eia.doe.gov/emeu/cabs/ukraine.html*), while Georgia is said to owe Russia USD 90 million (*http://www.eia.doe.gov/emeu/cabs/armenia.html*).

43 See Russia Country Analysis Brief, USA Energy Information Administration, October 2001, *www.eia.doe.gov*.

44 Under the Blue Stream project signed in 1997, Moscow and Ankara agreed to

build a pipeline to transport Russian natural gas to Turkey via the Black Sea. It is anticipated that once the pipeline reaches full capacity Gazprom will be able to deliver 16 billion cubic metres of gas per annum (*http://www.gasandoil.com/goc/company/cnc22698.htm*).

45 According to the International Institute of Strategic Studies, the Soviet Union/Russia's share of the global arms market plummeted from 35.6 per cent of total (second only to the United States) in 1988 down to 8.6 per cent in 1996, behind the USA (42.6), the UK (22.1) and France (14.1) – see *The Military Balance 1997/98* (IISS/Oxford University Press, Oxford, 1997), p. 265.

46 According to a very well-placed Asian source, the Russian S-300 system was superior in range and reliability to the American Patriot missile, as well as being considerably cheaper. However, political realities, including pressure from then Secretary of Defense Bill Cohen, ensured that Seoul bought American.

47 In November 2000 the Russian government publicly repudiated the 1995 Gore–Chernomyrdin agreement on Russian arms sales to Iran (see note 21, chapter 3).

48 See Henry Meyer, 'Russian Arms Sales Hit Record 4.4 Billion Dollars in 2001', AFP report, 26 December 2001, *www.spacedaily.com*.

49 Putin's Open Letter to the Russian Voters, *http://www.putin2000.ru/07/05.html*.

50 See Edward L. Morse and James Richard, 'The Battle for Energy Dominance', *Foreign Affairs*, vol. 81, no. 2, March/April 2002, p. 17; also Isabel Gorst, 'Burying the Hatchet', *Petroleum Economist*, vol. 69, no. 7, July 2002, p. 6.

51 As formalized in the Russo-Chinese 'Joint Declaration on a Multipolar World and the Formation of a New International Order' – *Rossiiskie vesti*, 25 April 1997, pp. 1–2.

52 Witness the continuing difficulties over construction of the Kovykta gas pipeline, intended to carry oil from Angarsk in the Irkutsk region to Daqing in northeast China. Currently there is not even agreement over the routing of the pipeline, with Russia wanting to build it through Mongolia and the Chinese preferring instead a longer route bypassing the latter (see 'Russia, China eye pan-Asian oil bridge', Sergei Blagov, *Asia Times Online*, 26 June 2002, *http://www.atimes.com/c-asia/DF26Ag02.html*).

53 For example, with Malaysia – see Lyuba Pronina, 'Weapons Sales: The Peace Dividend's Evil Twin', *St Petersburg Times*, 26 November 2002, *http://gvnewsnet.com/html/worldreacts/alert55.html*.

54 It was the historian Richard Pipes who used the term, 'patrimonial mentality', to describe Moscow's assertive behaviour with the newly independent former Soviet republics – 'Is Russia Still an Enemy?', *Foreign Affairs*, vol. 76, no. 5, September/October 1997, p. 73.

55 Another example of Russia using economic methods for political leverage is the ongoing threat to build a new gas pipeline from Russia to Poland via Belarus (thereby sidestepping Ukraine).

56 Perhaps the most signal demonstration of the growing closeness of American relations with several of the CIS states was the attendance by the leaders of the GUUAM (Georgia, Ukraine, Uzbekistan, Azerbaijan and Moldova) sub-regional group at NATO's 50th anniversary summit in Washington in April 1999. Their presence at the summit was all the more galling for Moscow given the ongoing NATO military intervention over Kosovo and Russia's consequent refusal to attend the celebrations.

57 In September 1994, Azerbaijan and a group of Western oil companies (including British Petroleum and Amoco) signed a production-sharing agreement to develop Azerbaijan's oil reserves in the Caspian Sea. This was in open defiance of the then Russian (Foreign Ministry) position which insisted that the energy resources of this 'inland sea' – 'indivisible' and 'under common ownership' – could only be developed with the agreement of all the littoral states (Russia, Kazakhstan, Iran, Turkmenistan, Azerbaijan) or not at all. In effect, Moscow was insisting on a right of veto. Subsequently, it agreed to a compromise whereby Lukoil increased its stake in the enterprise and much of the oil produced would be transported to the West via southern Russia (see Georgii Bovt, 'V politike nichya chasto oznachaet pobedu', *Kommersant-Daily*, 10 October 1995, pp. 1, 4).

58 The main difficulty with the Baku–Ceyhan option is the sheer expense involved in building the pipeline through rugged mountain terrain.

59 The term 'regional superpower' is used by Leon Aron in 'The Foreign Policy Doctrine of Postcommunist Russia and its Domestic Context', in Michael Mandelbaum (ed.), *The New Russian Foreign Policy* (Council on Foreign Relations, Brookings, Washington, 1998), p. 33.

60 For example, Putin insisted to US media bureau chiefs in June 2001 that investment conditions should be 'equal' for foreign and domestic investors alike: 'we cannot place our national market participants in worse conditions … The terms for production sharing must be universal, they must be accessible to Russian entrepreneurs as well' – *http://www3.itu.int/MISSIONS/Russia/Bull/2001/25-2106B.htm*.

61 During 2002, the Russian government opposed EU proposals for even a relaxed visa/permit regime for travel to and from Kaliningrad on the grounds that this would infringe the basic rights of Russian citizens to move freely within their own country, and thereby constitute an attack on Russian sovereignty itself. See, for example, comments by Kasyanov – 'PM rejects EU visa proposal for Kaliningrad', *The Russia Journal* (online edition), 27 September 2002, *http://www.russiajournal. com/news/cnews-article.shtml?nd=27419*. The matter was only resolved – for the time being – at the EU–Russia summit in November 2002, when Putin assented reluctantly to a system of expedited travel documents for Russians travelling to and from Kaliningrad via Lithuania.

5 Security and geopolitics

1 Bobo Lo, *Russian Foreign Policy in the Post-Soviet Era: Reality, Illusion and Mythmaking* (Palgrave Macmillan, Basingstoke and New York, 2002), p. 99.

2 The liberal historian, Yuri Afanasyev, refers in similar terms to the 'foxhole mentality' – 'Russian Reform Is Dead', *Foreign Affairs*, vol. 73, no. 2, March/April 1994, p. 23.

3 For example, it was the Foreign Intelligence Service which, under Primakov's leadership, presented the first significant detailed criticism of NATO enlargement and its allegedly adverse effects on Russia (see Yevgenii Primakov, 'Opravdano li rasshirenie NATO?', *Nezavisimaya gazeta*, 26 November 1993, pp. 1, 3).

4 'Vladimir Putin, Russia's post-cold-warrior', *The Economist*, 8 January 2000, p. 45.

5 The 2000 version of the National Security Concept began with a conceptual discourse on the nature of the global environment. It describes the latter as being characterized by two 'mutually exclusive tendencies': the first, supported by Russia

and a significant number of states, was towards the establishment of a multipolar world; the second, based on the domination of the United States and its Western allies, advocated unilateralism and the application of military force 'in circumvention of the basic norms of international law' ('Kontseptsiya natsionalnoi bezopasnosti Rossiiskoi Federatsii' – *Nezavisimoe voennoe obozrenie*, no. 1, 14–20 January 2000, p. 1).

6 It is true that Putin secured Duma ratification of START-2 and the Comprehensive Test Ban Treaty (CTBT) in April 2000. However, the government's prime motivation here appears to have been to preempt criticism of Russian disarmament efforts by the Non-Nuclear Weapons States (NNWS) at the Sixth Non-Proliferation Treaty (NPT) Review Conference in New York later that month. Certainly, Russian ratification of the CTBT, belated though it was, contrasted favourably with the US Senate's resounding rejection of the same in October 1999.

7 See Sergei Agafonov, '10 dnei chuzhoi voiny, kotorye potryasli Rossiyu', *Novye izvestiya*, 2 April 1999, p. 1.

8 The well-known commentator Andranik Migranyan remarked, in the context of the NATO military intervention over Kosovo, that only its failure would ensure that the West retained some respect for Russia 'as a country that still matters' – 'Nuzhno li nam pomogat Yugoslavii?', *Nezavisimaya gazeta*, 28 April 1999, p. 6. In similar vein, Alexei Pushkov observed, following settlement of the conflict, that Washington 'would have shown more regard for Russia's interests in Europe only if it had achieved less during its operation …' – 'Sindrom Chernomyrdina', *Nezavisimaya gazeta*, 11 June 1999, p. 3.

9 See 'Vladimir Putin Believes in Positive Development of Russian-US Relations', 24 December 2001, *http://english.pravda.ru/world/2001/12/24/24294.html*.

10 At the NATO–Russia summit in May 2002, Putin and the leaders of the 19 alliance member-states issued a formal declaration, 'NATO–Russia Relations: A New Quality'. Although the document deals mostly in generalities, it also identifies a number of areas for enhanced cooperation, including the struggle against international terrorism, crisis management, non-proliferation, and arms control and confidence-building measures.

11 'Joint Declaration on a Multipolar World and the Formation of a New International Order', Yeltsin-Jiang summit statement, *Rossiiskie vesti*, 25 April 1997, p. 2.

12 According to a 1998 study by Dean Wilkening, the Russian strategic force would be 'largely obsolete by 2005, with the exception of the bomber force' – 'The Future of Russia's Strategic Nuclear Force', *Survival*, vol. 40, no. 3, 1998, p. 101. See also Joseph Cirincione with Jon B. Wolfsthal and Miriam Rajkumar, *Deadly Arsenals: Tracking Weapons of Mass Destruction* (Carnegie Endowment for International Peace, Washington DC, 2002), pp. 108–9.

13 At the 1815 Congress of Vienna following the defeat of Napoleon, the ('Concert' of) major powers – Russia, Britain, Prussia, Austria-Hungary – agreed to divide up Europe and work together in preserving autocracy and Christianity against reformist/revolutionary tendencies on the continent.

14 It is ironic that Kozyrev, not Primakov, was the first major Russian advocate of multipolarity, believing, furthermore, that it had already emerged – see 'Rossiya i SShA: Partnerstvo ne prezhdevremenno, a zapazdyvaet', *Izvestiya*, 11 March 1994, p. 3. The difference between the two, however, was that Kozyrev's vision of multipolarity was cooperative rather than competitive or 'counterbalancing'.

15 See Sergei Karaganov, 'Novaya vneshnyaya politika', *Moskovskie novosti*, no. 8, 29 February–6 March 2000, pp. 5, 11.

16 In his April 2002 address to the Federal Assembly, Putin took the opportunity to announce the end of Cold War confrontation: 'After 11 September of last year, many, very many people in the world understood that the Cold War is over. They saw that we have other threats now, that a new war is on, a war against international terror' (*http://www.great-britain.mid.ru/GreatBritain/prezident.htm*).

17 Under Article I of the 2002 Strategic Offensive Reductions Treaty, both parties undertake to reduce the aggregate of strategic warheads to 1,700–2,200 by 31 December 2012. The fiction of the 'binding' nature of the agreement is exposed, however, by the provision in Article IV that '[e]ach Party, in exercising its national sovereignty, may withdraw from this Treaty upon three months written notice to the other Party.'

18 The demographic imbalance along the Russian–Chinese border is generally estimated to be around 6.8 million people (and declining) in the Russian Far East against 130 million inhabitants in the adjoining Chinese provinces.

19 The 'Shanghai Five' agreement involved the states along the old Sino-Soviet border – Russia, China, Kazakhstan, Kyrgyzstan and Tajikistan. In April 1996, these countries undertook not to use force against one another or engage in aggressive military actions. The agreement was formalized one year later in the margins of the Yeltsin-Jiang summit in Moscow. Confidence-building measures (CBMs) included ceilings for ground troops and certain types of military equipment. The Shanghai Five was renamed the Shanghai Cooperation Organization in June 2001 with Uzbekistan's accession to the group.

20 See Zbigniew Brzezinski, 'The Premature Partnership', *Foreign Affairs*, vol. 73, no. 2, March/April 1994, p. 74; also Richard Pipes, 'Is Russia Still an Enemy?', *Foreign Affairs*, vol. 76, no. 5, September/October 1997, p. 71.

21 During a visit to Uzbekistan in December 1999, Putin explicitly denied that Russia viewed the former Soviet Union as a 'sphere of influence' – see Arkady Dubnov in *Vremya MN*, 16 December 1999, p. 6 (in *The Current Digest of the Post-Soviet Press*, vol. 51, no. 50, 1999, p. 16).

22 Especially notable in this regard were the reciprocal visits between Putin and Polish President Alexander Kwasniewski in 2001. Putin described his visit to Warsaw in January that year as a 'decisive turning point towards developing a platform for moving our relations forward (*http://news.awse.com/17–Jan-2002/Politics/7316.htm*).

23 Thus, Presidents Putin and Kuchma have met officially on around 20 occasions; Russian capital dominates the Ukrainian economy; and pro-Russian (and anti-Western) views are increasingly aired on television and even in official statements. See Nigel Pemberton, 'Russia and the West Compete over Ukraine's Foreign Orientation in the Post-Kuchma Era', *RFE/RL NEWSline*, 29 March 2002, *http://www.rferl.com/newsline/2002/03/5–NOT/not-290302.asp*.

24 See Dmitri Trenin, 'After Putin Has Spoken', *Helsingin Sanomat*, 1 October 2001 (*http://www.carnegie.ru/russian/attack/experts.htm*). By this time, the leaders of the frontline Central Asian states – Uzbekistan, Kyrgyzstan and Tajikistan – had already indicated to Washington that they would welcome an American military presence in their countries.

25 The 2000 Military Doctrine noted, for example, that 'the threat to Russia and its allies of direct military aggression in its traditional forms had diminished thanks to positive changes in the international situation' – 'Voennaya doktrina Rossiiskoi Federatsii', *Nezavisimoe voennoe obozrenie*, no. 15, 26 April–11 May 2000, p. 4.

26 As reflected in the struggle over spending priorities during 2000–01 between the then Defence Minister, Igor Sergeev, and the Chief of the General Staff, Anatolii Kvashnin. As a former head of the Strategic Missile Forces, Sergeev strongly favoured maintaining and upgrading Russia's nuclear weapons capability; Kvashnin, in charge of the North Caucasus military district during the 1994–6 Chechen war, instead emphasized the importance of building up the country's conventional military capacities which had become severely degraded since Soviet times.

27 The Russian General Staff's planning for military exercises in the spring of 2001 was based on the traditional scenario of a large-scale, multi-front war against the United States and its allies in Europe and Asia. See Alexander Golts, 'The Russian military's exercise in futility', *The Russia Journal* (online edition), 24 February–2 March 2001, *http://www.trj/ru/weekly/pdfs/100_18.pdf.*

28 See Ivan Rybkin, 'O kontseptsii natsionalnoi bezopasnosti Rossii', *Nezavisimaya gazeta*, 29 April 1997, pp. 1–2.

29 See 'Kontseptsiya natsionalnoi bezopasnosti …', *Nezavisimoe voennoe obozrenie*, no. 1, 14–20 January 2000, p. 1.

30 In September 1999 two massive bomb attacks took place against apartment blocks in south Moscow. In both cases, the buildings collapsed with major loss of life. Although no clear proof of Chechen involvement was produced, Russian elite and public opinion united in blaming Chechen terrorist groups for the incidents.

31 Among the more vivid (and ugly) examples of Putin's sensitivity on this issue was his tirade at a press conference following the EU-Russia summit in November 2002. Asked whether innocent Chechen civilians might suffer as a result of Moscow's anti-terrorist campaign, Putin responded: 'If you want to become a complete Islamic radical and are ready to undergo circumcision, then I invite you to Moscow. We are a multi-denominational country. We have specialists in this question. I will recommend that they carry out the operation in such a way that, afterward, nothing else will grow' (cited in Gregory Feifer, 'Putin's Statements On Chechnya May Reflect Public Opinion', *Radio Free Europe-Radio Liberty*, 13 November 2002, *http://www.rferl.org/nca/features/2002/11/13112002160541. asp*).

32 Following a meeting with Russian security chiefs in Sochi on 22 September 2001, Putin asserted that Russia had been the first to propose that the global community unite in the fight against international terrorism. See *http://english.pravda.ru/ politics/2001/09/22/15922.html.*

33 This motif was popular well before 11 September 2001. In an address to the Council of Europe in January 2000, Igor Ivanov depicted Russia as the defender of Europe's 'common borders' against 'a barbarian invasion of international terrorism that is persistently and systematically working to create an axis of influence: Afghanistan, Central Asia, the Caucasus, the Balkans' – see Dmitrii Kosyrev, 'PACE dala Rossii ispytatelny srok', *Nezavisimaya gazeta*, 28 January 2000, p. 6.

34 In addressing the German Bundestag on 25 September 2001, Putin emphasized the universal nature both of international terrorism and the means that should be employed to confront it (*http://english.pravda.ru/politics/2001/09/26/16209.html*).

35 In a speech in Washington in January 2002, Grigory Yavlinsky, head of the liberal Yabloko parliamentary faction, claimed that Putin's pro-Western choice after 11 September 'was made despite the views and the position of the majority of the Russian political elite.' He described a meeting in which Putin had canvassed views from 21 representatives from the Duma and the Federation Council. According to Yavlinsky, one person (rumoured elsewhere to be Zhirinovsky) advocated supporting the Taliban, two (said to be Yavlinsky and Nemtsov) called for 'unconditional support' to be given to the anti-terrorist coalition, while the remainder argued that Russia should adopt a neutral position – see Grigory Yavlinsky, 'Domestic and Foreign Policy Challenges in Russia', Carnegie Endowment for International Peace, *http://www.ceip.org/files/events/Yavlinsky transcript013102.asp*.

36 At Putin's invitation NATO Secretary-General Lord Robertson visited Moscow in February 2002.

37 Putin has given conflicting signals regarding Russia's interest in NATO membership. In a well-publicized interview with the BBC's David Frost in March 2000, he indicated that Russia would not rule this out at some unspecified time in the future and under certain conditions. In retrospect, this seems to have been something of a stunt to test the West's interest in reviving Russia–NATO cooperation and, more generally, its attitude towards the new Kremlin leadership. Putin's actual position, as reflected in the Russia–NATO Council, is that Russia's interests are best served by maximizing cooperation with NATO on an 'equal' basis, rather than as an outside supplicant subject to alliance dictates and rules (see 'Putin Says Not Interested In NATO Membership', *Radio Free Europe/Radio Liberty*, 22 November 2001, *http://www.rferl.org*.

38 It is interesting to compare the wording of the relevant sections in the 1997 Founding Act and the 2002 Rome Declaration. The former speaks of providing a 'mechanism for consultations, coordination and, to the maximum extent possible, where appropriate, for joint decisions and joint action with respect to security issues of common concern' (*Founding Act on Mutual Relations, Cooperation and Security between the North Atlantic Treaty Organization and the Russian Federation*, 27 May 1997, p. 5). The more ambitious Rome Declaration states that '[t]he Members of the NATO-Russia Council … will take joint decisions and will bear equal responsibility, individually and jointly, for their implementation' (*NATO-Russia Relations: A New Quality*, p. 1).

39 Interestingly, Kozyrev argued this point in relation to the first wave of NATO enlargement – see 'Partnership or Cold Peace?', *Foreign Policy*, no. 99, Summer 1995, p. 12.

40 See Jean-Christophe Peuch, 'Duma Backtracks On Georgia But Maintains Pressure', *Radio Free Europe/Radio Liberty* report, 6 March 2002, *http://www.rferl.com/nca/features/2002/03/06032002092252.asp*.

41 See Alexei Arbatov, 'A Russian-U.S. Security Agenda', *Foreign Policy*, no. 104, Fall 1996, p. 107.

42 See note 61, chapter 4.

43 See Igor Ivanov's comments to the press following discussions with the EU 'troika' in Madrid, 2 April 2002 (*Diplomaticheskii vestnik*, no. 5, May 2002, p. 21).

44 Andrei Kokoshin, Deputy Defence Minister under Yeltsin, has noted that in the 1980s Soviet military planners were already moving away from the principle of

exact 'military-strategic parity' towards more general ideas of 'strategic stability' based on adequate deterrent capabilities – see Andrei Kokoshin, *Soviet Strategic Thought, 1917–91* (The MIT Press, Cambridge, MA and London, 1998), p. 141.

45 During 1999 MFA officials consistently indicated to me that the Russian government would be pleased to see a START-3 benchmark as low as 1,000 warheads. Unfortunately, the Americans had shown little interest in such proposals.

46 See Alexei Arbatov, *The Transformation of Russian Military Doctrine: Lessons Learned from Kosovo and Chechnya*, Marchall Center Papers, no. 2 (George C. Marshall European Center for Security Studies, Garmisch-Partenkirchen, 2000), p. 16.

47 During 1999, my MFA sources consistently dismissed the possibility that American deployment of a national missile defence system could materially affect the Russia–US strategic balance.

48 Putin has been very careful to avoid any suggestion that China could emerge one day as a major nuclear weapons power (and therefore directly threaten Russia). Instead, he has pitched the argument in positive terms – The Russia–China relationship as a crucial element in an 'arc of stability' involving the United States and Western Europe as well. See interview with the *Jianmin Zhibao* newspaper on 4 June 2002 (*http://www.putin.ru/status.asp*).

49 Thus, in his first press conference as foreign minister, Primakov listed the defence of territorial integrity at the head of Russia's foreign policy priorities – 'Primakov nachinaet s SNG', *Moskovskie novosti*, no. 2, 14–21 January 1996, p. 13. See also the 'General Propositions' section in the 2000 Foreign Policy Concept ('Kontseptsiya natsionalnoi bezopasnosti ..., p. 1).

50 Following the Khasavyurt accords of August 1996, Chechnya became independent in all but name, a state of play that lasted until the second post-Soviet Chechen campaign was launched in September 1999.

51 Since the end of the Second World War, Russia and Japan have been embroiled in a dispute over the sovereignty of several tiny islands – Kunashiri, Etorofu, Shikotan and the Habomais. Although the islands, known as the Northern Territories by Tokyo and the South Kuriles by Moscow, have been the subject of claim and counter-claim for at least a century, the territorial dispute came to a head when Stalin exploited Russia's late (July 1945) entry into the war against Japan to reacquire the islands by force. As a result of this annexation, Russia and Japan have yet to sign a peace treaty and remain, technically speaking, in a state of war. At a more practical level, the failure to reach a territorial accommodation has been a major impediment to the development of economic and political ties between the two countries.

52 It used to be argued that the disputed islands were of key strategic importance in that their possession allowed the Soviet/Russian Pacific nuclear submarine fleet safe passage in and around the Sea of Okhotsk. These days, however, such considerations are no longer relevant, and are notably absent in Moscow's arguments for retaining the islands.

53 Vladimir Lukin made this point to the author in early 1999.

54 In 1956 Nikita Khrushchev indicated that the Soviet Union would be willing to return Shikotan and the Habomais in return for a bilateral peace treaty, the restoration of full diplomatic relations and the development of economic cooperation. The terms were the subject of a joint Soviet–Japanese declaration in October that

year, but did not lead to anything more substantive. Subsequently, Moscow toughened its position by making the partial return of the islands conditional on Japan's withdrawal from its (1960) military and security treaty with the United States.

55 This concern dates back a century. Petr Stolypin, Prime Minister under Tsar Nicholas II, was especially mindful of the problem and sought to alleviate it by actively encouraging migration to the RFE. See Alexander Lukin, 'Rossiya-Kitai', *Mezhdunarodnaya zhizn*, no. 12, 2001, p. 80.

56 Under the 1860 Treaty of Peking China formally ceded most of the southern part of the Russian Far East (Khabarovsk, Primorye, Amur, Birobidzhan regions).

57 See Dov Lynch, *Russian Peacekeeping Strategies in the CIS: the Cases of Georgia, Moldova and Tajikistan* (St Antony's, RIIA, Macmillan Press and St Martin's Press, Basingstoke and New York, 2000), p. 4.

58 The 'format-20' idea is essentially about enshrining Russia's 'equality' within the Russia–NATO Council; this in lieu of the old 19 + 1 formula which Moscow (rightly) saw as excluding it from NATO decision-making processes.

59 The presence of important Russian economic interests in Iraq makes a flexible stance even more imperative. After all, Moscow wants to be able to work with whatever regime is in power in Baghdad.

60 See 'Kontseptsiya natsionalnoi bezopasnosti ...', p. 6.

6 Identity, values and civilization

1 Given its central location between Europe and Asia, it may be more accurate to speak in Huntingtonian terms of Russia being situated along a civilizational fault-line rather than on the periphery as such.

2 The expression 'moral-civilizational mainstream' is of course somewhat arbitrary. Here it refers to the loose amalgam of Western humanistic beliefs and values originating in the 18th-century Enlightenment.

3 At various times in Russian history, there have been experiments in what might very loosely be called 'democratization', most notably the establishment in 1864 of the *zemstva*, or local assemblies of self-government. Yet these were hardly democratic institutions in any meaningful sense, being dominated by the local nobility as well as facing constant checks on their functions from the central authorities. See Orlando Figes' *The People's Tragedy: The Russian Revolution 1891–1924* (Penguin Books, Harmondsworth, England, 1998), pp. 39, 51–2.

4 The 1917 Revolution is perhaps the one example in Russian history where one can make a (partial) case that popular power overthrew a ruling regime. It is worth pointing out that in post-Soviet Russia, unlike in Ukraine, the opposition has never managed to defeat the incumbent power – quite a notable non-achievement in light of the political and socio-economic troubles of the past decade.

5 The notion of 'confidence in tomorrow's day' (*uverennost v zavtrashnem dne*) was a very common theme of the Brezhnev period, contrasting the stability of Soviet life to the uncertainty and hardship of the masses in capitalist countries – see Leonid Brezhnev, 'Delo Lenina zhivet i pobezhdaet' (speech on the 100th anniversary of Lenin's birth), *Pravda*, 22 April 1970, p. 3.

6 In a 1993 nationwide survey conducted by Igor Klyamkin, the majority of respondents identified Yurii Andropov and Margaret Thatcher as their 'ideal' political

figure – see 'Tetcher, Pinochet ili Andropov?', *Izvestiya*, 4 November 1993, p. 4. The pollster Yuri Levada has shown that the popular desire for authoritarian or 'strong' rule has, if anything, increased over the course of the post-Soviet period. In 1995 some 66 per cent of respondents agreed with the proposition, 'A strong leader can give the country more than the best of laws', as against 24 per cent disagreeing (the rest being 'don't know'). In 1997 the respective figures were 72–20; in 1998, 78–21; and in 1999, 76–15 ('Civil Society: Hopes and Obstacles', Moscow School of Political Studies, *http://www.msps.ru/eng/libr/rr/r_un_r10.html.*

7 Such stereotypes are reinforced by the Russian literary canon, which abounds in idealistic but ineffectual characters.

8 See Isaiah Berlin, *Russian Thinkers* (Penguin Books, Harmondsworth, England, 1994), p. 118; also Vladimir Lukin, 'Our Security Predicament', *Foreign Policy*, no. 88, Fall 1992, p. 75.

9 Lukin, 'Our Security Predicament', p. 65.

10 There are many references by Putin to Russia's essential European-ness, but perhaps the most notable examples are (i) the comment in his quasi-autobiography, *Ot pervogo litsa* (p. 156), that '[w]e are a part of Western European culture. In fact, therein lie our values. Irrespective of where our people live – in the Far East or in the South – we are Europeans'; and (ii) his address in German to the Bundestag on 26 September 2001 during which he described Russia as a 'friendly European country' and 'a most dynamically developing part of the European continent', and emphasized that it was pinning its hopes on European integration (see *http://english.pravda.ru/politics/2001/09/26/16209.html*).

11 In noting that Russia 'stands on the boundary between the post-modern and modern and even pre-modern world', Dmitri Trenin argues that its 'only rational option is to fully stress Russia's European identity and engineer its gradual integration into a Greater Europe … a clear pro-Europe choice would facilitate the country's modernization, its adjustment to the 21st century world' – *The End of Eurasia: Russia on the Border Between Geopolitics and Globalization* (Carnegie Moscow Center, 2001, p. 319).

12 See 'EU-Russia Economic and Trade Relations: An Overview', European Commission, Brussels, 21 May 2001 – *http://europa.eu.int/comm/trade/bilateral/russia/rus_ovw.htm*.

13 It is worth recalling in this connection Charles Krauthammer's distinction between 'real' and 'apparent' multilateralism. Whereas the former involved a 'genuine coalition of coequal partners of comparable strength and stature' (as with the Allies during the Second World War), the post-Cold War environment was characterized by 'pseudo-multilateralism', in which 'a dominant great power acts essentially alone, but, embarrassed at the idea and still worshipping at the shrine of collective security, recruits a ship here, a brigade there, and blessings all around to give its unilateral actions a multilateral sheen' – 'The Unipolar Moment', *Foreign Affairs*, vol. 70, no. 1, 1991, p. 25.

14 While Europe is Russia's largest energy client, the United States – and its dominating influence in the global energy market – remains the key player for Moscow in this as in other fields.

15 See Thomas Graham, 'U.S.-Russian Relations', Wilton Park conference paper, 15 March 2001, pp. 3–4.

16 See note 39, chapter 2.

17 See, for example, Putin's comments on the subject in his Bundestag speech of September 2001 – *http://english.pravda.ru/politics/2001/09/26/16209.html*.

18 In an interview with American media bureau chiefs on 18 June 2001, Putin complained that Moscow had many times attempted to establish a dialogue with the Chechen leadership, but with no success whatsoever: '… Maskhadov governed nothing. All of [Chechnya] was divided into separate pieces by areas … Simply there's no one to talk to' – *http://www3.itu.int/MISSIONS/Russia/Bull/2001/25-2106B.htm*. Significantly, the Kremlin held Maskhadov directly responsible for the Moscow hostage crisis of 23–26 October 2002 in which 128 civilians died. See comments by Yastrzhembsky (in Sarah Karush, 'Russia Arrests Alleged Terrorist', *Johnson's Russia List*, 31 October 2002, *http://www.cdi.org/russia/johnson/ 6525-16.cfm*).

19 Even liberal commentators have been inclined to see Western government criticisms of the Chechen war as being largely for a domestic audience – see Maksim Yusin, 'Golos Ameriki – "Rossiya dorogo zaplatit" za Chechnyu', *Izvestiya*, 8 December 1999, p. 1.

20 See Elena Korop, 'A klimat u vas khoroshii', *Izvestiya*, 1 October 2002, p. 6. Despite the improved business climate, however, annual foreign direct investment remains very low and even declined in 2001 to US$4 billion (compared to USD 4.4 billion in 2000) – 'The Russian Economy in June 2002', Russia-Eurasia Program, Center for Strategic and International Studies (CSIS), *http://www.csis.org/ruseura/rus_econ0206.htm*.

21 Such as the 11th-hour exclusion of Alexander Rutskoi from the Kursk gubernatorial elections, and the transfer of the infamous governor of Primorskii krai, Yevgenii Nazdratenko, to head the State Fisheries Committee in February 2001.

22 See, for example, comments by Igor Ivanov cited in Dmitrii Gornostaev, 'Eltsin nameren ubedit zapad', *Nezavisimaya gazeta*, 18 November 1999, p. 1.

23 There is a common perception in Moscow that the main reason why Putin targeted Boris Berezovsky and Vladimir Gusinsky was that they were intimately involved in politics, unlike the other big oligarchs. Berezovsky played a king-making (or preserving) role with Yeltsin and in supporting the Putin succession, while Gusinsky's media outlets – in particular, his television channel NTV – had greatly irritated the President with its critical coverage of the Chechen war during 2000.

24 See note 22, chapter 2.

25 The emphasis on law, order and control has been a dominant theme in Putin's speeches from the outset, in fact, while he was still putative President-to-be. In his Open Letter to Russian Voters during the presidential campaign, he spoke of the 'dictatorship of the law' and asserted that '[t]he stronger the state, the freer the individual' – *http://www.putin2000.ru/07/05.html*. His 2002 address to the Federal Assembly called for the 'modernizing' of the system of executive authority and demanded that the executive structure be 'logically and rationally organized.' Putin's comments on the functioning of the judiciary acknowledged the need for 'protection of the individual's rights' and 'more humane' penalties, but nevertheless laid primary emphasis on efficiency: 'An effective judicial system is also needed so that both domestic and foreign companies have no doubt about its authority and efficiency' – *http://www.great-britain.mid.ru/GreatBritain/ prezident.htm*.

26 This judgment may seem harsh on some of Russia's self-styled liberals who claim the attainment of a civil society as a cherished goal. It is worth emphasizing, however, that the focus of mainstream Russian liberalism during the post-Soviet period has been overwhelmingly economic. A civil society, or what passes for it, is principally a means to achieve a liberal (or neo-liberal) economic vision, rather than an end in itself. In this connection, one of the more striking features of post-Soviet liberalism towards the end of the 1990s – and now into the new century – is the emergence of a hybrid species that combines a liberal economic agenda with support for a strong state and an assertive foreign policy. A liberal friend of mine described the typical representative of this tendency as a liberal-*derzhavnik*, while one commentator resorted to the somewhat sinister sobriquet of 'national liberalism' (Andrei Kolesnikov, 'Pokolenie "P"', *Novoe vremya*, no. 8, 27 February 2000, p. 9). More generally, if we understand a civil society as meaning the primacy of laws over the exercise of arbitrary power or covert and shady (*na levo*) practices – in practice and not just in theory – then it is apparent that few in Russia's elite understand or support the notion, at least in its Western humanist guise.

27 The notable exception to this general rule-of-thumb is the continuing American criticism of religious restrictions in Russia.

28 Vladimir Baranovsky refers in this context to Russia's 'instinctive impulse to re-establishing itself as a special player, "not-like-the-others"' – 'Russia: a part of Europe or apart from Europe?', *International Affairs*, vol. 76, no. 3, 2000, p. 451.

29 Some Bush administration officials have admitted privately to concerns about the 'reversibility' of the recent progress in Russian–American relations.

30 In this connection, a senior Foreign Ministry official emphasized to a Western diplomat of my acquaintance the importance of 'expectation management', including being able 'to agree to disagree in a civilized way'.

31 As Sergei Ivanov put it, '[t]he essence of our proposals consists of creating a new mechanism of equal relations between the NATO countries and Russia' – see Kathleen Knox, 'Officials Call For Shift In Relations With NATO', *Radio Free Europe/Radio Liberty*, 21 November 2001.

32 Although it is perhaps unlikely that Moscow would be inclined to use such powers (even if feasible) in the case of an American attack on Iraq, there are other situations where the question would be much more problematic, for example, in the Balkans or with Iran.

7 11 September and after

1 Dmitri Trenin, '"Osennii marafon" Vladimira Putina i rozhdenie Rossiiskoi vneshnepoliticheskoi strategii', *Brifing Moskovskogo Tsentra Karnegi*, 15 November 2001, p. 6.

2 Boris Yeltsin, 'Obshchee prostranstvo bezopasnosti', address to the Budapest OSCE summit, *Rossiiskaya gazeta*, 7 December 1994, p. 1.

3 As one senior MFA official put it, he was now experiencing his fourth détente in Russia–West relations – the first being the original Nixon-Brezhnev détente of the early 1970s; the second, Gorbachev's 'new thinking' in foreign policy; and the third, Yeltsin's pursuit of 'strategic partnership' following the collapse of the Soviet Union.

4 See Grigory Yavlinsky's speech at the Carnegie Endowment, Washington (note 35, chapter 5) – *http://www.ceip.org/files/events/Yavlinskytranscript013102.asp*.

5 See text of Putin's televised speech on 24 September 2001 – *http://english.pravda.ru/politics/2001/09/25/16106.html*.

6 See Trenin, 'After Putin Has Spoken', *Helsingin Sanomat*, 1 October 2001 (note 24, chapter 5).

7 In his speech at the Carnegie Endowment, Yavlinsky remarked: '… for Mr Putin to make the consensus is not a very difficult thing. He's simply saying, this is the consensus … And this is the consensus. The same with Gorbachev. The same … with Yeltsin. This is the Russian tradition …' – *http://www.ceip.org/files/events/Yavlinskytranscript013102.asp*.

8 One need only recall Yeltsin's active role in the 1997 Krasnoyarsk and 1998 Kawana summits with Japanese Prime Minister Hashimoto. On his moderating impact on Russian policy over Kosovo, see Gennadii Sysoev, 'Rossiiskie generaly protiv mira v Yugoslavii', *Kommersant*, 5 June 1999, p. 1.

9 A senior Western diplomat in Moscow has suggested to me that the MFA has sought to portray Putin as being under greater anti-Westernist pressure than is in fact the case. The reasoning behind this tactic is to pressure the West into offering more generous concessions for fear that failure to do so could lead to a change in the Kremlin's Westernizing policy. Whatever the truth of the matter, it is certainly true that such thinking was common in the 1990s. For example, the Yeltsin administration attempted to dissuade NATO against eastwards enlargement by arguing that this would cut the ground from beneath right-thinking liberal and democratic opinion (see Vyacheslav Nikonov, 'Rossiya i NATO', *Nezavisimaya gazeta*, 14 September 1994, p. 4), and used 'implosion' arguments more generally to extract additional political and financial support (see Boris Yeltsin, 'Strategicheskaya tsel – sozdat protsvetayushchuyu stranu', address to the Federal Assembly, *Rossiiskaya gazeta*, 25 February 1994, p. 1.

10 Witness the equal status of Sergei Ivanov and the MOD in the joint ministerial group on strategic security – see note 8, chapter 3.

11 Remarks at a joint question-and-answer session with George W. Bush at St Petersburg University, 25 May 2002, *http://www.putin.ru/status.asp*.

12 *http://www.great-britain.mid.ru/GreatBritain/prezident.htm*.

13 *http://www.great-britain.mid.ru/GreatBritain/prezident.htm*.

14 At the joint press conference on 24 May 2002 following the Russia–USA summit negotiations, Putin insisted that Russia's nuclear cooperation with Iran was 'not of such a nature as to undermine the non-proliferation process. Our cooperation … is focused exclusively on problems of an economic character' – *http://www.putin.ru/status.asp*.

15 Whereas under Yeltsin the official Russian and Iranian positions on exploitation of the Caspian Sea's energy resources coincided – namely, regarding the principles of 'indivisibility' and 'common ownership' – the present administration's energetic pursuit of Russian economic interests in the region have led to growing differences and tensions between Moscow and Tehran. Interestingly, in the lead-up to the Caspian Sea summit in Ashgabat in April 2002, the Russian press was notably critical of Iran's hardline position and aggressive behaviour. See, for example, Vladimir Georgiev, 'Kaspiiskaya neft pakhnet porokhom', *Nezavisimaya gazeta*, 11

April 2002, p. 3, and Usina Babaeva, 'Pyat stran – pyat pozitsii', *Nezavisimaya gazeta*, 18 April 2002, p. 6.

16 See Zbigniew Brzezinski, 'The Premature Partnership', *Foreign Affairs*, vol. 73, no. 2, March/April 1994, p. 76.

17 It is notable, for example, that Moscow has sought to justify recent aggressive behaviour towards Tbilisi – threatening Russian military intervention in the Pankisi gorge – on the grounds that this may be the only way to deal with the problem of 'international terrorists' (i.e., Chechen guerrillas) on Georgian territory.

18 Presidential spokesman Yastrzhembsky noted that the world had 'not always listened to Russia … but it has now become clear that only through joint, coordinated actions can we counter this threat which Russia has frequently spoken and warned about and against which it has proposed concerted action. Mikhail Margelov, Head of the Federation Council's International Affairs committee, remarked in similar terms: 'Those who before the tragedy in the USA did not believe Russia's words that international terrorism constituted a threat to all countries must rethink their position.' See 'Kreml prizyvaet k obedineniyu', *Vremya novostei*, 12 September 2001, p. 2.

19 The contrast with the approach of the Yeltsin administration to NATO enlargement and the Kosovo crisis could hardly be more striking. In both these cases, the Kremlin threatened all sorts of 'counter-measures' but in the end did – and was seen to do – virtually nothing.

20 See note 17, chapter 5.

21 At a seminar at the Carnegie Moscow Center in May 2002, Vyacheslav Nikonov made the point that even a 'Potemkin' agreement, i.e., one containing little or no substance, had considerable symbolic importance. The existence of such a document amounted to formal American recognition of Russia's special status as a world power.

22 The declaration, 'NATO–Russia Relations: A New Quality', is less than three pages long, and sketches areas of cooperation and joint decision-making in only the most general of terms. The latter, for example, is to be 'in a manner consistent with [the parties'] respective collective commitments and obligations' (p. 1) – a get-out clause that allows NATO ample room for manoeuvre in deciding what areas and issues will be subject to joint decision-making.

23 An additional, if secondary, consideration here was the perceived Islamic threat emanating from Central Asia, in particular from the Taliban regime in Afghanistan.

24 This is true even in the economic sphere, where the Putin administration views WTO accession – in which Washington is the chief external actor – as more important than its substantial (and growing) trade with the EU.

25 The latest encouraging development for Putin has been a marked softening in the French government's position following a meeting between Chirac and Putin at Sochi on 19–20 July 2002. See Marie-Pierre Subtil, 'M. Chirac abandonne toute critique de la guerre en Tchetchenie', *Le Monde*, 21–22 July 2002, p. 2.

26 I am indebted to Timofei Bordachev for drawing my attention to this apt term.

27 Doorstop interview in the Duma, 19 September 2001.

28 This was particularly evident in the wake of Communist and nationalist successes in the December 1993 Duma elections.

Index

Index